EVERYTHING
THEY HAD

EVERYTHING THEY HAD

SPORTS WRITING
FROM
DAVID HALBERSTAM

Edited and with an Introduction by
GLENN STOUT

HYPERION

NEW YORK

Copyright © 2008 The Amateurs Ltd.

Library of Congress Cataloging-in-Publication Data
Halberstam, David.
  Everything they had : sports writing from David Halberstam/David Halberstam ; edited and with an introduction by Glenn Stout.
      p.   cm.
   ISBN 978-1-4013-2312-7
  1. Sports journalism—United States.   2. Halberstam, David.   I. Stout, Glenn.   II. Title.
   PN4784.S6H35   2008
   070.4'49796—dc22   2008004440

Book design by Karen Minster

FIRST EDITION

10 9 8 7 6 5 4 3 2 1

FOR ALL HIS EDITORS

CONTENTS

INTRODUCTION

BY GLENN STOUT

MANY READERS MAY BE SURPRISED TO DISCOVER THAT AS an undergraduate at Harvard University, David Halberstam, who would become the most honored journalist of our time, began his journalism career in the press box. As a staff writer for the *Harvard Crimson* he covered intramural basketball and the freshman baseball team before matriculating to varsity football. For a time he even wrote a sports column for the *Crimson* inventively titled "Eggs in Your Beer." One of the pleasures of editing this volume has been the discovery that over the ensuing five decades, through stints at newspapers in Mississippi and Tennessee and the *New York Times*, and assignments in the Congo, Vietnam, Poland, and Paris, and then after leaving daily journalism to write books, he never strayed from the sports page for long. While working for the Nashville *Tennessean* from 1956 through 1960 he once covered opening day of the baseball season and reported on a high school student who would soon win several Olympic medals named Wilma Rudolph. After he joined the *New York Times* in 1960, his first byline for the *Times* was not about any great issue of the day, but, of all things, about a ski jumping exhibition held in late November on man-made snow at Central Park's Cedar Hill.

This is, I think, telling. He once wrote of his sports titles that "[they] are my entertainments, fun to do, a pleasant world and a good deal more relaxed venue," less pressured and more enjoyable than his heavier and more lengthy books about what he termed "society, history and culture." Yet I do not think he viewed writing about sports as necessarily something lesser, for he also wrote that sports were "a venue from which I can learn a great deal about the changing mores of the rest of the society." He recognized that sports are important because sports matter to people, and that sports, and how we relate to sports, say something of value about ourselves, our society, and our history and culture, one of the rare places where citizens of differing creeds, classes, and races come together.

David Halberstam was, at his core, a reporter, and even when he was writing about sports he was reporting on the world—they were not separate. In a story he wrote as an undergraduate for the *Harvard Alumni Bulletin* about sculling on the Charles River, the first story reprinted in this book, he also managed to capture a bit of the Cold War fear that was then wreaking havoc upon the postwar psyche. His brief report on Wilma Rudolph's track squad provided Halberstam himself with a lesson in racial progress, or the lack thereof. His editor excised his use of the term "coed" in his description of the runners—at the time the term was reserved for white students only.

This background in sports does not make David Halberstam particularly unique. A number of great American writers were, at one time or another, sportswriters, ranging from Ernest Hemingway to Jack Kerouac, Hunter S. Thompson, James Reston, and Richard Ford. What is unique, however, is that David Halberstam, while moving beyond sports, did not, I think, move past sports. While he never elevated sports out of proportion, sports never ceased to be important to him and he never cast sports aside as insignificant, once writing that "I do not know of any other venue that showcases the changes in American life and its values and the coming of the norms of entertainment more dramatically than sports."

One reason that he felt that way may be because he found those who wrote about sports among the best teachers of writing in all journalism. In his introduction to a collection of work by W. C. Heinz entitled *What a Time It Was*, Halberstam credits Heinz, who is best known for his sportswriting, as "one of those people who made me want to be a writer," someone who "helped teach me what the possibilities of journalism really were." Gay Talese's famous profile of Joe DiMaggio, "The Silent Season of the Hero," written in 1966 for *Esquire*, had a similar impact. For Halberstam, Talese's sober, nuanced portrait of DiMaggio simultaneously exposed the limits inherent in newspaper journalism and the creative possibilities of magazine work, which promised what Halberstam called "the greatest indulgence of all for a journalist, the luxury of time." Over the years he regularly noted the influence of other writers like Red Smith, Jimmy Cannon, Jimmy Breslin, Murray Kempton, and Tom Wolfe on his own work. Smith, of course, was a sports columnist, and while Breslin, Cannon, Kempton, and Wolfe wrote of many topics, all considered sports a valid subject upon which to exercise their unique creative talents.

It was, in fact, the influence of these talented writers that caused Halberstam to look at his own work and career and, shortly after Talese's story about DiMaggio appeared in print, to ponder leaving daily journalism. Despite winning the Pulitzer Prize in 1964 for his reporting on the Vietnam War, he began to find daily journalism too rigid and confining.

His frustration with daily reportage and his desire to say more is apparent even in his earliest work and is apparent even when he wrote about sports. In March of 1961 Halberstam wrote a brief story for the *Times* about the Washington Redskins' new football stadium, which was being built as part of the National Capital Parks system and therefore fell under the jurisdiction of the Interior Department. In the story, U.S. Interior Secretary Stewart Udall warned Redskins owner George Preston Marshall, a notorious bigot who at that point had yet to put an African American player on the field in a Redskins uniform, that if he continued to discriminate in his hiring practices, the new stadium might not be available to the Redskins.

The story is unremarkable except for the ending. Halberstam interviewed both Udall and Marshall for the story, and the Redskins owner offered up his usual excuses for not employing any African Americans, telling Halberstam that Redskins fans were mainly from the south and therefore the team recruited players from southern universities, which just so happened to field all-white football teams, a transparently cowardly posture that ignored the fact that there were already African American collegiate players in black colleges as well as African American players in the NFL available by trade. Yet Marshall told Halberstam, "I don't know where I could get a good Negro player now—the other clubs aren't going to give up a good one."

Reading the story today, one can almost feel Halberstam bristling at Marshall's unapologetic bigotry and insensitivity. As the reporter of a news story, he simply did not have the latitude to take Marshall directly to task on the topic, an experience he must have found frustrating.

Yet still, he did find a way—through simple reporting. Immediately following Marshall's quote, Halberstam added one single, concise fact, one small *"take that"* of a sentence that said everything, writing simply, "The Redskins won only one game last year and finished last in their division."

Several years later, when Halberstam was serving as a foreign correspondent for the *Times* in Warsaw, Poland, the paper sent staffers a memo requesting that they write stories exactly 600 words long. In response Halberstam wrote his now famous letter to his fellow correspondent and former staffer at the *Harvard Crimson*, J. Anthony Lukas, in which he stated, "There are only two kinds of stories in the world: those about which I do not care to write as many as 600 words, and those about which I would like to write many more than 600 words. But there is nothing about which I would like to write exactly 600 words."

One of those stories that he found that he wanted to write more than 600 words about was at the racetrack in Poland, in the company of two Poles, Tadeusz and Zygmunt, whom he trailed for a day as they watched the races and placed their bets. It is a simple, understated story, one that easily could have been nothing more than a pleasant little diversion, yet Halberstam, by actually reporting what took place, manages to reveal a thing or two or three about daily life in Poland, making deft note of the underground economy, entrenched corruption, the continued existence of class in a supposedly classless society, and the genuine affection between his two subjects. But the opportunities to write such stories were few, and two years later, following an unsatisfactory assignment in Paris, he left the newspaper business altogether, joining *Harper's Magazine* in 1967 and, in 1969, pursuing a career primarily as an author of books.

This collection does not include excerpts from his many sports titles. All are still widely available and deserve to be read in full, rather than in any abbreviated fashion. Instead, this collection is built from his lesser-known writing on sports: the essays, articles, and columns that he wrote over a lifetime, most of which will be new to even the most dedicated reader. I have chosen to start this volume with two early pieces—his column on rowing on the Charles and his day at the racetrack in Poland—not only because of their historicity, but because each of these early stories demonstrates something that differentiates David Halberstam, the sports writer, from so many other writers better known in other genres who sometimes write about sports.

He was no dilettante. He never dipped his pen into the world of sports and then simply walked away, treating it as, in the parlance of the newsroom, simply the "toy department." Sports was a lifelong subject of interest to him, a place he valued and considered worthy of his attention, and where over time I think he discovered that some of his larger concerns—the checkered history of race relations in this country, for example, or the value of friendship and camaraderie—were sometimes played out in a more concentrated, more accessible form. No matter the subject, his approach never varied. He never wrote just to fill up a page or spoke to fill a screen at a time when other writers preferred to talk than write. His commitment to the craft of writing was always apparent.

It should have come as no great surprise that after the towering success of *The Best and the Brightest* in 1972 and *The Powers That Be* in 1979, his next book would be his chronicle of the 1979–80 season of the NBA's Portland Trailblazers, *The Breaks of the Game*, published in 1981. For throughout the 1970s, even as he earned a reputation as the preeminent journalist of our day, he continued to write about sports in publications like *Harper's* and *New York Magazine* and in newspapers. The real surprise is not that he chose to write a book about sports, but that he took so long to do so. Sports had always been part of his own personal beat. It was only natural that he would one day write one or more books in that genre.

The success of that book, a bestseller and still, I think, the single best chronicle of a season in sports, spawned many imitators. In short order a host of writers successful in other genres, ranging from political columnists, newspaper journalists, novelists, and pundits, tried to duplicate his success and chose to turn their attention to sports, rashly deciding, after a lifetime of writing about something else, that what they really wanted to do was write about baseball or some other sport. Many such books, even those that have sold well, have not been very satisfying, for very few of the authors brought the same skills of reporting and level of respect to their task as David Halberstam did to his. In the hands of these less skilled craftsmen, their sporting subjects were often made to seem small and insignificant, even disposable. In Halberstam's hands, that was never the case.

This may be, in fact, precisely what differentiates his work from that of those sports writers who followed in his wake. "Big games, and late innings and fourth quarters . . . that's when the test is real," he once wrote, and in his own work he sought to find those moments in a subject that similarly revealed when the test was real, when it mattered. He was not awed or overwhelmed by big themes and big subjects. And when he found a worthy subject, he often probed it repeatedly, returning time and time again, ferreting out more and more each time, as he did with Michael Jordan, for example, first in a number of articles and finally in a book, or with Ted Williams, or with fishing. His vast knowledge of American history and culture allowed him to place sports both within a larger landscape and in perspective, helping us see what we had not seen before, and by articulating what he saw in a subject, teaching us.

There is a wonderful logical progression in much of his work that contains lessons for any writer. He reports first, slowly adding layers of fact and observation, before reaching conclusions that simultaneously seem both revelatory and completely evident and obvious. I suppose that is the rough guideline I have used in selecting the articles and essays that grace this volume. Each, in some way, brings us to a place of knowledge and a level of understanding we likely would not have reached without his guidance—wisdom we would not have otherwise gained. Even better, he manages to teach without preaching, and like any truly good teacher, makes each lesson somehow feel like ours alone.

That appears to be something of a family tradition. His mother was a teacher, and so too is his daughter, Julia, and that is one of the small pleasures of this book—while reading about sports we also learn quite a bit about David Halberstam himself. In his sports writing he was often much more personal and revealing than he was when writing about other subjects. There are probably many reasons for this, but most important, I think, is that he recognized that sports is one of the ways in which we come together, both as a nation and as individuals. The reader will notice that in these selections we meet many of his subjects not as remote figures whose deeds are far removed from our lives, but as friends, and to show us them, Halberstam sometimes had to show us himself.

And so we also meet David Halberstam, not merely as a figure on a book jacket, but as a kind and decent person who wasn't much of an athlete while growing up, but enjoyed fishing for bass on small Connecticut ponds with his father and brother and going to the occasional baseball game at Yankee Stadium and Fenway Park. A person who called his friends "pal," liked the camaraderie of men, marveled at and appreciated those who gave their task everything they had, and was sometimes frustrated by those who did not. A man who enjoyed the process of his work as much as the product, and found peace and comfort on the water and with his family both in New York and on Nantucket, and about whom his wife, Jean, said, "[he] would like to be remembered as a historian and particularly remembered for his generosity to his peers and young people choosing the field of journalism."

That he will certainly be. I did not know David Halberstam well, but over the past twenty years was fortunate enough to give him some small assistance with several of his projects and then had occasion to collaborate with him on several others. Our encounters, I think, are revealing, and I am grateful that now I have the opportunity, in some small way, to repay him for that generosity.

We first met when I was working at the Boston Public Library and David Halberstam was researching the book that would become *The Summer of '49*. I was one of those young people, a fledgling writer who a few years earlier had started mining the newspaper microfilm and special collections of the BPL for help in writing stories on local sports history, primarily baseball. Soon after I began publishing these stories in *Boston Magazine* I started to hear from sports writers, most of whom wanted me to look something up on their behalf either in old newspapers or in the library's archives. One of them must have tipped David off to the fact that I had become the de facto sports archivist at the library. One day I returned to my desk, and a note telling me to call David Halberstam was taped to my phone.

No "while you were out" message has ever done more for a person's self-esteem. I remember that I left it on the phone and then went to lunch, just so it would stay there a bit longer. I spoke to him later that day, and he made an appointment to visit the library a few days later.

Most other sports writers who had contacted me before wanted me to look up material for them, and frankly, many treated me as if I were some kind of chambermaid. Not Halberstam. Not only was he extremely considerate, but after I set him up in a back room he wanted only minimal assistance and pored through the archival boxes himself. He was politely curious about me, and when I told him I had written an article about the Red Sox 1948 playoff game with the Cleveland Indians, and had been the first writer to interview Boston pitcher Denny Galehouse since he gave up the winning run more than forty years before, not only did he want to see the story, he wanted to talk. Thereafter he spoke to me as an equal, as a colleague, and as he continued his research over the next few days, we held several lengthy discussions about Boston, the Boston press, and the history of the Red Sox and Yankees. In the wake of our conversations I felt like the rookie hitter who discovered he could hit big league pitching; David Halberstam made me feel like I belonged.

A few years later I was offered the opportunity to serve as series editor for the inaugural edition of the annual collection *The Best American Sports Writing,* the first book project of any kind I had ever been asked to be involved in. My editor at Houghton Mifflin asked me who I thought should serve as guest editor. I knew from the start that the collection should not be confined simply to the compound word "sportswriting" but should also include "sports writing," the best writing on sports, a somewhat different thing. Halberstam's work was already the best example of this. With *The Summer of '49* still on the bestseller list, and the earlier successes of *The Breaks of the Game* and *The Amateurs* still fresh, he fit the criteria perfectly. I immediately suggested that we ask Halberstam to serve as the first guest editor.

My suggestion was, I recall, greeted with some skepticism. Not that my editor didn't think Halberstam would be perfect for the job, but I do not think he believed that a writer of Halberstam's stature would have any interest in serving on such a project, particularly one not yet out of the box. Naively perhaps, I thought otherwise. I boldly told my editor that I knew Halberstam from the library, and that when he contacted him, he should mention my name.

A few days later my editor called with the happy news that David was on board. Moreover, he told me that the clincher had come when he told David that he would be working with me, providing me with yet another boost. Although many of the guest editors for *The Best American Sports Writing* make their selection *in camera*, which is their right and privilege, David was different. During the selection process he wanted to discuss the stories and solicited my input. That was a kindness I have never forgotten, for I think that together we created a sturdy template for the series, one that otherwise might have been less assured and lasting.

I soon began to write books myself—primarily illustrated biographies and histories with photographs selected by my colleague and friend Richard Johnson. On several occasions we asked David to contribute an essay. He almost always agreed, asking only if he was being paid out of our own pockets or that of the publisher, and adjusting his fee accordingly.

We worked together one last time in 1999, when my publisher decided to publish a collection entitled *The Best Sports Writing of the Century*. David Halberstam was my first and only suggestion to serve as guest editor. This time I was allowed to make the call, and again, the only question he asked was whether we would be working together or not.

I cannot overstate how much that query meant to me, both personally and professionally. Once again he turned the editing of the book into a collaboration. Each time I sent him a bundle of material, I would soon receive a phone call from David wanting to discuss the stories. He seemed to know every writer and story already, and in conversations that were, in turn, sometimes funny and earthy but always profound, I felt as if I were the student at a private journalism seminar as he would deftly dissect a piece I liked that he did not, and, more often, show me why he liked the stories that he did. In one of those conversations, as we discussed the stories of W. C. Heinz, David openly wondered if Heinz was still living. I answered that I did not know, and over the next few minutes I could tell that David was intrigued by the possibility that he was—as I have already mentioned, Heinz had been an enormous influence on his career, but the two journalistic giants had never met or spoken.

A few days later I received another call, and without even saying hello, David blurted out, "I just got off the phone with Bill Heinz," and he proceeded to tell me all about it, speaking with the unbridled enthusiasm of a young boy who had just attended his first big league baseball game. His curiosity, combined with the selection of a few Heinz stories in the book, sparked something of a W. C. Heinz revival and introduced his work to an entirely new generation of writers, a true and lasting gift.

It was during this time, as we spoke often and sometimes at length during the several months it took to put the book together, that I really began to comprehend the central role that sports—and sports writers—played in David Halberstam's own personal biography. They were important to him and, to borrow a metaphor, he already knew the players without having to look at the scorecard. There truly was no one better equipped to serve as the captain of such a book than him.

Later, after the book came out and he either referenced it in something he wrote or spoke of it in an interview, he nearly always mentioned that I did all the "heavy lifting," an acknowledgment I cherished, for I knew that he was sincere. Like me, as a young man he had labored as a construction worker. Hard work was something he treasured and appreciated, and no writer I have ever encountered has matched his considerable work ethic. Yet as much as I appreciated the compliment, it also made me smile, because how could working with David Halberstam ever be considered "heavy lifting"?

In the ensuing years before his passing we spoke only a few more times, primarily about another collaboration that never quite came together. The title of this book, in fact, stems from those conversations.

We envisioned putting together a book we hoped our daughters would read, a collection of sports writing solely about female athletes. The working title we agreed upon was *Everything She Had,* a phrase that seemed to acknowledge a quality that David Halberstam admired not only in athletes, but in anyone who strove to succeed.

When I was asked to recommend a title for this volume, I immediately suggested *Everything They Had.* I believe the title recognizes that not only did David Halberstam value those who gave their task everything they had, but that inside these pages he responded in kind, with his own best effort. For David Halberstam wrote about sports with the same veracity with which he wrote about everything else, once summing up his approach to all his work by quoting none other than basketball legend Julius Erving, who said, "Being a professional is doing the things you love to do, on the days you don't feel like doing them." Here, in *Everything They Had,* I believe we gain a sense that David Halberstam himself was perhaps the best example of many of the qualities he admired most in others.

Although I don't believe I spoke to him at all over the last four or five years or so, that was fine. We were professional acquaintances, and I never felt comfortable contacting him unless it was absolutely necessary. Yet when I asked him once how I should respond if I was ever asked by anyone how to contact him, he told me simply, "Oh,

I'm in the phone book." On a few occasions when I encouraged trusted younger writer friends to contact him about projects or issues where I thought he might be of some help, he was, every single time.

I was honored one last time when his editor at Hyperion, Will Schwalbe, contacted me about serving as the editor of this volume. Will described the circumstances of the project and then added that David's wife, Jean, suggested that I serve as this book's editor. There are no words to describe the degree of gratitude I feel toward her for allowing me to share the byline of this book.

So once more I have been given the privilege of doing what David Halberstam would have described as the "heavy lifting," again selecting the best of the very best from among the essays, features, columns, and other sports writing that David Halberstam produced over the course of his distinguished and inimitable career. Although, given the circumstances, part of that task was done with a measure of sadness, the burden, of course, was not really heavy at all. Like the writing that graces these pages, it was joyful and real, enriching, uplifting, and true.

EARLY DRAFTS

In the spring of 1953 and 1954 people would turn to me and say:

"Look, if sculling's that dangerous, if people are always throwing at you and trying to sink you, why not quit? Why do you do it?"

"Escape," I would answer.

DEATH OF A SCULLER,
IN THREE ACTS

Harvard Alumni Bulletin,
April 23, 1955

DEATH OF A SCULLER, IN THREE ACTS

From the *Harvard Alumni Bulletin*, April 23, 1955

HARVARD'S SANITARY ENGINEERING DEPARTMENT RECENTLY recorded 1,000 times the normal radioactivity in Cambridge water. "When we put our Geiger counter to some Cambridge water," Harold A. Thomas, associate professor of Sanitary Engineering, admitted, "it sounded like a bobcat caught in the bushes."

This discovery marks, not as some immediately imagined, something strikingly new on the local scene, but rather another step in an age-old unceasing struggle—that between man's progress and the single sculler on the Charles River.

To understand this conflict, one must realize that through the ages the shape and form of the single scull have changed remarkably little. True, from time to time artisans have managed to make them thinner and lighter, and this year the boathouse has added a fiberglass shell. But the basic concept of rowing has not changed.

On the other hand, as man has progressed, the opposition to the sculler has armed itself with newer and more dangerous weapons. The cycle of the opposition's development, historians note, falls roughly into three overlapping periods.

The first of these is the stone age. If the stone age was at first simple, it was nonetheless irritating. Little boys stood on the bank of the Charles and threw rocks at the moving sculls. It was something of a game, with the sculler's sanity the stake. Simple in its pure form, even the stone age underwent some modernization.

First, the scullers learned to spot the little boys and row on the opposite side of the river. But the urchins were not to be fooled—they took to hiding on top of bridges and dropping rocks down on the passing shells. Since there always appears to be an abundance of little boys and big stones, this practice is employed even today.

The other day I was rowing under the Weeks Bridge when two juvenile delinquents fired.

"I got him," said the first.

"Nah, I got him," said the other.

"You both got me," I said, tossing two enormous rocks out of the scull.

Thus you see that while the stone age belongs to the past, in one form at least it is dangerously close to us today.

The second part of the anti-scull cycle is best termed the machine age. Even the most accurate of rock throwers had to remain stationary on the river side. But with the advent of Robert Fulton, the Charles River mechanized. Motor boats, big and small, appeared, oblivious to the frail Harvard students and their frail craft. If formerly one had only to row to the other side to escape a rock, now the boats and their over-present waves were all over the river. To add to the sculler's confusion, there are several types of motor boats.

First of all, there is the Chris Craft pleasure boat, which contains at least one blonde and one hairy chest. While you row they come zooming by, within sinking distance, pull out the throttle, and yell: "Hey, kid, row that boat." In order to stay afloat, of course, you must stop rowing.

Even more dangerous than the floating leather-jacket set are the sight-seeing excursion boats which look like leftovers from the Mississippi River. For something like a dollar you can get on down in Boston and travel past Dunster House, all the way up to Watertown. It is a round trip, so you actually can see Dunster House twice.

It also means they can tip the scullers over twice. The river boats, for that is what they are called on the Mississippi, have a ratio of almost two children to every adult. Since there are no rocks on the ship, they are very good-natured children.

"Look at the rowboats," they invariably shout, and then wave energetically. Since you have only as many hands as oars, it is almost impossible to wave back. Nevertheless, friendly passengers or not, it is a scientific fact that at least once this spring you will be tipped over by the excursion boat.

This brings us to man's final attack upon the sculler, the nuclear age as evidenced by the Sanitary Engineering Department's discovery. Perhaps for the first time the sculler has no chance. Previously impervious in the face of rock and Evinrude, he bravely fought back, head over shoulder, his eyes peeled for trouble. That was in the old days. Now trouble is all around him, he is rowing on trouble.

In the spring of 1953 and 1954 people would turn to me and say:

"Look, if sculling's that dangerous, if people are always throwing at you and trying to sink you, why not quit? Why do you do it?"

"Escape," I would answer. "No problem of coexistence on the river. No Iron Curtain, only the Lars Anderson Bridge. Why, for all it matters, the Czars might still be ruling Russia."

That was in the old days. Now atomic fission is everywhere. Nowhere is the conflict between East and West, Communism and Democracy, so clearly outlined as on the Charles River. A nightmare is haunting today's single sculler: the vision of a motorboat filled with little boys. The little boys are armed with rocks, and they pursue him relentlessly until he is capsized into the nuclear waters of the Charles, Cambridge's first casualty from radioactivity.

HORSE RACING IN WARSAW: SPORT OF THE PEOPLE

From the *New York Times*, June 13, 1965

"DUMNA," SAID TADEUSZ, "MEANS 'THE PROUD ONE.'"

The American suggested they bet the horse since they had lost in the first three races and they needed all the pride they could get.

"There will be some money on Dumna," said Tadeusz, who considered himself a professional at the Sluzewiec track but claimed that in his later, less revolutionary, years he had found the will power to break the habit. "The sire of Dumna was a famous horse who won the Derby here 10 years ago. I am positive that I won on his father many times."

The American, who knew nothing about Aqueduct, let alone about racing in this Communist country, said Dumna sounded fine.

It was a windy Wednesday at the races. The sun had been out earlier in the day but it had gone now, for the races on Wednesday are held in the late afternoon so the workers can come out and bet after the job. During the 74-day season in Warsaw the races are held on Wednesday, Saturday and Sunday, but it is on Wednesday afternoon that the real bettors, the real faithful, gather.

Saturday and Sunday, Tadeusz noted with a slight measure of contempt, brought out women, people who think the race track is a place for a picnic, and rich peasants from the surrounding countryside who sell vegetables to Warsaw.

"Often their children are quite plump," he said.

He was right in his estimation of the crowd. There were about 3,000 people there (as many as 10,000 on a good Sunday) and they were almost all working men in their 50's and 40's.

"There are few young people here anymore," he said. "Now they don't want to spend their money on the races. They want to buy a car or a record player or take their girl to some student cellar and buy a bottle of wine."

Before the war, he added, there were men with their sons. "And there were always lots of Jews, too, from the Nalewki section of Warsaw, tailors and shoemakers, and they were the ones who taught me about horses, but now there are not many of them left in Warsaw," he said.

The people who go to the races now are often poor, he said, and they take the races seriously and play the long shots.

The cheapest bet is 20 zlotys (the zloty is officially valued at 24 to the dollar) and one can also bet at a 100-zloty window. This is a Communist country and though horse racing and betting on the races are not necessarily the kind of thing that Communist officials see as part of a workers' paradise, racing continues to thrive here. One reason is that it is a major source of income. Not only does the State get a percentage of all admissions but it gets 22.5 per cent of everything bet at the track.

The rough estimates are that between two and three million zlotys are bet every day at the track here and that on Derby days the figure may go as high as four or five million.

The Government theoretically runs and controls all betting and the grandstand is ringed with betting windows. But there are the inevitable entrepreneurs, some working at the track, some filtering in and out of coffee bars downtown.

One tout suggested to Tadeusz quite modestly that he had a sure thing in the fifth.

Tadeusz listened dubiously. The tout assured him that he couldn't go wrong. "Bet wisely and buy one ticket for me. That's all

I ask. One for you and one for me," the tout said. But it was not Tadeusz's kind of horse.

Another reason that racing continues here is that it is deeply ingrained in the Polish blood. Poland has been known for fine Arabic horses for several centuries and racing has been going on here for more than 120 years. Before the war, when there were 16 race tracks in Poland, Polish cavalry regiments had their own racing stables and the breeding of horses was a specialty of Polish noblemen.

Now the noblemen have gone but the horses remain. In many cases the breeding of horses, which is run by the State, is done by some of the same families that did it before the war.

After some talk of the success of breeding horses here, Tadeusz took the American on a tour of the track to see the regulars: a blind man who comes all the time "and sometimes even wins"; a 20-year loser who regularly sinks deeper into debt and lives off his wife; a police captain who fought in the 1944 Warsaw uprising alongside Tadeusz; a man in a flashy sports shirt and sunglasses who was a big bettor until recently "and who now bets less but wears fancier clothes to disguise the fact that he does not have so much money."

Just then one of Tadeusz's friends arrived. He introduced the new Pole proudly. "This is one of the survivors of Auschwitz." The survivor, Zygmunt, rolled up a sleeve to show the concentration camp number on his arm. Then there were more serious things to attend to. He quickly began to argue with Tadeusz on behalf of the favorite, a horse named Arbiter.

"Dumna looks nervous and edgy," Zygmunt said.

"That's good. A little fire," said Tadeusz.

"Maybe you should wait a few races before you bet Dumna," said Zygmunt.

Then the two Poles began a furious argument. Zygmunt went away somewhat embarrassed. The American asked what had happened. "He started to tell me that this is an honest year at the track," said Tadeusz.

The race came and the odds dropped on Dumna from 4 to 1 to 2 to 1. Nearby, two other Poles were talking. It was clear that there was interest only in three of the five horses running. They decided to make a 50-zloty bet on the two other horses, the winner being the one that finished closer to the front.

The trouble with the races here, said Tadeusz, "is that everyone knows all the horses. They know some of the horses better than they know their wives."

The race was a good one, Arbiter and Dumna fought side by side and Arbiter won in the last few yards.

Zygmunt immediately materialized, magnanimously praising Dumna, claiming that the race showed both that the horse had a bright future and that the track was honest. Tadeusz was pleased, too. He had bet the horses one-two and in a situation like this it does not matter which is first and which is second. He had three tickets. He won 200 zlotys.

And so it went. It was a pleasant afternoon. The winnings were small but they were at least winnings. In the last race the favorite was a horse named Brama and the betting was very heavy.

At the start Brama was, incredibly, 20 lengths behind. The favorite finally was third. The crowd booed and jeered and threw paper. The public address system announced that the jockey had been suspended for five racing days. Tadeusz beamed, congratulated himself for having broken the habit and went off joyously to find Zygmunt.

THE LONGER VIEW

I like wearing the two hats. The first hat is ostensibly the more serious one, and my larger books on politics tend to take some five or six years; the other hat as a sportswriter I wear more lightly, I think. The books are shorter and I do them more quickly. I've come to see these books as a form of relaxation. College professors get sabbaticals, self-employed writers do not, so I see them as a form of partial sabbatical. They are work but they are pleasure.

SPORTS AS A WINDOW
OF SOCIAL CHANGE

The Sporting News,
May 23, 1994

INTRODUCTION

From *The Best American Sports Writing 1991*

I GREW UP AS A SEMI-RED-BLOODED ALL-AMERICAN BOY. That is, I loved sports, and like most true-blue American boys I followed almost all sports faithfully. This meant following baseball in the summer, football in the fall, and basketball in the winter; my only exemption was professional hockey, a sport I simply did not get then and do not get now. Following all sports was not as time-consuming an avocation in the forties, for those were the arid years of American sports, before the arrival of television and before the coming of the contemporary sports glut. As I write today in the spring of 1991, I can watch some eight professional basketball play-off games on the weekend, an equal number, it seems to me, of professional baseball games, as well as college baseball championships, a summer football league with teams from Europe, golf championships, and for those who feel that a summer football league is an inadequate substitute for professional football, some six hours of live coverage of the first round of the professional football draft. Less generous people might speak of this as an addiction.

As a worthy and rather typical member of my tribal species, North American, male, middle twentieth century (roots in radio sports rather than television sports), I did then, and still do, duly open the paper each day and turn first to the sports page; in the instance of tabloids, the first love of the tribe, this of course means reading from back to front. Cultural anthropologists may make of this what they wish. As an all-American boy, therefore, so far so good. Where I failed in my youth as a prototype of the species was in a number of things: I was not big and strong, at least not then; I wore glasses, which in the forties and fifties was a sign of nonathleticism; and worst of all, I displayed a premature and clearly unhealthy interest in that day's sportswriters, as well as the athletes. Even at the age of ten and eleven I checked out bylines, and I came to know and recognize certain ones. I loved the early, feisty work of Dick Young, whose reporting semed to burn with a toughness and candor unmatched elsewhere (as he turned meaner and more bitter in his later years as a columnist, I came to detest his work), and I was fascinated by Red Smith and Jimmy Cannon and Leonard Gross: Smith because he wrote so beautifully, indeed so delicately; Cannon because he provided a rare sense of immediacy in an age before television when cameras did not do that—a Cannon story always seemed to take the reader right into the clubhouse; and Gross because of his unusual sensitivity to the athletes themselves, and because he instinctively understood that sports was the first showcase of a broader Civil Rights revolution which was just beginning in this country.

When I was young there was no *Sports Illustrated*, which eventually became the most serious bastion of sportswriting as literature, but like a lot of my colleagues who later made our reputations in the great breakthrough in nonfiction letters of the sixties, I read the old *Sport* magazine carefully and I loved it. There was some very good writing in it, it was one of the first places where the writing seemed more serious, and one could sense the beginning of a literary touch, and an attempt to break out of the routine format of magazine writing of the day. (I was hardly the only young teenager affected by it; Dick Schaap, who went on to become one of the preeminent print and television journalists of this generation, likes to recall that there was a letter to the editor of *Sport* published years ago from a teenage boy named Gay Talese, singling out a piece he enjoyed and asking for more articles like it.)

If *Sport* was the monthly bonus, then I devoured every day if I could Smith, Cannon, and Gross. Smith, of course, was the great sportswriter of the time, the acknowledged champion, because of the fresh, graceful way he wrote, because it simply was not in him to offer up anything clichéd. I can remember, as a freshman in college, taking one of Red Smith's early collections, *Out of the Red*, from Harvard's Lamont Library and keeping it so long that I had to pay $13 in library fees, no small sum in 1951 dollars (the equivalent of four or five meals in Boston's Chinatown with my fellow editors of the *Harvard Crimson*). I can also remember a piece by W. C. Heinz, who was one of my favorite writers and who never quite got the acclaim I thought he deserved (it was his misfortune to work for a paper that was in faster decline than the tabloids I favored); it was about Pete Reiser, the great Dodger player known equally well for his extraordinary talent and for his penchant for crashing into outfield walls and thereby prematurely ending otherwise promising seasons. The piece was done, I believe, for the old *True* magazine, and it contained a memorable scene: it was spring training and a few Dodger players were sitting around talking about the season ahead. "Where you think you'll end up?" they were asked. Most said first place, a few said second. Finally it was Reiser's turn. "Brooklyn Memorial Hospital," he answered. In retrospect, told some forty years later in a time of endless breakthroughs in nonfiction writing, it does not seem so world shattering a bit of writing, but the important thing is that four decades later I still remember it, remember that it was Heinz's way of saying that he was there, that he was going to quote these men as they actually spoke, not as writers thought they should speak, and I also remember that I wanted to be able to write like that.

I was not the only one who loved the work of Bill Heinz. Al Silverman, who edited *Sport* in the sixties and later became the editor of the Book-of-the-Month Club (and is one of the nicest men in this business), tells the story of being at a bar in New York in the sixties when Jimmy Breslin, by then a star columnist with the *Daily News*, was proclaiming that a piece by Heinz in *Sport,* on a fighter named Bummy Davis, was the best sports story of all time. Breslin was making this point with considerable enthusiasm and decided he needed some final bit of proof. "Hey, Rosemary," he yelled to his wife, who was at the other end of the bar, "what's the best sports magazine piece of all time?" "Bummy Davis by Bill Heinz," she immediately answered back. Wonderful, thought Silverman, but too bad it was *True,* not *Sport,* that published it.

When I think of the early influences on me and many of my contemporaries, I think of men like Smith, Cannon, and Heinz. They were the writers who we as young boys turned to every day, and they were the ones experimenting with form. They were all very different, they were all very good, and what made reading them exciting for a generation of young men and women wanting to go into reporting was that they were changing the rules, not accepting the bland, rigid, constricting form of journalism. They gave the reader a sense of what really had happened, what an important sports event had felt like to those most deeply involved, what the jocks had really said. In truth, they were all in different ways the children of Hemingway, profoundly influenced by him, trying to apply the lessons learned from him—the modernization of the language and the use of realistic dialogue—to the small piece of territory given to them each day on the sports page. Hemingway, in turn, so admired Cannon, who was, of course, the purest of the Hemingway disciples, that he had Cannon's paper, the *New York Post,* flown in every day to his home in Cuba. Since Cannon was very close to DiMaggio, and since Hemingway was a major DiMaggio fan, and since DiMaggio was the Hemingway hero incarnate, reading Cannon allowed Hemingway to keep up with his favorite baseball player.

IF WRITERS LIKE THAT WERE my first heroes, for a time I did not emulate them. Instead, I went straight, finished college, went off to the South and busied myself reporting on the beginnings of the Civil Rights revolution. I covered very little in the way of sports, although at least once I covered opening day of the Nashville Volunteers, in the Southern Association. The Nashville Vols played at a wondrous old ballpark called Sulphur Dell. There where right field should have been were the old L&N railroad tracks, in effect decapitating right field and making it, as I recall, about 250 feet at the foul pole. In order to give the right fielder a chance, the architects of the park had *landscaped* right field so that it rose ever higher, and the fielder, not unlike a Swiss mountain climber, had to play on an incline. It was a disaster for some young left-handed Nashville hitters who, because of the temptation posed by the wall, developed what became known as the Sulphur Dell chop, a quick, controlled upswing at an unusually sharp angle, which, if the hitter connected, almost guaranteed a home run, but which finished the hitter forever with line drives.

So my life in my early twenties had very little to do with sports. Perhaps, my family hoped, I had finally grown up. A few years later I arrived in New York as a newly minted *New York Times* reporter (first to be a Washington bureau reporter and soon afterward a foreign correspondent) and I met Jimmy Cannon, then in his early sixties, and spent a pleasant evening with him. He after all had been a hero of mine and had covered my other heroes: the great DiMaggio, the sturdy Henrich, the powerful Keller. I was stunned by the almost unbearable quality of his loneliness. If there is such a thing as the beginning of the end of innocence for a young man, then it comes at moments like that of seeing someone who had been a hero, indeed perhaps a role model, and knowing instantly that there is something dreadfully wrong with the way he has lived, that the price was too great.

In the unofficial pecking order of the *Times*, foreign correspondents ranked above national correspondents, who ranked above city-side reporters, who ranked above sportswriters. In those days, the *Times* did not pay much attention to its sports page. It was mostly an afterthought, and the predecessors of today's fine columnists—Dave Anderson, Ira Berkow, and George Vecsey, and now once again Bob Lipsyte—were not, to be as generous as I can, very good. The transcendent skills of Red Smith in the rival *Trib* were a source of constant embarrassment, if not to the editors of the paper, then at least to most of the reporters who worked there. That being said, there was nonetheless at the *Times* a magnetic attraction that pulled some of the best-known journalists of our age back to the sports department to talk to the sportswriters. I can remember Homer Bigart, the great reporter of two generations in American journalism, a Pulitzer Prize winner as a war correspondent in World War II, a Pulitzer Prize winner as a war correspondent in Korea, almost a Pulitzer Prize winner in Vietnam, a Ruthian figure, sidling back to the sports desk to talk to the beat men who covered the Yankees and the National League teams, and I could sense in him and others, and indeed in myself, a certain envy. We did what we did, and were duly honored for it, we were the paper's stars, but there was an undeclared and gnawing sense that the sportswriters had more fun, and also that they were allowed to earn a living and remain—as most people in the city room, for all of their fame, could not—little boys.

At that time, sportswriters, the good ones on the good newspapers anyway, seemed to have had more freedom to *write*, and generally the best writing in most metropolitan papers during the fifties and sixties was done on the sports pages. That freedom reflected in part the curious double standard of American journalism: because the editors of most important papers did not take their sports departments or the lives of athletes very seriously, and because the sports page therefore was not deemed a serious place, writers who worked there could experiment, they could be irreverent, they could tell stories about athletes they could never tell about, say, a mayor or a congressman. Sportswriters could write more realistically and with more candor than their colleagues in the city room or on the national desk. After all, the sports department was still known on major papers as the toy department.

There was a reason only sportswriters enjoyed this freedom: the more highly regarded the paper, the more reverential its tone toward important political, social, and cultural figures of the day. A good example are stories about Yogi Berra that appeared in the *New York Times*. Certainly there were, in New York politics in the fifties, politicians as colorful as Yogi who used the language with almost equal skill, but the *Times* did not write about them as it wrote about Yogi. As the paper became more influential in the sixties and seventies, it became even more reverential. The problem, of course, is that good writing demands irreverence, skepticism, a certain *edge*. It was all right for a reporter to be irreverent about what he had discovered at a baseball park or a football field on a given day, because he wasn't writing about serious people (athletes were perceived as entertainers), but it was not acceptable for him to be equally skeptical about politicians. The world of politics clearly was not viewed as entertainment, though that strikes me as increasingly debatable.

Another reason that the writing on the sports page tended to be livelier was the drama inherent in the world of sports: the action and flow of a contest, the obvious winners and losers. It was and remains a world in which the value system, the purpose, and the pain are all comprehensible, and comprehensible even to relatively young reporters. Most other journalistic assignments are mundane and by their nature resistant to almost any instinct to indulge in literary tendencies. The one exception is war, which is graphic and can be readily and movingly described, and to which ambitious young journalists have always been pulled. The drama of war, like the drama of sports, is self-evident. The reporter not only set out to move his readers; he was moved himself.

The drama of the rest of life is a great deal more subtle, less easily revealed, and more resistant to the quick assaults of deadline-propelled journalists. The real world is more unruly and complicated; the increments of victory and defeat in ordinary people's lives are infinitely smaller and lend themselves more to the eye and talent of a skilled novelist than a young and eager sportswriter in his or her twenties. In addition, sports reporting is easier to master, so it is easier to add authority to the writer's voice, which is also important. Good writing is first and foremost authoritative; the writer must be sure of the terrain.

It is not surprising, therefore, that so many of the writers who became part of the flowering of nonfiction letters in the sixties, called the New Journalism, had some roots in sportswriting. There, writers could experiment, find their voice, and be rewarded for breaking out of form (after all, a beat writer who covered 154 baseball games using the same form every day was not only boring his readers, he was boring himself). When I think of the pioneers of New Journalism, I think first of the trinity of my early heroes: Red Smith, Jimmy Cannon, and Bill Heinz.

If those early pioneers influenced some of the more important nonfiction writers of the sixties and seventies, then the circle was unbroken; these nonfiction writers continued to experiment with form, to write books, and as they did, they influenced younger writers still working on newspapers. It struck me, as I put this collection together with Glenn Stout, that sportswriting is alive and well in magazines and newspapers, that the coming of television has changed the role of the print reporter and made the good writers ever more nimble. After all, the day when print was the prime carrier and the fastest carrier of news is long over. The job of the skilled sportswriter is to go where the cameras can't go, to find out exactly what hungry readers who already know the outcome need to know, and to beat television at a story it thinks it has already covered.

Some people bemoan the fact that we don't have a Red Smith anymore, and believe that because he is gone, sportswriting is in decline. I do not agree. There may not be one or two writers who stand out among the pack, as Smith and Cannon did in their time, but one reason is simply that there are so many other sportswriters on so many papers who are writing well, who have learned to break out of the old-fashioned form, slip inside the locker room, and give the reader an extra dimension of what has happened in a sport just witnessed by millions, and to do it with some measure of literary grace.

Sports as a Window of Social Change

From *The Sporting News*, May 23, 1994

I AM AT A NEW YEAR'S EVE PARTY IN WASHINGTON TO START this year. It is at the Georgetown home of Ben Bradlee and Sally Quinn, he the former editor of the *Washington Post* and arguably the best American editor of his generation, she the talented former writer for the paper's Style section and now novelist. It is an A-list party. Larry King is near the door as my wife and I enter. Colin Powell, who had recently finished his tour as Chairman of the Joint Chiefs of Staff, is in the next room to the right and 20 yards off is Bruce Babbitt, Secretary of the Interior and quite possibly future Supreme Court member. Lloyd Cutler, veteran Washington insider (and soon to be summoned to investigate the Whitewater affair), is moving deftly through the party. Senators abound. White House aides, past and present, are commonplace.

Major figures of the media, like Bob Woodward, Sam Donaldson and Bill Safire, are plentiful. James Carville, most certifiably the season's most important power figure, spots me and comes over to talk. He is wearing a bow tie with the stars and stripes of American flags on it. Does he want to talk about the hot subject—the President and the press, and the book I wrote 15 years earlier on the subject, *The Powers That Be*? No, Carville, the hottest political spin doctor and consultant in the country, wants to talk about Matt Batts, whom I had written about and he had admired as a boy.

Matt Batts? Matt Batts was the backup catcher on the 1949 Red Sox team that went down to the final day of the season in a heroic battle with a much deeper Yankees team. He is a lovely man, and he, like Carville, is from Baton Rouge, La., where he now runs the Batts Printing Company. One of the most pleasant professional days that I have spent in years was spent sitting in his office six years ago interviewing him for a book I wrote on that season, *Summer of '49*. We had never met, but he sat me down, and gave me a Coke in a bottle from a Coke machine (which won me over from the start, Coke does taste better in a bottle).

Then he started talking. He was immediately warm, generous and wondrously funny. Out came story after story of those days, lovely anecdotes of Ted Williams and his teammates. It was a glorious morning and when I left I thanked him and told him it was one of the best days I had had in years.

"Well, it's been nice for me too," he said, "you got my mind off other things." I asked, what other things? Well it turned out, on that day he had been sitting around waiting to hear from his doctor if he had prostate cancer, and reminiscing with me about the old days had taken his mind off it. Two days later I called him from New York and asked what the medical report was. False alarm, he said, just a mark where he had been bruised 40 years earlier as a catcher. We became friends, and we have stayed in touch and when there was a publication party in New York for my book, Matt Batts got in his car and drove to New York to attend.

I told all this to Carville, and we cemented our new instant friendship as we might well not have been able to if the subject had been politics. Politics is always much edgier; I spent some 40 minutes with Carville and we never talked about the Clinton White House. We were in our first meeting, united in our admiration for Matt Batts, and not divided over an issue of politics. I quite preferred that beginning: He did not have to spin me and I did not have to spin him.

I WEAR AT THIS MOMENT rather late in my career two hats, one as serious journalist-historian of American politics and the other more recently as sports writer, or more accurately, writer of sports books. Rarely do my two worlds connect: Few of the people in the sports world have read my political-social books, although most of the people in the political world know of the sports figures I write about, and I can feel on occasion the palpable envy of some of my literary peers because of my association with athletes who were stars when my friends were little boys.

Some six years ago when I was at a dinner party in New York at the home of Roger Altman, a friend who is now Deputy Secretary of the Treasury, a dinner filled with top political people and media stars, wealthy and accomplished men and women, I let the others have their ego time, one after another one-upping each other on what they had done lately and which important person they had just interviewed. I waited patiently all evening, like a great poker player holding the perfect hole card, and then late at night I played my card, saying (quite casually, of course) that the next day I was flying to Islamorada, Fla., in the Keys, to interview Ted Williams. All conversation stopped, and I owned that dinner party and it struck me that at the moment if I had wanted to auction off a job as my assistant—not unlike Tom Sawyer, that is, someone to carry my notebooks and tape recorders while I spent the day with Ted Ballgame—I could easily have gone to five figures.

As I write this I have just finished up *October 1964*, the fourth of my sports books, and the bookend to *Summer of '49*; it is the story of the 1964 season and the seven-game Cardinals-Yankees World Series that year, and the end of the Yankee dynasty. I had a wonderful time doing it.

I spent two days in Omaha with Bob Gibson and found him (as I suspected I would) utterly admirable, a man whose intellectual, physical, and spiritual abilities seem to be in almost perfect proportion, and the component parts not merely for a dominating athlete, but an imposing person. Bill White, then in his final days as National League President, was filled with laughter and a sense of amusement about life's contradictions, and he had an inner richness all his own. Tim McCarver was a writer's perfect interview, combining an exceptional love of language with an equally remarkable love of the game. Dick Groat talked the way he played, ever the strategist, each play from that season still fresh in his mind as it was 30 years ago, each one a situation, calling for its own strategy. Lou Brock was the ultimate student of the pitchers and base stealing; what came through was his hard work and discipline as well as his passion and hunger to excel.

Among the Yankees, Al Downing was a wonderful interview, analytical, candid, thoughtful. Steve Hamilton, now the athletic director at Morehead State, was bemused, and self-deprecating (albeit appalled when my car, which had been parked outside his office, was towed away and I was stuck with a $40 ticket—"We don't usually treat our visitors quite this way," he said). Mel Stottlemyre, 30 years in baseball, then pitching coach of the Mets, a sad team it seemed to me, filled with largely overpaid and quite (at least to me as the two of us were talking and the Mets players turned up their boom boxes to make the interview more difficult) surly players, became once again the cool fearless rookie who had saved the Yankees when he came up in August of 1964 and went 9–3. Pete Ramos, who was coaching at Miami-Dade Community College (Wolson campus), was delighted to summon me before his players as living proof that in that season when he had come to the Yankees late in the pennant race (too late to pitch in the World Series) and had made 13 appearances, he had an earned-run average of 1.25 and had not, despite all the pressure on him in big game after big game, walked a single batter. And Bobby Richardson, despite the considerable gulf between his personal politics and mine, treated me with great grace and generosity, had me in his home and took me with his extended family to lunch and recalled the season with singular irony.

That I eventually gravitated to writing books on sports is not so surprising. I had always been a serious sports fan, and as a college student I had covered sports for the *Boston Globe* to help pay for my tuition, and as a young reporter in the South during the early days of the Civil Rights movement in the mid- and late Fifties, I had been fascinated by the coming of the first generation of black athletes in big-time American sports and my instinctive sense that a revolution was taking place in America, and that it was taking place most notably and quite possibly first in the world of sports.

So it was that I gradually and tentatively ventured out 15 years ago to do my first sports book. I did it almost because I needed to: In 1979 I had finished a long book on the media which had taken six years; it, together with a book on the origins of the war of Vietnam, *The Best and the Brightest,* meant that I had spent 11 years on two books, and I was tired both physically and mentally, and I badly needed a break. I was a serious professional basketball fan, had become a friend of coach Jack Ramsay, had loved his 1977 championship Portland team, and by chance had been in Portland on a book tour the day Bill Walton announced that he wanted to be traded. Instantly I envisioned a book on a season in professional basketball, and in particular how the coming of ever-larger salaries (in those more innocent days, $300,000 for a star player was still considered an outlandish salary) and the increasingly litigious nature of the society had begun to change sports. I thought it could be a good book, and could be a welcome change of pace after almost 25 years of covering politics. So I went out and did it (*The Breaks of the Game*) and had a glorious, if exhausting, time.

I liked the world of sports and I liked many of the people I met and I came to cherish the friendships I made in the doing, and the passion, intelligence and, on occasion, inner purity of the different athletes I met, basketball players, baseball players and rowers, many of whom who still remain in my life. (Just last year Bill Walton decided to expand my cultural horizons and took me and my family to a Grateful Dead concert at the Meadowlands, thereby gaining me a new level of esteem in the eyes of my then 12-year-old-daughter.)

I like wearing the two hats. The first hat is ostensibly the more serious one, and my larger books on politics tend to take some five or six years; the other hat as a sportswriter I wear more lightly, I think. The books are shorter and I do them more quickly. I've come to see these books as a form of relaxation. College professors get sabbaticals, self-employed writers do not, so I see them as a form of partial sabbatical. They are work but they are pleasure: It is a world that is, for me at least, as witness my meeting with Carville, generally more pleasant and less adversarial than that of politics.

Graham Greene, the great British novelist, would alternate his serious novels with detective novels, which he came to call his "entertainments," and in some way these sports books are my entertainments, fun to do, a pleasant world and a good deal more relaxed venue, and yet a venue from which I can learn a great deal about the changing mores of the rest of the society. (I should admit that in baseball I have the luxury of interviewing athletes who played 30 or 40 years ago rather than those who play today, something I am not sure I would enjoy nearly as much.) If I did these books at first because they were fun and in some ways less demanding, then I have been surprised by their increasing commercial success—and the expanded constituency they have brought me, that is, readers who have come to my other books because they first read one of my sports books.

In addition, sports has been an excellent window through which to monitor changes in the rest of the society as we become more and more of an entertainment society. I do not know of any other venue that showcases the changes in American life and its values and the coming of the norms of entertainment more dramatically than sports. We can learn as much about race from sports as almost any subject and we can learn what the coming of big money does to players and to lines of authority more from sports than anything else. When I wrote *Summer* I did it because I wanted a book on the last moment of the old era in baseball, when the game was played on grass, in the daytime, when the teams traveled by train, and when the games were broadcast by radio, when owners held dictatorial power, and when above all else, both teams, the Yankees and the Red Sox, were still lily white.

October 1964 catches baseball midway through the dramatic changes that have taken place since World War II: By 1964 baseball is a television sport, expansions have come, because of television ever bigger money is moving into the game (the Astrodome is just being completed at $30 million) and although the new money has not yet reached the players it is already affecting the nature of the game and its ownership.

Above all, by 1964, baseball reflected a larger slice of America: In the critical last game of the 1949 pennant race, four of the starting nine players on the Yankees—Raschi, Rizzuto, DiMaggio and Berra—were of Italian-American descent, whereas in the critical seventh game of the 1964 World Series, four of the nine Cardinals—Gibson, Brock, White and Flood—were black. The Yankees, of course, could have extended their dynasty, they could have signed Ernie Banks and other great black stars, but George Weiss, their general manager, did not think blacks were as talented or as mentally tough as whites and he gave for far too long orders to his best scouts not to sign them. All of that came to a head by 1964 as Mantle and Ford and others wore out; the Cardinals that fall, it seemed to me (and I was a Yankees fan), represented not just a larger slice of America, but a more just America. That, I suppose, was the answer I had been looking for when I started the book.

A Dynasty in the Making

Introduction to *ESPN Sportscentury*, 1999

AMERICA ENTERED THE NEW CENTURY ON THE VERY THRESH-
old of becoming a great power. Barely more than a century old, it
was already moving at an astonishing rate from agrarian to industrial society, and from rural to urban society. With a population of
roughly 70 million, the nation was becoming urbanized at an accelerating rate; indeed tensions between the new immigrants who
lived in the cities and were often Catholic, and people who were na-
tivists, that is the older stock Americans who lived in more rural
areas, would dominate the country's politics for the first third of a
century.

More than a third of the population made their living from
farming. The pace of life was slow; for every 1,000 Americans, there
were only 18 telephones, most of these in businesses. No one spoke
of disposable income or the entertainment share of the take-home
dollar—take-home dollars were too scarce. Sports, both amateur
and professional, had a limited importance; ordinary people lacked
the time to play them, and more important, the time and money to
watch them.

But the country would become the most dynamic society in the
world. In a century of stunning advances in technology, no country
was so systematically on the cutting edge like America, not only in
inventing new and critical scientific breakthroughs, but in bringing
them to market as devices to be enjoyed by simple working citizens.
If there was one great American revolution, created by hundreds of

smaller inventions, it was a revolution which created the good life for ordinary working men and women. It was a revolution which in sum made the worst kind of physical labor less harsh, paid workers a fairer share for their labor, gave them a decent wage, and allowed them not only great personal dignity and economic independence with an increased amount of disposable income, but more leisure time. How America spent both that leisure time and disposable income—the rise of an entertainment society and its effect upon the world of sports—would be one of the most dramatic by-products of what was often called the American Century.

By the end of the century, it had become America the affluent, a place where ordinary families owned two and sometimes three cars, one and sometimes two houses, took long, expensive vacations, and spent a vast amount of the GNP on the search for pleasure. In the process—in part because of its wealth, in part because of the direction the new technology took it—America had morphed itself from a grim, often joyless, rather Calvinist society to a modern mass-production industrial society. By the Sixties, it changed again, into a communications society, to finally, by the end of the century, an entertainment society in which images replaced print as a principal means of communication.

In all of this change sports—amateur and particularly professional—would be among the main beneficiaries. By 1998, America's most famous athlete, Michael Jordan, a young black man from North Carolina, made some $78 million a year in salary and endorsements, and certain professional sports franchises, like the New York Yankees and the Dallas Cowboys, were said to be worth close to a billion dollars.

Rarely had the beginning of a century in one nation seemed so distant from the end of the same century. In January 1900 the country was barely a generation removed from a bitter and exceedingly violent civil war, yet from that war were the beginnings of American power, dynamism and industrialism first fashioned.

But that was yet to come. If the Civil War had been fought to end slavery, then there was in the Reconstruction era, as the true political price of reunion emerged, a resurgence of racism, slavery replaced by legal racism, and fierce continued suppression of the children of slaves. If, in Lincoln's phrase, a house divided against itself cannot stand, then America as the century began was neither a house divided nor a house unified. In the new century, one of the great struggles played out would be that of black Americans struggling for full citizenship. And no arena would showcase this battle in a series of stunning and often bitterly divisive increments, or reflect the true talents of black America more clearly, than the world of sports.

THE CENTURY WOULD BEGIN with what was virtually a national attempt to limit the possibilities of a great black fighter, Jack Johnson, because he was considered uppity and was far too often seen with white women. Special laws were passed as a means of entrapping Johnson and ending his right to be seen as the heavyweight champion of the world. It was just the beginning. The struggle of blacks in the century ahead would be an ongoing source of national tension and debate.

But for those who weren't bound by race (or gender), the country was still a land of promise, the place where the past could be shed and a man could start anew. America offered the concept of hope—if not for yourself, for your children, the place where in one generation change could be wrought. The most telling comment on that American ideal came when I. I. Rabi, the distinguished scientist, won the Nobel Prize for physics. A reporter interviewed him that day and asked him what he thought. "I think that in the old country I would have been a tailor," he answered.

No one would illustrate that unique American social fluidity more than most of the best-known athletes of the century, each with their own very American drive to excel. Babe Ruth, born of a troubled, shaky family. Joe DiMaggio and Johnny Unitas, each the son of immigrants. Muhammad Ali and Michael Jordan, descendants of slaves who would become special American icons. All of them were in different ways driven by the unique forces which created America—the combination of prejudice inflicted on those who had gone before them, and yet the belief that in the lives of their children things would get better. More, the world of sports offered the ideal arena for new Americans, or black Americans whose forebears had been suppressed by racism, to show their strengths and their talents. Only the U.S. military was in any way nearly as democratic a venue.

America was, of course, almost without knowing it, a favored nation. The quality and energy and passion of its immigrant citizens and the part they were to play in the successes of the coming century were not to be underestimated: They were to become inventors, scientists, workers, farmers and exceptional citizens. "Give me your tired, and wretched and poor," Senator Daniel Patrick Moynihan once said, ironically mocking the words taken from Emma Lazarus and engraved on the Statue of Liberty, then adding himself, "Some wretched, some poor." What Moynihan meant, of course, was that America was getting the cream of the crop, though when they had first arrived they did not look like the cream of the crop—all they carried were their hopes and ambitions, and their desire to be not just Americans but good Americans.

This explosion of affluence and power and confidence connected directly, it would turn out, to the world of sports; more, the world of sports would serve as an almost ideal window through which to watch the profound changes taking place elsewhere in the society. Was the country more confident, more affluent, and did its citizens have more leisure time? Then they would show it by becoming more addicted to their games.

No one signified the coming of power quite like Babe Ruth. He changed the very nature of sports. He was five years old when the century began (or at least he so believed, since it was also possible that he was four years old). Because his deeds were so awesome, particularly when measured against the existing dimensions of what passed for power, his name was almost immediately turned into an adjective. Long drives, more than half a century after he played his last game, are said to be Ruthian. He was the perfect figure about whom to create a vast assortment of myths and legends, some of them true, some of them not, though it meant little if they were true or not, because the ones which had been made up seemed just as true as those which could more readily be documented.

RUTH WAS BIG, JOYOUS and seemingly carefree. Rules were made to be broken—he had spent much of his childhood in an orphanage not because his parents were dead but because they could not control him. That sense of him, as a kind of all-American Peck's Bad Boy, seemed to endear him to many of his fellow citizens, more trapped by all kinds of rules in their lives than he was in his. If editorial writers on occasion thundered against his childlike and occasionally boorish behavior, the same antics seemed to charm millions of ordinary American sports fans.

He brought drama to everything he did. He was not just a great athlete, he was a show, fun even when he struck out. He became a phenomenon. Ordinary people longed to read about him. The outrages he committed socially were the outrages of the common man, the ordinary American catapulted to an elite world by his athletic success, but unspoiled in his heart. After he had signed for $80,000, a salary greater than that of President Herbert Hoover, and a reporter questioned him about it, he had said, "Why not? I had a better year than he did." When he met Marshal Foch, the commander of the French forces during World War I, he had said, "I suppose you were in the war."

If Ruth was the most egalitarian of sports heroes, then this was the most democratic of lands, the nation where mass production—and a new kind of economic democracy that went with it—was born. It was not by chance that the new century was perfectly designed for America, and indeed was often known as the American Century. That was a partial misnomer. In truth, it was the Oil Century, as the Japanese intellectual Naohiro Amaya called it, for it was a century in which gas-driven machines would replace coal-driven machines, with an explosive increase in productivity. In the oil century productivity flowered; it could generate products enough for everyone—not just for the handful of rich. The oil culture because of the nature of the fuel created vastly more wealth, a wealth so great that it was shared by ordinary people. And of all the industrialized nations poised for the start of a new era, America, with its rich indigenous oil deposits, was uniquely well-positioned for the new age.

In the oil culture, because oil produced so much more in the way of goods, the workers became prosperous, too. The oil century produced, it would soon become clear, workers who would become consumers; and the more they consumed, the more they created work for others. It was the dawning of a culture in which ordinary people achieved not merely middle-class status, but an elemental social dignity which had in the past been reserved for a tiny number of people. This was an American invention—a nation with something new, a mass middle class. The citizens in this new society gained dignity, confidence, leisure time and, in time, disposable income. That alone was to have a profound effect on the rise and the obsession with sports in the century ahead.

If there was one key figure who represented American genius in the first half of the century, and gave a sense of what America was to be—a mass-driven society with mass-produced goods, all those forces which would make America an economic superpower—it was the first Henry Ford. He was the architect of the most powerful of American ideas which drove the century and made American economic democracy unique—the worker as consumer. He brought the concept of mass production to its height with his River Rouge plant, and turned the auto from an item available only to the rich into something that all Americans could own. In time he came to love the assembly line—the true diamond in his eye—more than the car itself.

Almost from the start, sensing that his workers were his real customers, he began to put most of his energy into what was his production line, to build more cars faster, to meet the unparalleled demand, and at the same time to keep reducing its price. Because the car was already so simple and well-designed there was not much to tinker with in the car itself, he poured most of his energies and his special genius into the production line.

The cars poured off the line, soon more than a million a year. The speed of manufacture meant he was selling that many more cars per year and could cut the price per car accordingly. Ford loved making a car that benefited working people. "Every time I lower the price of a car $1," he said, "I can get 1,000 new customers." In its early incarnation, in the 1910–11 fiscal year, the Model T had cost $780; a year later with the production ascending in amazing increments, the price had dropped to $690 and then to $600, and on the eve of World War I, it was down to $260. What he had wrought was the beginning of a revolution—the good life for the common man.

And so early in this century America became a vastly more dynamic, vastly less class-dominated, infinitely more open society than competing nations. Its people were busy; they were on the move, driving all the time now, it seemed, prosperous, and ever more confident. Its love of sports became a parallel force. The more confident and affluent Americans were, the more they became sports nuts. In addition, other inventions were taking place which would not only bind America together more as a nation, but make sports an ever more important part of the fabric of the society.

It was not just the games themselves that were about to change and become more important. It was the delivery system—the coming of modern broadcasting, first radio, then network television, and then satellite television—which was going to change the way Americans felt about sports; for the new, more modern delivery system was about to make the games more accessible (and thus more important) and make the athletes themselves infinitely more famous, and soon, infinitely wealthier. In the beginning, there was radio. It would help usher in what became known as the Golden Age of Sport. In 1923 the Yankees defeated the Giants in the World Series in six games. Ruth hit three home runs, was walked constantly and scored eight times. It was a noteworthy series, not the least of all because it was the first time the World Series was broadcast across the country on radio. The principal voice at the microphone was that of a young man named Graham McNamee, and the fact that this was broadcast to millions of Americans made the Babe's fame—and the importance of sport within the culture—that much greater.

For it was not just the game itself which was changing, it was the amplification system in a country so vast, which for the first time was becoming linked as one by a new and powerful broadcasting system. On a vast, sprawling land mass where the connection of ordinary people to each other had often been tenuous, big-time sports, broadcast to the entire nation at one time, giving the nation shared icons, was to prove immensely important. It was not just a shared moment of entertainment, though that was critical in the rise of the popularity of sports, but it was to be an important part of the connecting tissue of the society, arguably more important in a country so large where the population was so ethnically diverse—and new—than it might have been in a smaller country with one dominating strain of ethnicity. Sports in some way united America and bound Americans to each other as other aspects of national life did not—it offered a common thread, and in time a common obsession. Americans who did not know each other could find community and commonality by talking of their mutual sports heroes.

ALMOST OVERNIGHT Graham McNamee became a major cultural figure. In January 1927 he worked the first true national sports hookup, broadcasting the Rose Bowl game. He did every World Series game from 1923 through 1934. He covered the first political conventions broadcast live. On the occasion of Lindbergh's triumphant inaugural flight to Paris, the voice that most Americans heard the news from was that of McNamee. He was very good at what he did. "The father of broadcasting," the distinguished broadcaster Red Barber called him. In the early days of broadcasting, there were no radio booths. So the announcers had to work in an open stadium and do their work in the most primitive of all possible settings. McNamee, Barber noted, "walked into the stadium, sat down . . . and told the nation what it was waiting to hear and had never heard before . . . told them about 10 different sports. I concentrated on two—baseball and football—and I thought I had my hands full. . . . His sign-off was distinctive: 'This is Graham McNamee speaking. Good night, all.' "

Thus was the audience increased, and thus was sports made more important. Americans by means of radio could now monitor its sports heroes as never before. Events in the world of sports seemed to be ever more important and hold the attention of the public that much more. The resulting popularity of sports was amazing, as was the resilience of its appeal throughout the Depression. On the eve of World War II, baseball seemed to be poised at a level of almost unique preeminence. The 1941 season was a historic one: Joe DiMaggio hit in 56 consecutive games and Ted Williams hit .406. Soon both were in the service, and baseball, like other sports, went on essentially a four-year vacation.

If World War I had been the first act of America's emergence as a world power, World War II would be the defining act. If there had been fears in America on the eve of the entry of the United States into the war that a democracy might not be able to stand up to powerful totalitarian military powers, those fears soon proved completely invalid: Rarely had a democratic society's power been so brilliantly mobilized. America rose to true superpower status during the war; its industrial base, secure from enemy attack because of the two oceans, became the arsenal of democracy. When the war was over America stood alone, rich in a world which was poor. The change in the balance of power had taken place with a startling swiftness.

For the war changed the balance of power in the world with a certain finality: In Europe the old powers had been bled white by two wars; America, by contrast, had been brought kicking and screaming to the zenith of its power. No bombs had fallen on America; its losses—roughly 350,000 men on two fronts—were slight in comparison with other nations.

All of these factors had given the nation a startling boost in affluence, household by household, and equally important, a critical increase in personal confidence. Not only had America as a nation played a decisive part in the war, not only had it been, in contrast to most wars, considered a good war, but millions of Americans, whose professional careers might in an earlier part of the century have been proscribed by class, had left their small towns, had learned that they could lead men, and now had a chance to continue their careers through the G.I. Bill. If one of the things which distinguished America from the old world was its concept of social fluidity—the fact that in only one generation ordinary citizens could rise significantly above the level attained by their parents—then nothing made that concept more muscular than the G.I. Bill.

IN THE POSTWAR ERA America had to face the domestic consequences of its own wartime rhetoric. For the war had generated its own powerful propaganda, that of the democracies taking on two totalitarian powers, Germany and Japan, and in the case of Germany a racist, genocidal nation. But there were important domestic consequences to that. If America was the driving force of a new, more democratic world, then it was still a nation divided racially, not just in the South, where feudal laws imposed state-sanctioned legal and political racism, but in the North as well, its major professional sports events still lily white. In the courts a large number of cases trying to end the doctrine of separate but equal were working their way to the Supreme Court. But it would be the world of sports that became the most important postwar laboratory of racial change and where black Americans finally got their first true chance at showing their real talents. That their sports were segregated was singularly unjust, and no one knew this better than the professional baseball players themselves. For they often barnstormed with black players from the Negro League after the season, and they knew exactly how good the black ballplayers were, that only racial prejudice prevented them from playing.

JACKIE ROBINSON, whose terrible responsibility it was to be the first, the man in the test tube, his abilities and conduct to be scrutinized by an entire nation—was nothing less than history's man. He was a superb athlete, strong, quick, and wildly competitive. He had been a four-sport star at UCLA before he played professional baseball, and he could probably have played professionally in three major sports. Before he entered the service in World War II, though professional basketball and football were still quite embryonic in the West, he played with semi-pro teams in both.

He brought with him a rare on-field and off-field intelligence, and exceptional mental discipline and toughness of mind, an ability to restrain himself despite extreme provocation (and control his hair-trigger temper). He resisted, as he promised he would, the temptation to lash back for a long time despite the constant taunts of fans and opposing players. "Mr. Rickey, what do you want?" he had asked the Brooklyn Dodger boss at their fateful first meeting. "Do you want a player with guts enough to fight back?" "I want a player," Rickey had answered memorably, "with guts enough not to fight back." He might rage inside, but he remained true to the challenge offered him by Rickey. Throughout his career, Robinson remained aware that the spotlight was always on him, and that the challenge to excel on field and behave with dignity off it was singular in his case. Few Americans were ever subjected to such relentless scrutiny in so public a manner; it is doubtful if any of his fellow citizens ever endured such relentless pressure with such sustained excellence.

If American society, in the oddly pious-but-shrewd incarnation of Branch Rickey, was looking for the perfect candidate to undergo so withering a test as being the first black to play in the major leagues, then it could not have done better than Jackie Robinson. He was intelligent, purposeful, resourceful, modern; he played at a brilliant level, and he did not back down when taunted racially. He was fast and strong: clothed in his loose-fitting baseball uniform, he did not look particularly powerful, but there is one photo from those days of him alongside Joe Louis, both men stripped to the waist, where Robinson looks every bit as muscled and powerful as the heavyweight champion. Above all, Robinson was nothing if not a man. Everything about him demanded respect. He had played in endless integrated games as a collegian, and he had no illusion, as many blacks less privileged might have, that white athletes were either smarter or had more natural talent than blacks. White people to him were not people you were supposed to shuffle around who had superior abilities; they were just people, people who because of their skin had gotten a better deal than blacks.

It was a great experiment, and it took place in 1947, seven years before *Brown v. Board of Education*. In a way, what Jackie Robinson did, performing in the most public arena in America, was every bit as important as that Supreme Court decision in 1954. His arrival in the big leagues had been the ultimate test of something that most Americans prided themselves on—the fairness of their country, that in this country the playing field was somehow supposed to be fair. In a way it was an experiment which put America itself at a crossroads between two powerful competing national impulses, one impulse reflecting the special darkness of racial prejudice and historic meanness of spirit which had begun with slavery, the other the impulse of idealism and optimism, that a true democracy offered the children of all American citizens a chance to exhibit their full talents and rise to their rightful place. What he was contesting was the worst myths of the past, for in the particular cruelty of the time, America had not merely barred blacks from its professional leagues, it had said it was barring them because they were unworthy. Yes, the rationale went in those days, they could run fast, but they lacked guts and heart, and they would fold in the late innings in big games, and, of course, by the way, they were lazy—everybody knew that.

By midseason the argument was over. Robinson was a great player—clearly on his way to becoming rookie of the year. He had brought life and speed and intensity to an otherwise more passive Dodger team. He was an American samurai, the baseball player as warrior, and the other Dodgers became more like him—they were with his arrival much more a warrior team that fought you all the time than they had ever been in the past, and they would remain that way for the duration of his career. As a player no one was more explosive. Pitchers in particular feared him once he was on the base paths because of his explosive initial burst of speed. Years later, the Yankees pitcher Vic Raschi, talking about how he had lost a 1–0 game in the 1949 World Series by giving up a hit to Gil Hodges, said that it was Robinson, bluffing a dash from third toward home, who had beaten him. "I had just never seen anything like him before, a human being who could go from a standing stop to full speed in one step. He did something to me that almost never happened. He broke my concentration, and I paid more attention to him than to Hodges. He beat me more than Hodges."

IF ROBINSON'S STUNNING SUCCESS against the myths of the past marked the first great breakthrough of the postwar era, then the second one was driven by technological change. It was the coming of network television and it started as a true national phenomenon roughly a decade after the end of the war. It inaugurated nothing less than another golden age in sports. For in truth the world of sports as the postwar era started actually had two golden ages ahead, both of them driven by technological breakthroughs, the first one wrought by the coming of network television which dramatically boosted football as a sport, especially the professional game, and the second some 25 years later with the coming of satellite transmission, which created the world of cable television and aided all sports, most particularly basketball.

It was the power of an instrument—the power of the camera—which now revolutionized American society. Nothing changed the culture and the habits of Americans more than the coming of television. Television had a kind of greenhouse effect on the society around it: What the camera liked grew and prospered beyond anyone's expectations (often growing too quickly and too large for its own good, of course); what the camera did not like just as quickly withered.

In particular, the camera liked professional football. What the camera caught and savored about football, which radio had always missed, was the speed of the sport, and, above all, the violence. For the camera more than anything else loved action. Football—fast, balletic, often brutal, with its bone-crushing hits—was made to order for the camera. Baseball, with its slow, leisurely pace, a sport which had its roots in an agrarian America where the pace of life was slower, had been perfect for radio, where an announcer could paint a gentle portrait and measure his cadence to the casual pace of the game.

Before the coming of television, professional football was, in comparison to baseball, virtually a minor league; it was a very good game, indeed a connoisseur's game, played by immensely talented athletes before passionate, diehard fans, but it had somehow never quite broken out of its rather narrow place in the sports spectrum. Radio revealed neither the talent nor the fury with which it was played. To the degree that ordinary sports fans committed their time to football on fall weekends—it was on Saturday when they could pick up a Notre Dame or Michigan game on the radio, not Sunday.

Sunday became in the new televised age the day which was set aside in the fall for American males. It introduced the pro game to a vast new audience, and the pro game began to enter the consciousness of average sports fans as never before. Very quickly in the mid- to late Fifties, as the country was wired nationally for television, pro football went on a dizzying rise to a point where it began to rival professional baseball as the national sport. In those days not that many people owned sets, and many young American males would agree to meet at a neighborhood bar to watch and eat and drink. The sense of a sport on the rise was obvious—and nowhere was that more obvious than in New York, where the football Giants began to become something new in pro football ranks, media celebrities. Football stars like Frank Gifford, movie-star handsome, were doing commercials (for very little money, mind you), and being welcomed as never before in bars like Toots Shor's, where baseball players, fighters and jockeys had held forth. The game was coming of age.

WITH THE COMING OF network television professional football became a truly national game, with a national constituency. A fan did not have to live in Baltimore to be a Unitas or a Colts fan, or for that matter to live in New York to root for the Giants defense led by middle linebacker Sam Huff. Millions of sports fans who cared nothing about Pittsburgh, had never been to the University of Louisville, and had no intention of ever visiting Baltimore turned on their sets on Sunday to watch the daring exploits of a young quarterback from Pittsburgh who had gone to the University of Louisville and now played for the Baltimore Colts. The camera, it turned out, was quite dazzled by Johnny Unitas, the least likely, it would seem, of American media heroes.

In a way his career marked America in a cultural and economic transition. He grew up under the worst hardships inflicted on blue-collar America in the Depression and post-Depression years, living in a home which received almost no protections from the government, and yet he became one of the early celebrities under the gaze of a new and powerful medium which was going to change the nature of the economy and make part of the society infinitely more glitzy. He knew all too well an America which was tough and poor, and he was largely unmoved by his place in this new America which was more affluent and more celebrity oriented. Unlike Namath (and Ali), who came after him and understood intuitively that in the new sports world created by television, it was always both sport and show, he always thought it was merely sport. His values had been set in that earlier age. Yet Unitas became the first superstar of the new age, the signature player of an old sport amplified by a new and loving medium, the perfect working-class hero for a sport just beginning to leave its working-class roots behind.

To the degree that radio liked football, it loved offensive stars—quarterbacks, running backs and wide receivers. But television was different, it had eyes for the defensive stars as well. Fans loved not only the long passes and the brilliant broken-field runs; they loved the savagery of clean hits. In this new era, living in the media capital of the world, Huff had become the first great national celebrity on defense. CBS did a documentary on him, "The Violent World of Sam Huff," and *Time* magazine put him on the cover. Giants fans cheered more loudly when their defense came on the field than when the offense took over. "Our offensive unit was not highly regarded," Kyle Rote remembered, years later. "When the offensive unit went out on the field, the defense shouted, 'Get in there and hold them.'" Because of that new rivalries developed and flourished: If New York against Baltimore was not necessarily a historic rivalry, then that collision of the Colt offense against the Giant defense, a matchup perhaps without historic roots, was one the knowing fan could readily anticipate.

In 1958, in what was later called the greatest game ever played, Unitas led the Colts to victory in overtime in the championship game against the Giants. He did it with two spectacular long drives, one at the end of regulation, the other in the sudden-death overtime. It was a signature game. Ewbank, not known for his pregame inspirational speeches, really pushed his players before the game. "In 14 years," defensive end Gino Marchetti said about pregame pep talks, "I heard 'em all. 'Win for Mother,' 'Win for Father,' ... 'Don't disappoint all those people watching on television.'" Sometimes, Marchetti said, "they even tried to tell you how to act: 'Don't piss in the air with forty million people watching.' But that day Weeb really put it to us. He went up and down the roster, name by name: 'Donovan, they got rid of you—too fat and slow . . . Ameche, Green Bay didn't want you.' Yeah, he named me, Unitas . . . he didn't miss anybody."

On that December day the Colts, because of Unitas, were the favorites, and they took a 14–3 lead. At one point in the third quarter the Colts had a first down on the Giant three, and a chance to put the game away 21–3. But the Giants held and began to turn it around. They came back to take a 17–14 lead in the fourth quarter. With 1:56 on the clock, it was Unitas time. The Colts got the ball back on their 14. Unitas missed on his first two passes, and then he simply took over. He connected on four passes, three of them to Raymond Berry. When the drive was over, the Colts were comfortably poised for the tying field goal on the Giant 13. That drive and a comparable one in the overtime, when the Colts marched for the winning touchdown, were like works of art. "The man was a genius," Huff said later. "I never saw a quarterback that good on those two drives." The Colts were the winners, but when the game was over, the real winner was the game of football itself.

Professional football ascended in popularity like a comet. In 1960, a second league was founded, and its star quarterback Joe Namath, coveted by both leagues because he had star quality, signed for $400,000. In just a few years more, the leagues merged, and played the defining event of America the Superpower in the Super Century, the Super Bowl.

The rise of the nation in the postwar era to this pinnacle was constantly contentious. Isolationist before the war, it was now a leading international power. On the way the debate over race had become ever more barbed. In the early Fifties there had been a powerful challenge to the existing Jim Crow rules in the South. By the late Sixties, the existing laws had fallen, but the mood of American blacks was changing, and there were constant signs of the powerful alienation just under the surface. The black power movement began to flourish in the late Sixties—its slogan was black is beautiful, and in northern cities, the old religious ties which had been so important to black life in the South had begun to wither. A new movement, that of black Muslims, seemingly threatening to whites—its principal leaders spoke of white people as devils—had taken root among the deeply embittered blacks of the nation's northern cities.

THAT MEANT THAT a young man named Cassius Clay, who rose to fame as a heavyweight boxer, was to become at once the most dazzling, and the most controversial athlete of his era, a symbol of all the powerful societal forces let loose in the Sixties.

He also in some way understood that television had changed the nature of sports, and no one, it would turn out, was a better entertainer; no one knew better how to hype his own fights. He was, he understood, as much actor as he was fighter, and he was exceptionally skilled at casting not just himself, but his opponents to his specifications. He himself, he liked to proclaim, was beautiful. His opponents were not. Sonny Liston, the most threatening of men until Ali completely defanged him, was too ugly, he boasted, to be the champ.

He was the most volatile of superstars, joyous, talented, angry. Sportswriters, at least the younger ones, loved him, but Madison Avenue avoided him like the plague. He was the perfect figure to illuminate the contradictions of America in the late Sixties, as it surged past mere superpower status, and became even more affluent: Yes, the nation was making great progress in ending age-old racist laws, but no, the progress was never fast. Yes, the country was a bulwark against a totalitarian power in Europe, but yes, too, it had become an anti-revolutionary force fighting on the wrong side in a war of independence in Asia. He touched all of our fault lines and it was not surprising that attitudes toward him on the part of sportswriters and sports fans tended to divide along generational lines—a reflection of an America which was fighting a war not so much against the Vietnamese, but against itself, a great power with a fractured soul.

Ali was not going to be like Joe Louis, or for that matter Floyd Patterson, the benign black fighter who knew his place, was grateful for his opportunity, was respectful to all in authority around him, no matter how sleazy they were or how tenuous their hold on a position of authority, and watched carefully what he said and did. Ali represented a new and angrier generation of more alienated blacks: A lot of damage had been done over centuries of slavery and neo-slavery, and a lot of anger had been stored up.

In the end he was a marvel, a figure not only of sports but, like Jackie Robinson, though in a different way, of history itself. The day after he became heavyweight champion, he had announced that he was a Muslim and that his name was Muhammad Ali. A few years later, because of the war in Vietnam, he refused induction into the army, citing his religious principles. So it was that he lost his crown—and the ability to fight—for more than three years.

Politically, time worked on his side: By the Seventies, the Muslims were perceived to be less menacing. Dissident, and alienated, certainly, as blacks who lived in the poorer parts of America's cities might well feel alienated and dissident, but not that threatening. As for the war in Vietnam, that became something of a badge of honor, that Ali had dissented, and acted upon his dissent; he, it turned out, had paid the price for others on a war which was something of a scar on the national conscience.

In time he regained his crown. Older now, several critical years wasted, he returned, his conscience having been served, to fight better than ever, to demonstrate in his fight with Foreman in Zaire and in three wondrous battles with Joe Frazier his true greatness.

HIS WAS A SOBERING CHALLENGE to America's self-image at a volatile and emotional time. He, the most marginally educated young man, barely able to get through high school (he got his high school degree only because the officials at his school realized that he was going to be the school's most famous product, and that it would shame the school rather than Clay if he did not graduate), had turned out to be right about a war about which the most brilliant national security advisers who had gathered around the President—including the Dean of Harvard College, the former head of the Ford Motor Company, and the former head of the Rockefeller Foundation—had turned out to be wrong. That was sobering, a reminder that America at the height of its affluence and power in this century had lost sight of what its true meaning and purpose was. The arrogance of power, the head of the Senate Foreign Relations Committee, Senator William Fulbright, called it. Ali would never have been able to come up with a phrase like that—instead he simply said, "I ain't got no quarrel with the Vietcong." He had acted upon conscience; the advisers, even when they were later burdened by doubt as the war went forward, had not. He had paid the price for his actions when he was young; they, the architects of this disaster, would pay it when they were older. That, for a nation which in its increasing power had become too prideful, too sure of its value and its rectitude, was a sobering lesson. No wonder, then, by the Nineties he had become something of a beloved national figure.

The success of Ali, the quality of his singular struggles, so much of it political, makes a sharp contrast with that of the final surpassing athlete of this era, Michael Jordan. The two had much in common: Both were supremely talented, both were black, both with their looks, their talent, and their style transcended their sports, appealing to millions of Americans who nominally had little interest in either boxing or basketball.

There the comparisons end, and the Americas they performed for differ. They are produced by different Americas: Ali by an America which seemingly closed off all of its benefits to a young talented black man from the South, other than the most brutal, primitive road to fame, boxing; Jordan, born in a time which made him a beneficiary of all the modern civil rights struggles. He was born in 1963, a year before Ali as Clay won the heavyweight title. He went to integrated public schools and was able to go on and star at North Carolina, a school which only recently had been closed to black undergraduates and which at the time of his birth still had not fielded a black basketball player on its team. His parents were comfortably middle class, his father by dint of victories in another hard-won battle—that of blacks in the American military. At Carolina Michael received the kind of great education and exceptional coaching that had been denied black athletes in the past.

Jordan was the most charismatic athlete of his era, and he was the best big-game, fourth-quarter player of a generation. He helped carry a team which often in other ways seemed somewhat ordinary to six world championships. He was the perfect figure for the American communications and entertainment society as the century came to a close, the first great athletic superstar of the wired world, arguably the most famous person on the planet. In his last season as a player, he earned some $78 million, $33 million in salary and $45 million in endorsements. It seemed only proper that as the century ended, he was engaged in serious negotiations to buy a large part of an NBA team.

He was a new world prince, graceful, beautiful, but a warrior or samurai nonetheless, and easily recognizable to the rest of the world as such. He arrived, unlike those before him, such as Robinson and Mays and Aaron, in a nation which had begun finally to realize that it was not a white nation, and as much as any other American he was proof that America, in some way, despite all its ethnic and racial divisions, was moving toward the beginning of a universal culture.

He gave the nation nothing less than a new concept of beauty. Not surprisingly, his comfort zone was singularly high. He was gifted, he worked hard, and was beautiful in a nation which was now willing to accept a more complicated definition of beauty. America, after some 30 years of racial turbulence, was delighted to have a gifted young black man who seemed to be smiling back at it. If he endorsed sneakers, millions of Americans bought them, and in time he sold hamburgers and soft drinks and underwear and sunglasses and batteries and a telephone company.

As the century ended, he was known everywhere in the world, for the sport he played, basketball, was easily understandable, and traveled smoothly across borders in a way that American football and baseball did not. For in the new age of inexpensive satellites, America exported not its autos or its machine tools, but its culture—its music, its sports, and finally, the informality of its lifestyle. And Jordan was the most luminescent figure of the new world, his deeds the easiest to comprehend and admire.

IT HAD BEEN, all in all, an astonishing century for America. No other country had ever changed so much in so short a time—rising to a position as a monopoly superpower, gaining steadily in power, affluence, and innate self-confidence. In this period much of the change, and the interior struggle, could be witnessed in the world of sports. It was not so much a metaphor for the society as a window on it—the tension, the conflicts, and the constant progress had often taken place first (and been witnessed more widely) in the world of sports. That was true, whether it was the rise of black athletes or the greater independence of the athletes themselves as they enjoyed greater personal freedom. Throughout the century, sports had served as a remarkable reflection of the strengths and weaknesses of the nation—its diversity, its hungers, its excesses, its rank commercialism. But above all the fact that the athletes always seemed to get bigger and stronger and faster, and the games themselves better.

Sports Can Distract, but They Don't Heal

From ESPN.com, September 10, 2002

THE QUESTION BEFORE US TODAY IS SPORTS AND TRAGEDY, most particularly Sept. 11. Is there a connection, and how important is it? Does the world of sports heal, and does it make us stronger, and give us precious, badly needed relief from the darker concerns and burdens of our lives, as so many people (most of them connected to the world of sports, and therefore with no small amount of vested interest) keep saying?

I have my doubts . . . strong ones, as a matter of fact. Serious readers of this space will note that I disappeared from it for some 10 months after Sept. 11, largely because I could not find it in me for a long time to want to write about sports. That world seemed to shrink on me overnight. Instead, I wrote about the men of our local firehouse, 12 of whom had perished on that apocalyptic day. So, along with my doubts, I have my prejudices.

I like sports, enjoy the artistry of them enormously. I love to watch great athletes compete against each other in big games or matches, like Sampras beating Agassi in the U.S. Open final. But I think there is an important faultline out there somewhere: The world of sports is the world of sports, and reality is reality.

Sometimes sports mirrors society, sometimes it allows us to understand the larger society a little better. But mostly, it is a world of entertainment, of talented and driven young men and women who do certain things with both skill and passion. I am always amused at playoff time by those obsessive superfans, who cast the players from their home team as the good guys, and the visitors as evil—they hate the opposing players and do not understand that, in most circumstances, the players they root for are closer to the players they hate than they are to their adoring fans, and would almost surely rather go out for dinner with the alleged enemy than they would with the home-team fans.

I am wary, as well, of those people who say after a given World Series or Super Bowl victory that it saved the city, made it whole and healed deep-seated racial grievances. When I hear things like that—and I often do—I usually think, "I'll give it about two weeks before it all unheals." In truth, if making your city whole demands a World Series victory on behalf of athletes who more often than not flee the city the moment the season is over, then your problems are probably harder to solve than you realize.

Nor did I think, during the Vietnam years, that the link between the NFL and the Pentagon (all those jet fighters flying overhead at the Super Bowl) greatly helped the war effort, nor factored into the NVA or the Viet Cong's schedules. I was not much moved by the Army's television recruitment commercials showing teamwork between NFL players, who most demonstrably had no intention of serving in the military.

So back to the question at hand—did sports help bind us in the days, weeks and months after Sept. 11? Did we need to be so bound? The answer to the first question is, I suspect, a little bit, and my answer to the second is, I fear, surprisingly negative. If, in the long run, you need sports to help you through a time of tragedy and to take your mind off a grimmer reality, then you are emotionally in so much trouble in not understanding what is real and what is fantasy that the prospects for your long-term emotional health are probably not very good.

Let me suggest that there are notable exceptions to this, and that many of us, at one time or another, have gotten some kind of lift—albeit usually a brief one—from the performance of a favorite sports team on an unusual roll. I am a New Yorker, and there is no doubt that in all the pain and grief that followed the assault on the World Trade Center, the last-minute run of the Yankees—particularly some of the late-inning rallies in the World Series—was unusually sweet, that for a short period of time, they lifted many people in the city, including a great number (such as my wife, who usually does not care very much). It was an aging Yankee team, trying for one last hurrah, the starting pitching was wearing a bit thin—as were some of the left-handed hitters—but it made one last wonderful run. I suspect the city boosted the team and the team, in turn, boosted the city. It surely made The Stadium a more difficult place to play for some of the visiting teams.

But for all the sportscasters who tried to push the point too hard, that the grief and passion of New York lifted the local athletes, we have these other reminders: the dismal performances of the Giants (just a year removed from a Super Bowl appearance) and, all too soon, the even more dismal performance of a Knicks team that openly cheated its fan base—the sorriest performance by a local basketball team in the 35 years in which I had paid attention.

So, if there is a connection, it is likely to be a thin one. In my own case, I can remember one particular time in my life when a sports team made something of a difference in my overall mood.

It was in September and October 1967. I was in Vietnam on my second tour as a reporter. More than 500,000 U.S. troops were in the country, and I was in a terrible mood. I thought the war was stalemated, which meant we were eventually going to lose because it was their country, and sooner or later we would have to go home—those of us who would be lucky enough to get that chance. More, I hated what I saw about me every day—all the lying from the Saigon press officers—and I hated what it told me about my beloved country back home, which was, for me, becoming harder to love at that moment.

That happened to be, by chance, the year that Carl Yastrzemski played so brilliantly in September to lead the Red Sox to the pennant.

So I would go every morning (there was, as I recall, a 12-hour time difference) to the AP office in downtown Saigon where the baseball news and box scores would come in, clicking slowly over the old-fashioned teletype. And I would watch for Yaz, and he never seemed to disappoint—3-for-5, one home run, three RBIs. And of course, a great catch.

I was joined there every day by Tom Durant, a Boston native who was over there working as a doctor. It was the beginning of a lifelong friendship with a man who was as close to being a contemporary saint as any man I've ever known. He devoted his entire career to bringing desperately needed medical care to people in Third World countries. Doc Durant died last year, and I, like thousands of others, mourned him; we were, it seemed, bonded by Vietnam, the 1967 baseball season and Yaz's ability, and thus able to feel a little better about our country. When we saw each other, even in the 1990s, we thought about Yaz in 1967. But moments like this are rare—a brief bit of sunshine in an otherwise difficult setting. If it's a fix, it's a momentary one at best.

That's what I think is at stake here. The parallel between what sports does for the country now and what it did during World War II is, I think, the wrong one. The America of 1941–45 was more of a Calvinist nation, with far less in the way of entertainment. Baseball—poorly played as it was, with aging veterans and lots of minor-leaguers—was a small bit of normalcy in a nation where almost everyone's life had been profoundly changed by the war. People's lives were much harder, and almost the entire nation was making a national effort which demanded considerable sacrifice. There was radio, but no television, and a family going off together to a movie was a rare treat. So it was completely different from the America that exists today. In those days, we badly needed every respite we could get from the reality of the war, especially in the first year when the news was systematically bad. We needed some limited degree of diversion.

But today it's completely different. We live in an entertainment society. There is little around us but diversion—even people trying to broadcast the news have to make it ever quicker, simpler and more entertaining in order to compete with rival channels. Many people have television sets with 200 channels. Video games and computer games abound. The sports glut remains exactly that—a glut. We watch what has become a never-ending season—football in the summer, baseball in November, basketball, it sometimes seems, throughout the year.

We lead lives surrounded by diversions. The manufacturers of our fantasies—in Hollywood with movies and television, and of course in the world of sports—are more powerful and influential than ever. Keeping the nation tuned to serious concerns is infinitely harder than it was 60 years ago. Diversion comes more readily.

After Sept. 11, there was a relatively short span of time when people cared about foreign news and were momentarily weaned away from their more parochial concerns. But now it's largely back to normal. There might be, in the back of the minds of millions of people, a certain uneasiness a year after Sept. 11, because we know that America is no longer invulnerable, and that we can be attacked.

But in truth, the events themselves touched a very small percentage of the population. Unlike World War II, we operate with an elite, highly professional military that comes from very few homes. Almost no one else has been asked to sacrifice—there is no rationing, and the contemporary U.S. economy is so different from the one 60 years ago that the president's main request to the American people was to ask us to travel more, presumably because the airline industry was so shaky.

As for the families who were actually touched by this tragedy, I would not presume to speak for them—they are eloquent enough in their own behalf. But the idea that their lives are in any way better because of what a given sports team did in the following months is barely worth mentioning.

In truth, our lives are what we make of them. We work hard and, at the end of the day, in a world that is often mundane, the ability to watch one or two sports games a week is a kind of blessing, a relief from what is often a difficult routine. But if we want any kind of real emotional balance, we must get it from our loved ones, family, friends, co-workers.

I am made uneasy by those who seem to need sports too much, these crazed superfans who bring such obsessive behavior to games where complete strangers compete. There is an equation at work here: The more obsessive they are as fans, the emptier I suspect their real lives are.

And so let me descend in advance from all the sportscasters and all the blathering that's going to go on in the next few days about the importance of sports after Sept. 11. Many of these sportscasters will push the importance and restorative qualities of sports. Let me suggest that we will do well in the current and difficult crisis not because the 49ers, Cowboys or Patriots do well, but rather if as a nation we are strong, wise and patient. That's all it really takes.

BASEBALL

I am also moved again by a sense of the timelessness of baseball. More than any sport, it summons the past. In football, photos from another era look dated, the helmets too dinky, the players too small; in basketball, the players look too white. But in baseball it is as if there is a linear path. It is where, in our society, yesterday and today collide: the boy is thinking of the power of the young Kevin Maas, the father, looking at Maas, is seeing the same compact stroke and thinking of Roger Maris. The son sees the awesome power of Doc Gooden and thinks there has never been a power pitcher like him; the father sees Gooden and thinks of Bob Gibson, and the grandfather sees the same players and thinks of Bob Feller.

INTRODUCTION TO *BASEBALL*:
THE PERFECT GAME

BASEBALL AND THE NATIONAL MYTHOLOGY

From *Harper's Magazine*, September 1970

WE ARE A NATION GIVEN TO OUR MYTHS. SHORT ON HISTORY, short on national ties, still seeking an American culture, hardly rooted to village or church or an American past, we find comfort, sustenance, and indeed continuity in our myths. George Washington, honorable, steadfast in hardship, rallying his people; Abraham Lincoln, for men who like their myths a little darker in spirit and taste; handsome young Jack Kennedy, married to pretty young Jackie, a myth intensified by his murder in Dallas, celebrating him in death as never in life, the myth freed of the irritants of foot-dragging committee chairmen, anonymous bureaucrats in the State Department, primitive generals, and pesky newspapermen. So the myth lives or lived, shattered a little by the appearance of the Rich Short Greek. ("Did you hear the weather report?" my friend Dick Tuck said over the phone that day. "It's raining in Camelot.")

Given that Washington is not exactly the ideal place for Camelot, and that our politics are more given to venality, drudgery, boredom, and frustration than to beautiful people and soaring ideas, it is not surprising that we turn to sports for our myths. There we search beyond ourselves and our boredom and frustration for something that is different, more heroic, for other men never bothered by bills, who never argue with their wives, whose house painters show up on time (sober), who, facing adversity, always triumph. Baseball is, I suspect, our most mythological of sports; it has the longest history, it is by its own proclamation our national pastime, and it harbors, I think, our greatest mythological figures. Babe Ruth, so American that Japanese trying to infiltrate our lines summoned his name. Ruthian, gargantuan in feat and taste, lover of little cripples and orphans, sidelined—boys will be boys—for eating too many hot dogs (not for social disease). Lou Gehrig, gamely playing day after day, carrying finally a dread disease, modest and humble to the end. He and Gary Cooper teaching each other how to be laconic; one could see even now Gehrig as the sheriff of a bad Western town, cleaning it up, with a minimum of talk (Gehrig to Cooper: "Gary, you're a good fella, but you talk too much"); his records obscured only by Ruth's. Bob Feller, straight off the farm with farmboy virtues and a blazing fastball, all farmboys are pure and have blazing fastballs; Joe DiMaggio, the melting-pot candidate, the Fisherman's Wharf boy, son of poor but simple stock, only in America could he rise to such fame, always a gentleman, DiMaggio has class, entering the ultimate mythological marriage (only Jack Kennedy and Grace Kelly might have done better), nothing there about Joe being, well, a little surly from time to time and liking, well, sycophants around him; Joe never talked, because it was, well, beneath him, not because he had nothing to say. And of course, Mickey Mantle (most mythology is manufactured in New York about *American* virtues; thus the mythologists are from New York, but the mythologized are preferably from Commerce, Oklahoma, or Fisherman's Wharf), game Mickey, pure country boy (not so country that he didn't understand it and later exploit it, opening, upon his retirement, Mickey Mantle's Country Cooking Restaurants), great power in an injury-ridden body; no telling how great he might have been, the mythologist likes to dream, to let the imagination sweep, playing when mortals like you and me would be staying home from the office, gobbling aspirin, Mickey bandaged from head to foot, blood showing on the uniform, game to the end.

Now we have a new candidate for enshrinement, Mr. G. Thomas Seaver of Fresno, California, and the New York Metropolitans, Mister

Clean and Wholesome. Not only is he young and virtuous, but modern and "concerned," liking Negroes and opposing the war (though backing down somewhat on the antiwar stand, when there was a brief flap last fall). He is also the possessor of sound judgment, a fine fastball, and a lovely, clean wife, so wholesome and attractive that if *Playboy* ever decides to let a fully clothed girl pose in the center section I suspect Nancy Seaver will be the first. Both good young Americans who took with their good American agent to hucktering themselves for a postseason lecture tour, for those situations which call for the ideal young Mr. and Mrs. America situation; they are close to having a television show of their own where they will interview other clean young marrieds, particularly if Tom can keep the fastball down.

Tom comes to us now in the latest example of mythology, a book called *The Perfect Game,* in collaboration with Dick Schaap, published by Dutton. It is a terrible book, and Schaap in particular ought to do penance. Before he went into the publishing business and became an industry he was an intelligent writer who wrote a good and quite honest book with Jerry Kramer called *Instant Replay.* With Seaver he has kept the form and lost the substance. The point of the Kramer book was that perhaps someone who was not a national sports celebrity might be an intelligent, sensitive person and might bring insight to the inner world of sport. Having succeeded admirably with Kramer, Schaap broke his own rules, writing a predictably cheap book with Joe Namath, did an even cheaper television show with Namath (an interview show with lots of pretty young girls in very short skirts running around, the point being, I guess, to remind us that Joe has, well, a life-style). Now with Seaver, Schaap has lent his name to another cheap product, this one classically mythological, the selling of the perfect couple. I counted seventy-six references to Nancy. Nancy meets Donn Clendenon, Nancy asks for Sandy Koufax's autograph, Nancy fixes breakfast ("I went into the kitchen for breakfast and as I ate my scrambled eggs, bacon, and applesauce, I thought

about the rest of the Orioles, the hitters following Buford in the lineup. I didn't talk much with Nancy. I knew she'd be cheering for me to get them out, and knew she didn't particularly care how . . .").
There was no tension on the Mets, no player conflicts, and particularly no racial dissension, and those of you who remember Gil Hodges walking out to left field to pull Cleon Jones out of a game are mistaken, as are those of you who thought there had been a fight between Don Cardwell and Ron Swoboda, when Cardwell mocked the femininity of wearing beads (Gil was against the beads too, if my memory serves me properly. Not good for baseball's image).

IMAGE IS SOMETHING that baseball is particularly sensitive about these days because there is more than reason to suspect that its hold as a national pastime has slipped. Its largest crowds during most of the season these days are huckstered crowds, drawn by promotions. Like all American boys of my age I like baseball and played it, and I retain a love-hate relationship with it, willing even to bear with, Holy Cow! Phil Rizzuto as he broadcasts Yankee games (". . . Just like a ball player, he booted that one. . . . They have their good days and bad days. . . . After all they are human. . . . What a job Ralph Houk has done with this Yankee club. . . . This year and every year. If you can't play for Ralph Houk you can't play for anyone. . . . Michael's second error of the game. Those are the kind you boot. . . . They look too easy. You nonchalant them and boot them. But then you make a great play . . .").

It is a sport with its own rhythms and graces, its skills are more often than not highly specialized; what makes a great natural athlete does not necessarily make a baseball player. By and large it is the American sport that a foreigner is least likely to take to. You have to grow up playing it, you have to accept the lore of the bubble-gum card, and believe that if the answer to the Mays-Snider-Mantle question is found then the universe will be a simpler and more ordered place. It is in trouble these days for a variety of reasons, ball parks in racially decaying areas, the difficulty of television, but most of all I think because it has not kept up with the velocity of American life, the jet age, instant gratification, instant action, the way other sports have. Football televises particularly well (I once lectured in Miami the day the Jets played the Colts in the Super Bowl, and flew back to New York because I couldn't watch the action as well with my naked eye). Similarly professional basketball has become a superb sport, now nationally televised, attracting, I suspect, the most brilliant athletes in the nation, and putting them to the most severe physical test. Baseball seems to suffer sharply by contrast with both; there is nothing more striking than watching an NBA game at the tail end of the season, and then during the time out switching over to baseball, the contrast in velocity and quality of action is extraordinary: basketball, three scores, one brilliant defensive block, one steal; baseball, three chaws of tobacco, one genital scratch by the pitcher, one reminder by the announcer that the game isn't over yet. In addition, I think the coming of the Negro athlete into American sports has made a marked difference for football and basketball because these are sports which are designed above all for *athletes*, whereas the coming of Negroes to baseball has simply shown that a very high percentage of them can play very well. That is to say: Willie Mays is a superb baseball player, and a rare superb athlete in baseball, perhaps the best single athlete in baseball of the last fifteen years. In a given game, when he plays well he may make one spectacular catch and swing the bat well once. You get perhaps eight seconds of watching a great athlete perform. Compare this with watching Gus Johnson of Baltimore in an average game, or, better still, Johnson against Dave DeBusschere for a good forty minutes. Superb athletes going up against other brilliant athletes, each move unpredictable, one is always amazed and surprised. If you have seen someone like Johnson or Bill Russell or some of the professional football players play and you still go to a baseball game, then I think you are making what is essentially a journey into nostalgia, and I think this is why baseball owners have to work so hard to get kids into the parks these days.

Baseball is, I think, the sport in which illusion and reality are furthest apart. Its dependence upon statistics proves its need for mythology; the performance is not fulfilling enough; it must be shown in quantified heroics, records to be set and broken, new myths and heroes to replace the old. (In this, I think, it is sharply different from pro football and pro basketball, where statistics are kept but are quite secondary to performance; most hep basketball fans know the Chamberlain Syndrome—that it is extremely difficult to show the statistical value of a player and his effect upon the team.) The height of the mound is to be tampered with if the records slip and there aren't enough .300 hitters around. A team with two .300 hitters is a team with heroes, but what myths can spring up about a .275 hitter? This, I think, was the dilemma for Roger Maris in 1961 and his remarkable unpopularity. He was breaking the record of one great mythological figure, the cripple-loving Babe, which was bad enough, but what was worse, he was doing it when the fans, led by the New York sportswriters and media, had been carefully indoctrinated to think that if the record fell it should go to Mantle, who if not orphan-loving was at least game-but-injury-prone, whereas Maris was still regarded as a Kansas City exile, openly sullen, lacking the requisite boyish grin. When Maris, alas, broke the record with sixty-one home runs and an asterisk, it was a dilemma which neither the fans nor Maris could resolve until finally and mercifully he left New York for St. Louis and the two final happy years of his career where the fans would cheer him for bunting for singles.

NOW JAMES ALLEN BOUTON, of World Publishing, New York City, Cleveland, Seattle, Vancouver, Houston (earned run average 5.99, as this is written) has done it. He has written the best sports book* in

---

* *Ball Four: My Life and Hard Times Throwing the Knuckleball in the Big Leagues.*

years, a book deep in the American vein, so deep in fact that it is by no means a sports book.

It is a fine and funny book, done in collaboration with Leonard Shecter, written with rare intelligence, wit, joy, and warmth; and a comparable insider's book about, say, the Congress of the United States, the Ford Motor Company, or the Joint Chiefs of Staff would be equally welcome. What is particularly pleasant about the Bouton book is that it is written from the heartland of mythology. What is important about the book, and about the critics of Bouton (most sportswriters and announcers), the anti-mythologists and the mythologists, is that they are in essential agreement about a basic point: baseball is America, the great American game, a reflection of what we are and who we are. If you look up and find baseball virtuous you are apt to find the country virtuous as well. Bouton's point is that yes, indeed, it is America, and more often than not run by selfish, stupid owners, men who deal with their ballplayers in a somewhat sophisticated form of slavery, that despite the reputation of melting pot, baseball dugouts reek of the same racial and social tensions and divisions that scar the rest of the country, that the underlying social common denominator is fairly crude and reminiscent of nothing so much as one's high-school locker room. It is now part of the mythology that baseball can do what the society as a whole did not do, which was to bring black and white together; white boy meets black boy, doesn't like him; black boy doubles in white boy with two out in the bottom ninth; lasting friendship forged. It is now clear, reading Bouton and others, such as William F. Russell and Jack Olsen, both of *Sports Illustrated*, that white and black getting along is the exception, that which plagues us nationally plagues us in the dugout and locker room, that if a team is winning, racial tension ebbs, that if it is losing, the mistakes then become racial. Reading Bouton, the baseball players become what they are, not larger than life, but perhaps, if anything, a little smaller. One is not tempted to say: "Son, I'd like you to grow up to be like Joe Pepitone."

Significantly, Commissioner Bowie Kuhn, who censured Bouton for having written the book, is now compromised as the nation's top Gillette razor-blade salesman, having allowed Gillette to take over the polling for the all-star game, then lending his and baseball's names to Gillette's promotion ("Pick up an official all-star ballot where Gillette products are sold or at any major- or minor-league ball park"). Good for you, Bowie Kuhn, as fine a decision as the one you made earlier in the year, suspending Denny McLain for *half* a season, but then there are few white super-stars left in the game and it wouldn't do to keep a thirty-game white winner out of the September pennant race.

IT IS NOT SURPRISING that Bouton's book has incurred the greatest wrath for what he has written about Mantle (essentially that though Mantle could occasionally be joyous, he could also be rude and sullen, that he was, to use the vernacular, a great beaver-watcher and perhaps he would have endured less pain if he had gotten more sleep at night. The kid from Commerce, heh heh, liked the big evil city). The cry against Bouton on this point is intense. To attack Mickey after all he did for the team, for the league, for baseball, for the country, say it ain't so, Jim. (Typically, Mr. Pepitone: "I've seen Mickey break down and cry because he thought he wasn't doing enough for the team. He gives eight hundred per cent. He had an image and I don't think Jim should have torn it down like that. It wasn't necessary to say all those things. The kids will read all that about the guy they looked up to. What will they think? I just don't think it was necessary.")

Thus the myths. The outcry of course is not so much from the other ballplayers, but from the sportswriters and house announcers. They are, after all, the creators of the myths; heroes should be found with darker sides washed out, lighter sides filled in (Yogi Berra was to my sportswriting friends a crude and dull man, as apt as not to yell something foul from the Yankee bus at teen-age girls; but in print he was the cuddly Yogi, full of quips, one awaited the Bill Adler book, *The Wit and Wisdom of Yogi Berra*). The Bouton book naturally enraged sportswriters, personified in New York by Dick Young, the *Daily News* guardian of morals and behavior. Young has waged a one-man campaign against Bouton (in a recent column he had an exclusive interview with an unnamed Chicago bellboy who put Bouton down for failing to tip). To Young, Bouton and Shecter are "social lepers," and indeed he sounds astonishingly Spiroistic: "People like this, embittered people, sit down in their time of deepest rejection and write. They write, oh hell everybody stinks, everybody but me, and it makes them feel much better." Again as the book is deeply in the American vein, so is the reaction against it. The sportswriters are not judging the accuracy of the book, but Bouton's right to tell (that is, your right to read), which is, again, as American as apple pie or the White House press corps. A reporter covers an institution, becomes associated with it, protective of it, and, most important, the arbiter of what is right to tell. He knows what's good for you to hear, what should remain at the press-club bar. When someone goes beyond that, stakes out a new dimension of what is proper and significant, then it is not the ballplayers who yell the most, nor in Washington the public-information officers, but indeed the sportswriters or the Washington bureau chiefs, because having played the game, having been tamed, when someone outflanks them, they must of necessity attack his intentions, his accuracy. Thus Bouton has become a social leper to many sportswriters and thus Sy Hersh, when he broke the My Lai story, became a "peddler" to some of Washington's most famous journalists.

THE EDUCATION OF REGGIE SMITH

From *Playboy*, October 1984

HE CAME DOWN THE CLUBHOUSE RAMP AT KORAKUEN STA-
dium, limping slightly, his knee already bothering him, though the
season was still young. Once of the Boston Red Sox, then the St.
Louis Cardinals, the Los Angeles Dodgers and finally the San Francisco Giants, a veteran of seven all-star games and four World Series,
now the highest-paid baseball player in the history of Japanese baseball, Reggie Smith managed to look more than a little out of place.
A burly, powerful man in any setting, he seemed immense here
alongside his Japanese teammates, as if he were not just a bigger
ballplayer but of an entirely different species.

The prevailing hair style of his teammates, befitting the most
somber and most establishment baseball team in Japan, was a Marine Corps crewcut worthy of the early Pete Rose or the middle
Haldeman. Smith's was early Afro (circa 1967), though thinning at
the top. He wore a mustache, which was not unusual for a
ballplayer on most American teams, but this was the first mustache
ever sprouted by a member of the Yomiuri Giants. When Smith
was about to sign with Yomiuri, the mustache became the subject
of a great deal of discussion in the Japanese press. His contract, after all, was the largest ever signed in Japan by any player, American
or Japanese (between $800,000 and $1,000,000); Sadaharu Oh, the
great home-run hitter, had made only $400,000 and only at the tail
end of his career, and that had been the previous top salary. But the

Giants had never permitted facial hair in the past. In a country like this and on a team like this, which was the pride of Japanese baseball, rules were important; minor rules were the same as major rules; there was no difference. Otherwise, all the discipline of a team might unravel and the Yomiuri tradition would be despoiled; and, worse, all Japan might soon follow. But Smith had made it clear that the mustache stayed; it was a part of his personal statement as a man, and that was important. (Besides, during the 1978 World Series, when his old friend and nemesis Tom Seaver was announcing the games for ABC, he said on the air one day that he'd been trying to figure out why Reggie Smith seemed less intimidating in this series and had finally decided it was because he had shaved off his mustache. That act alone, Seaver said, had made him seem more benign. Since the last thing Smith wanted was to lose any element of intimidation, he had immediately gone back to the mustache.) He had let the Yomiuri executives know this: Facial hair was nonnegotiable.

The Giants had wanted him badly. They had not made the Japanese World Series in the previous year, and even more than the old New York Yankees, they were supposed to win. In the truest sense, they were Japan's team. Indeed, partisans of the other teams in Japanese baseball sometimes thought that the entire sport existed so that their teams could lose to the Giants. Once, in fact, when the Hiroshima Carp had won the Japanese championship, they were cautioned the following spring by their owner not to try quite so hard; the owner, it turned out, was a Giants fan at heart. So in the miraculous way that the Japanese do business, the subject of hair had come up but had also never come up, and Smith had been able to keep both the money and the hair.

Reggie Smith was 38 now; his son, Reggie, Jr., was 15, almost as big as his father was when he broke into the minor leagues. The father was in the twilight of a career, playing it out in Japan, where he was better paid and a good deal lonelier than if he had stayed at home.

He came out of the park and the Japanese fans, among the most intense in the world, began to follow him. A few young fans wanted autographs and he patiently signed them and then, suddenly, a young man crossed a certain barrier as the Japanese fans sometimes do, for foreigners are still regarded, if not as exotic, certainly as oddities, and he touched Smith as if he were something different and strange. It was not a pleasant moment and the player resented it, for the fans do not do this with their own players—they are cautious and respectful with them and do not take such liberties lightly. Smith very firmly removed the hand of the young Japanese. "I am not your damn freak," he said, giving vent to a feeling that many Americans, especially black Americans, have had about being in a country where foreigners are considered strange.

Smith was not in a good mood. His knee was hurting and he could not run full out. In addition, he was completely frustrated by his failure to see any fast balls. On this day, against the Hanshin Tigers, he had not seen a single one, and he had barely seen anything in the strike zone. Desperate to show these fans what he was capable of, he had swung hard anyway, raising two immense pop-ups and grounding out twice. He had also heard the Tigers' manager yell to his pitcher to walk Smith-*san* and to give him nothing to hit.

"I'm a fish out of water here," Smith told a friend. "They pay me all this money to do a certain thing and it's supposed to be something they love, and then they won't let me do it. I just don't know if I belong here."

He was facing this season with increasing melancholia. For although he had known that Japan would be different, he had not known, like many a *gaijin* (or foreigner) before him, that it would be *this* different, nor had he known that he might never again see a real fast ball.

The confrontation of baseball was what Smith missed most, a power hitter against a power pitcher. For him, that was the real excitement of the game, a challenge of the most personal kind. But he had come to believe that the Japanese game, like the society itself, was designed to avoid challenge and confrontation. If there were a way of avoiding a confrontation, the Japanese would find it. In his case, it meant throwing him junk balls out of the strike zone. Dinky shit, he called it. If he walked, so be it. No one threw him fast balls; no one threw him anything out over the plate. They walked him consistently. In the first weeks of the season, he walked three times with the bases loaded, twice on four straight pitches. All of that took a great deal of pleasure out of his work, for Smith, a proud, outspoken player, found that he could not do what he was supposed to do. It was as if they were paying him a great deal of money but in the process stealing something even more precious from him.

Often, now, he came to daydream about the past and, of all things, about confrontations with Nolan Ryan, Steve Carlton and Seaver, power pitchers all, men whom other hitters often feared to face and men who had given Smith as good as he had given them. He even recalled now a game in which Ryan, by then with Houston, had disposed of him with three pitches, each seeming to come in a little faster and each rising a little higher in the strike zone. The Dead Red, players called it, meaning pure heat. The third pitch had been blindingly fast and Smith knew he had been beaten by a master. He had screamed in a kind of instinctive primal anguish, then had tipped his cap to Ryan, who had tipped his cap in turn. The Houston bench had seemed surprised, not understanding this was a personal thing, a war within a war, and that on this occasion Ryan had won.

Batting against Carlton was equally challenging; he was so excellent and complete a player that he was known simply as Lefty, needing neither first name nor last. Carlton was simply the best pitcher in baseball right now, Smith believed, a man of supreme physical gifts and, perhaps more important, awesome mental ones. Lefty had an almost perfect harmony of mental and physical strength, Smith thought. His concentration was complete. That gave him a special spiritual toughness that was rare in any aspect of life, including baseball. Lefty, Smith believed, liked to control a weaker person and create a certain doubt in the hitter. The hitter came to bat knowing how strong Lefty was, and how smart, and knowing, too, that, unlike the hitter, Lefty knew exactly where the pitch would be. In most cases, that made for a mismatch, but Smith enjoyed the combat. He knew that when he beat Carlton, he had beaten the best.

But Lefty was back in Philly and Ryan was in Houston, both of them caught up in their own competition for the all-time strike-out record. And Reggie Smith was in Tokyo, looking vainly for a fast ball.

EARLIER IN THE SEASON, an opposing pitcher had mistakenly come into the strike zone with a nice fat pitch and Smith had hit a monstrous home run, and at the end of the inning, the Japanese pitcher, returning to the dugout virtually in tears, had to be consoled by his manager. It was very clear that the Japanese pitchers were under orders that this highly paid American should not demonstrate his power (and, thus, figuratively, American superiority) against them. So on this day, though it had been a big game— the hated Hanshin Tigers against the Giants, the huge stadium filled hours before the game—Smith's frustration did not abate. He simply could not find a pitcher to challenge him, could not get a pitch to hit.

"Small baseball," he said, "they play small baseball."

He did not say this disparagingly but as a statement of fact. He was, in truth, on his best behavior here, accommodating to the

Japanese press, careful and sensitive with his teammates, ready to give tips on hitting but careful, given the importance of the hierarchy in Japanese society, not to intrude on the territory of the hitting coaches, who were more numerous, more influential and more meddlesome here than in the United States. Jim Lefebvre, the former Dodger, had told mutual friends that Smith, who had a reputation for being at the very least blunt and outspoken (and, to some critics, a clubhouse lawyer), would not last four months here.

He was trying to be a good ambassador, a good baseball player and a good teammate, but it was getting harder all the time. In his mind, he was cooperating, trying to do his best; but the entire nature of the Japanese game, of small baseball, was stacked against him.

By small baseball, Smith meant a precise definition of the game. Small baseball was a game tailored to the needs, both physical and cultural, of the Japanese. Because the Japanese, by and large, did not have powerful throwing arms, they made the relays better than Americans, and they were very good at hitting the cutoff man. Because the society was oriented toward the group instead of toward the individual and because hierarchy prevailed, the manager and his strategy were far more important. There was much more playing for one run and, starting in the first inning, the infield always seemed to be drawn in, trying to cut off a run.

All baseball leagues had different styles, Smith believed. The American League, in his early years, was a slow, almost stagnant league, modeled on the great Yankee teams of the Fifties. Its stars were largely power hitters, they were white and their teammates waited upon their mighty swings. They did not, in his opinion, play a hard-edged game of modern baseball in which speed and power were combined. The prototypical American League star during the era when Smith broke in was Harmon Killebrew, a kind, gentle player who generated offense only through his awesome swing. By contrast, the National League was the blacker league. Its tempo reflected speed combined with power and, Smith believed, with a certain barely disguised black rage.

The typical National League player was Frank Robinson, who was intense about *everything*. Robinson helped transform the American League, Smith believed, when he was traded to the Orioles. He changed the Orioles, and as he changed them, the entire league began to change. There was something about Robinson—the ferocity with which he played the game and his attitude about winning—that was almost frightening. His was an unrelenting presence, and teammates and opponents alike feared to cross him. Once, when Smith was a young player with the Red Sox, he had watched Robinson run out a ground ball and, noticing the man's odd, almost spindly legs, had made a smart remark, "Pump those wheels." It was the way that black players often teased one another in those days. They were brothers, after all. But Robinson, enraged by the remark, had gone past the Boston bench on his way back to the dugout and had pointed a finger at Smith and said, *"You don't know me that goddamn well."* Later, after the game, Robinson came and told him that next time the teams played, maybe they could go to dinner. But there was no doubt of the warning that had been issued or of the man's transcending hardness.

To Smith, the National League was about power, complete power, the power to hit for distance and to run with speed. It was also about territory, each man's success—indeed, his edge—came at the expense of someone else, and it seemed to Smith that those edges, no matter how small, were more reluctantly conceded in the National than in the American League. It was a game far more exciting than the American League version, constantly pitting power against power.

The Japanese game, by contrast, seemed to avoid power, to avoid the confrontation between hitter and pitcher. Much of the game, Smith believed, was not so much assertive strategy and tactics as it was an attempt to avoid making mistakes or taking responsibility. It was a cautious game and it probably suited their physical and psychic needs, but it did not suit him. It was therefore small.

SOMETIMES, NOW, Smith wondered whether or not he had made the right decision in signing. Two years earlier, when he was a free agent, the Yankees had made a handsome offer, something well over $1,000,000 for three years. Although that would only have made him one of about five first basemen and seven designated hitters on the team, he had been tempted by the deal. There was, after all, enough doubt about his physical condition, particularly about his arm, to limit his bargaining power. But there was something about the negotiations, a certain imperiousness to the Yankee bargaining style, that put him off—that, plus George Steinbrenner's reputation for paying athletes well and then believing he was entitled to play with them.

In that sense, Smith thought, the modern owner was not unlike the modern fan; there was more psychic tension than ever before between him and the star player. The relationship was not as it had been in his early days on the Red Sox, a shared relationship between star and owner, but, rather, a new, instant relationship in which the owner shared the spotlight in the moment of signing and felt freer than ever to attack the star. If the star failed, it was not the owner's fault, for he could show how much he had paid; he remained a good owner who had hired a bad player.

In the end, Smith signed with the San Francisco Giants for the 1982 season and enjoyed a surprisingly good year, with 18 home runs and 56 R.B.I.s in some 350 at bats. After the season, he began negotiating with the Giants with marginal success, but they had their eyes on Steve Garvey. And when it became clear that the American Giants would pay Garvey more than three times as much as Smith, he began to take the Japanese Giants more seriously.

In the beginning, he was amused by the cultural differences when the Yomiuri representatives came to him and asked if he wanted to sign with them. He responded in the good American tradition by asking how much they were willing to pay. They, in turn, said, "Tell us whether or not you'll sign and then we'll tell you how much we'll pay." He responded that he wanted a close idea of their offer before he committed himself. They replied that they could not make him such an offer, because if they made it and he turned it down, they would lose face. "Man, I'm not ready for Japan yet," he told them. Then they began to negotiate in earnest.

Soon one of the Giants' negotiators told him they wanted him to have a very good year, to hit perhaps .270 with 20 home runs, but not to have a better year than their own stars, particularly Tatsunori Hara, their talented young third baseman, who had hit 33 home runs the previous season. "That's really weird," Smith had said. He enjoyed the negotiations, however. They went on for some three months and, as they got more and more serious, Smith noticed a certain cultural progression, most apparent in the ascending level of sophistication of the clothes worn by emissaries of the Giants. The sports clothes quickly gave way to suits. Then the suits got progressively darker, the shirts whiter and crisper, the ties more subdued. At the higher levels, the men began to wear leather watch straps. When he finally got to meet Toru Shoriki, the owner of the team, Smith was waiting in a lounge having a drink; suddenly, a Giants executive materialized out of nowhere and, without even asking, snatched the drink away. "You should not be drinking when Shoriki-san comes in," he said. Just then, Shoriki himself walked in, an elegant man in a beautiful, understated black suit and the most subtle white shirt Smith had ever seen. "That's the boss," he decided.

Now he was sitting around having a postgame drink with a man named Robert Whiting. Whiting, a young American who had gone to college in Japan, stayed around after graduation and, because, of his special interest in both Japanese culture and American baseball, ended up writing a book about Japanese baseball called *The Chrysan-themum and the Bat*, one of the best of all books on modern Japan. In it, Whiting details the hard times Japanese baseball has often inflicted upon its American participants, the *gaijins*, and the equally hard time the *gaijins* have inflicted on the Japanese—times so hard that some Americans have in recent years come to be known as Pepitones (a derogatory name in honor of the former Yankee first baseman Joe Pepitone, who took so much money, caused so many problems and played so few games that he became the dubious standard against which other ballplayers were measured). One of the high points of the Whiting book is a description of the 1965 season, in which Daryl Spencer, once a San Francisco Giant, was making a run for the Japanese Pacific League home-run title and virtually every opposing pitcher in the league began to walk him on four pitches. All of this, Whiting was now telling Smith, was a reflection of the schizophrenic Japanese relationship with the Western world. They wanted to be like the West—were, in fact, the world's foremost imitators of Western customs—and they wanted just as badly to be left completely alone, unblemished by foreign influence. So, Whiting said, they know they need the *gaijins* and want them, on occasion, to do well, but they do not want them to do *too* well. Of course, the *gaijins* are also very handy in case a team begins to do poorly. They can always be blamed. That, he noted, might become Smith's role if things did not go well this year.

Indeed, the real belief of the people who run Japanese baseball is that as long as there are *gaijin* players, Japanese baseball cannot really be considered first class. The current commissioner has asked all clubs to be rid of their Americans in five years.

"Last year," said Whiting, "Tony Solaita, the former Yankee and Toronto Blue Jay, had a great year. Everything went right. Led the league in home runs and R.B.I.s. Led the league in game-winning hits. In the second half of the season, he got 14 of his 17 game-winning hits." Whiting paused. "He finished a distant third in the

M.V. P. voting. His manager told all the writers to vote for one of the other guys. So I told Solaita what happened and he was really pissed and he called the manager, who said, 'I'm sorry; I didn't know you wanted it. Besides, you weren't here.' Solaita had a hard year. He was in the race for the home-run title, and the Japanese are still sensitive about *that* title, because it means power, and they're more touchy about power than about average. So in the last part of the season, the opposing pitchers started walking him all the time. He got desperate and asked his manager to argue with the umpires, and the manager did. Then he asked if Solaita wanted him to walk the other home-run hitter. Solaita said, 'No, it's unprofessional.' But in the last appearance of the last game, he took himself out."

Smith listened carefully as Whiting spoke. He had been warned.

A DAY LATER, Smith was frustrated even further. Sliding into third base, he hurt his knee badly. It would be at least a month before he could run hard again. If he were lucky, he would be able to pinch-hit in about two weeks. It would be even harder now to perform here the way he wanted.

A career for an athlete was an elusive thing, he thought. Only when it was virtually over, when the physical powers were diminishing, was it possible to have any genuine insight into what made a career—not a season but a complete career, the signature of a man. He saw himself now as a contemporary not so much of certain teammates from the Red Sox or Cardinals or Dodgers but, rather, of a handful of players who had entered the major leagues in one era, the mid-Sixties, and lasted through an entirely different one, the early Eighties. The first era had been harder, the game was tougher, the pay was smaller and a rookie was always a threat to a teammate's job. Smith himself had been paid $6500 in his rookie season. It was a world without guarantees. The players were forced to be much tougher, both mentally and physically (particularly, he believed, the black players, who had all spent time in vicious little Southern towns and who later, in the bigs, faced a more subtle kind of racism, an attitude that allowed a black player to be accepted as long as he was unquestioning of authority and was not different and did not complain. As long, in Reggie Smith's view, as he remained as white as he could be).

That era had gradually come to an end in the late Seventies with the advent of free agency. By the early Eighties, even mediocre players were signing huge contracts with so many built-in guarantees that the pressure on players to maximize their talents had eased. Only in exceptional cases, he believed, did pride goad a young player into higher levels of excellence. Hunger, he was convinced, had diminished.

He remembered, now, with almost astonishing clarity, the beginning of his own career—not just the hard times in Wytheville, Virginia, where he had encountered a racial prejudice unlike any he had known before, but far more clearly the time when he showed up at Red Sox spring-training camp in Scottsdale in 1964. He had been a rookie, and rookies were still almost subhuman in those days, referred to by the veterans as "Bush," existing to be seen but not heard. If, in conversation, a rookie volunteered some experience of his—a minor-league moment, of course—the veterans would say, "Yeah, Bush, you hit .300 in Appalachia. We *all* hit .300 back there."

Spring training with the Red Sox had been almost as much dream as reality. There had been Ted Williams prowling the field, his intensity and instinct for confrontation not dimmed by three years of retirement. It was amazing, Smith thought, that the man had been away from the game all those years and was still stalking pitchers. He noticed that wherever Williams went, the Boston players began almost unconsciously to edge away, particularly the pitchers. Williams liked to taunt pitchers; it was a challenge he carried over from his days as a hitter. Pitchers, he said, "couldn't goddamn help themselves. They're just dumb by breed."

Williams loved to study young hitters. He was like a drill sergeant and he taught them, above all else, concentration.

"Bush, where was that pitch?"

"It was outside, Mr. Williams."

"Where outside?"

"About two inches."

"What do you mean *about*? Don't you know?"

"Yes, sir."

"Bush," he would say in disgust, "you're too dumb to be a hitter."

That spring, Williams had told reporters that a kid named Reggie Smith looked like a ballplayer, and that had been sweet.

In some ways, the real education of Reggie Smith had begun in that, his 19th year. Boston had assigned him to room with Earl Wilson, the Red Sox' only other black player, an immense power pitcher. Wilson's legend preceded him; he was not to be trifled with. In the previous season, he had pitched a no-hitter, and he was said to have only marginal tolerance for rookies. On the first day of spring training, Smith, determined to be respectful and not to behave like a rookie, had carried his suitcases down the hall, practicing all the while how he would greet this legend. He would prove to Wilson that he was a serious young man, not some brash rookie, since he was in truth a brash rookie. He finally knocked on the door and a huge voice told him to come in.

"Hello, Mr. Wilson, my name is . . ." he began.

An enormous black form began to rise out of the bed. "Get the fuck out of here!" he shouted. "My name is Earl."

So Smith left the room, knocked again, entered and said, "Hello, Earl." With that, he decided many years later, his education had commenced.

Not until long after both he and Wilson left Boston did he truly understand how generous Wilson had been. For Wilson, virtually alone on a mostly white team, had taken him in hand and made sure that he did not waste such exceptional natural gifts, particularly in an organization that had not yet become an equal-opportunity employer. That was not always easy or painless, for Wilson was educating a relatively soft young man for a harder world.

"You're so young, Bush," he had said to him in that first week, "that you don't even have your man muscles yet."

That spring, Wilson was pitching batting practice to Smith, who had power but did not yet know how to pull the ball. Wilson threw an inside pitch and Smith hit it sharply through the box. Wilson just managed to duck out of the ball's way.

Dick Radatz, the mammoth relief pitcher, began to get on Wilson. "You going to let that little kid get away with that, Earl?" he shouted. The next pitch, very fast, hit Smith in the back.

"Now hit that one back the middle," Wilson said. So Smith started trying to hit everything through the middle and Wilson, in turn, finally threw right at his head. That made Smith even angrier, though his anger was directed at Radatz, who, he decided, had started all the trouble. Earl, after all, was his friend. So he started yelling at Radatz; then Wilson came in and grabbed him by the collar. A hand had never seemed so large.

"Hey, Road," Wilson said, using a nickname for a roommate, "you're out of line. This is the big leagues, and you've got to learn to pull pitches like that."

A few minutes later, Smith was sitting in the dugout still fuming, when a huge foot belonging to Radatz suddenly appeared in front of him, blocking all else from view. It was surely the largest foot that Reggie Smith had ever seen. "You mad at me?" a voice that was in some way connected to the foot had asked. This man, Smith thought, is huge. Just huge.

"No, I think I'm over it now," he answered.

"I'm very glad of that," the voice said, and both it and the foot disappeared.

Later that day at Korakuen Stadium, Smith recalled an incident from his boyhood in California, a very long way from Japan. He had been about 15 and was driving back from a semipro game with his father when they had spotted Willie Mays doing a promotion in a tire store. Reggie had walked up to Mays and told him that he, too, was a ballplayer. Mays, to his surprise, had not asked him whether he batted lefty or righty or which position he played. The only thing he had said was, "Do you know how to duck?" Now Smith finally understood what Mays had meant.

Earl Wilson understood, too, by the time he spotted the immense raw talent in Smith. "He's in the Clemente / Mays class," Wilson would say, and he loved, that first spring, to show him off. Once, when Boston played the Giants in an exhibition game, he went over to the San Francisco bench and took Mays aside. "Willie," he said, "you think you've got an arm. Now watch this kid." Wilson worried about Smith, about his instinct for defiance in a profession not much given to contention ("Reggie reminded me a lot of me," he later said), and he had worked to protect him. Smith remembered now how Earl had told him once, when the younger player was depressed, that he was not allowed to get down nor to let his temper diminish his talent. "Reggie," he had said, "you've *got* to make it. You are the best young prospect ever to come along in the Boston organization. You've got the best chance and so you've got to make it. Not just for yourself but for all of us."

IT HAPPENED VERY QUICKLY. By 1967, he was in his rookie season and having a wonderful year. At first, he'd taken pleasure from the status, from simply being in the big leagues, and he had done the usual rookie things: bought the requisite T-bird, endowed it with REGGIE plates and enjoyed it when he was recognized on the streets of Boston. He had learned to time it, to watch the excitement in the face of the surprised citizens, and had learned to be very cool under the glare of that attention.

His natural gifts had shown through from the start, and he loved it when opposing teams gathered in front of their dugouts to watch him throw from the outfield during pregame practice. Roberto Clemente, who had been one of his heroes, said that Smith had the best arm in baseball. Carl Yastrzemski had taken him under his wing that first year, and that had been both generous and unusual, since Yaz usually stood apart from the others. But in 1967, the ball club came together. It was a young team, and it did something no team had done in 20 years—it went from last place in one season to first place in the next one. Baseball was sheer pleasure for Smith, and it generated a sense of excitement he had not known before. He simply could not wait to get to the ball park every day. In the morning, there was always an impatience, a feeling that they should skip the pregame drills and just play the game.

That summer, he watched his friend Yastrzemski with an admiration that was complete. Yaz had always been an exceptional teacher, not so much by what he said as by what he did (the lessons were there if you wanted them, but you had to ask; he did not volunteer anything). From Yaz had come not only his own shrewd insights about hitting but the distilled lessons of Ted Williams as well, for Yaz had listened carefully to Williams and shared with him that intensity of concentration, as if in life, baseball alone mattered.

If that was normally true, then it was even more true in the summer of 1967. During the pennant run, Yaz started taking extra batting practice after home games, something he had picked up from Williams. Soon he asked Smith and a few others to join him, and there was a special pleasure in those hours, a rare sense of camaraderie among big-leaguers. There they were, staying behind after everyone else had gone home, men playing like boys, exulting in the dual pleasures of their manhood and their boyhood.

Eventually, Boston went sour for Smith. There were divisions on the team; he was in the Yaz group, and the people who did not like Yaz took out their frustration on him, not on the superstar. There were racial tensions with fans and sportswriters, for the Boston sports press in the late Sixties was not entirely ready for a brash young black player who seemed to lack what some sportswriters felt was the requisite gratitude of a black player to a white newspaperman. Then, in the early Seventies, there were the beginnings of his injuries, and with them he became more of a target for the Red Sox fans.

At the end of the 1973 season, he was traded to the Cardinals. He was glad to go, glad to get out of Boston, where he had stayed too long, he thought, and where there was still a curious reluctance to accept a black star. He was also glad to be going to the National League, where he was sure his game would be more natural.

He loved the National League immediately. It was a far better place to utilize his skills. He felt liberated there, able to play the game all out as he had not been able to in Boston. (With a similar number of games played in each league, Smith made the all-star team five times from the National League and only twice from the American.) Speed was of the essence here; he was aware of that the moment he walked into the Cardinals' locker room. No one symbolized it more than Lou Brock. He might seem like a perfect gentleman on the outside, but there was an intensity with which he exploited his speed and pressured the opposition with his running that was almost frightening. No one was going to stand in the way of what he wanted. Brock's preparation for a game reminded Smith of nothing so much as a razor being sharpened and then sharpened again. Brock had exceptional speed, but what gave him his edge—it was all about edge, no matter how small—was his intelligence and passion. Smith worked with Brock, helping time opposing pitchers and catchers on their moves, and he decided they were all part of the same generation. They were the lineal descendants of Jackie

Robinson, all in their own ways fighting the stereotype that blacks had talent but not intelligence. They were hard men, Smith decided later, because they were always proving themselves.

The Cardinals were an organization in transition, and Smith enjoyed playing there but eventually got into a contract hassle with Augie Busch and, to his delight, was traded to the Dodgers. He was pleased to be going back to California, which was his home, and delighted to be playing for the Dodgers. They were, he thought, just one player—and a certain amount of toughness—away from being a great team. He was fascinated by the Dodgers as an organization; it did all the little things well: It scouted the minor leagues carefully; it taught fundamentals; and it looked for the type of player who would fit in with the new clean-cut, California Dodger tradition, which was, of course, different from the older, flintier Brooklyn one, for the tradition must fit the locale. Dodger Blue—the idea that they were not only cleaner but somehow spiritually superior to other baseball players—sold well. The seats were always filled and the teams were good, albeit not quite good enough. They lacked the inherent meanness of some of their opponents. Tommy Lasorda was a good front for it all, a man of the organization who not only articulated the team's myth but propagated it himself. Walking Eagle, some of the older players called him, meaning that he was so full of shit he could not fly. It was a handsome new media team for the brave new media world.

Smith was always amused by the idea of Dodger Blue and Dodger harmony; in its own way, it was one of the most divided teams he had ever known, as much wrought with truly petty jealousies as any team could be. Still, he admired the organization, the sheer professionalism of it on every level. He knew that Al Campanis had understood free agency before any other general manager in baseball and had signed all of his relatively young players to what seemed like generous long-term contracts. Generous they were the day they were signed; but within a few years, $300,000 a year was what utility players were being paid. As the contracts were about to run out in the past year or two, Smith had tried to warn his friends on the team that the Dodgers would not re-sign them, that they would turn to the younger players they had been stockpiling in the minors. But none of them really believed him. They were *Dodgers*, men of the organization; Walking Eagle was their buddy and they had been good to the organization, and they were now sure that it, in turn, would reward them. Smith was right, of course, and the Dodgers did not even try to sign Steve Garvey when he became a free agent. Soon Ron Cey and Davey Lopes were also gone, as was Reggie Smith.

It was a tough, well-run organization, Smith understood, a place absolutely without illusion or loyalty.

A MONTH AFTER HE twisted his knee, it was still giving him a lot of pain. He was pinch-hitting now, which meant that instead of seeing bad pitches four or five times a game, he was seeing them only once. And that meant he was pressing even more.

The Japanese press was beginning to needle him. There were references to him as "the million-dollar pinch hitter." It was too bad, one sportswriter noted, that his body was so old, because he was certainly trying hard. "But, fortunately, our young Japanese players are so good that we do not need Smith-*san*."

"It's getting harder and harder for me," he was saying as he got ready to go to the ball park in Osaka. "I can't show what I can do. I keep wondering why they brought me here. Why did they want me so badly? If they want their Japanese counterparts to be bigger stars, then OK, but I could have stayed in America. I pop up now and they spend half the paper writing about it, discussing it, analyzing my swing." He paused. "You know, one of the reasons they told me they signed me was that they wanted to measure their best against genuine American stars. But then they back away from it. Sometimes

I think the most paralyzing thing in this game—probably in this country—is the fear of failure. They would rather not try at all than try and fail. But to be an *athlete*, I mean a real athlete, you have to have the courage to try, which means the courage to fail." He shook his head.

Hector Cruz, one of the three Cruz brothers and Smith's one *gaijin* teammate, met him in the lobby. They got into a cab and headed for the ball park. "Reggie," said Cruz, "you are the best I've ever seen at getting around in Japan. You never get lost. You just get in a cab and they look at you and take you to the ball park. Maybe it's the haircut."

Cruz was having an even harder time than Smith. Part of it was language. Smith spoke English and, thus, the interpreter could readily connect him to the team. But Hector spoke Spanglish, and on the way from his native Spanish to their Japanese a great deal got lost. Then there was the cultural difference exhibited in style, attitude and body language. The Japanese were formal, disciplined; indeed, tight. Their body language was unbelievably formal. Even the baseball players seemed as if they should be wearing blue suits. Cruz, by contrast, was loose. Everything about him was loose—his body movement, his attitude. Japan was not easy for Hector, nor, for that matter, for his brother Tommy, who had played the year before for the Nippon Ham Fighters. The time a batting coach tried to correct Tommy's swing, he simply looked at him, dropped his bat on the plate and left the ball park. On another occasion, there was some difference of opinion on whether or not the team was going to pay Tommy Cruz's utility bill, as his contract promised. He showed up for a game one night quite angry because the bill had not been taken care of. He would not, he insisted, play in the 6:00 P.M. game unless it was done. No one took him very seriously. At 5:45, he returned to the clubhouse, dressed and left the ball park. They caught up with him outside the park and persuaded him to come back. But Japan had not been easy on the Cruz family, nor had the Cruz family been easy on Japan. Hector had been injured early in the season, but now he was ready to play. The team was winning, however, so there was no need to replace a Japanese player with a *gaijin*.

Smith and Cruz arrived at the ball park already dressed; the facilities were too primitive to shower there. There were still more than three hours to kill before the game. The Japanese sportswriters filled the Giants' dugout, so Smith and Cruz sprinted to the outfield. The sportswriters were eager to talk with an American colleague about visiting baseball teams of the past, particularly the old Yankees.

"We were very excited when Mr. Yogi was going to come here," one of the sportswriters was saying, "because we heard a great deal about Mr. Yogi and how funny he was. But then he came here and we did not think he was very funny. We wanted him to say funny things, but mostly he told us to get out of his way. We do not think Mr. Yogi liked Japanese people."

Another sportswriter mentioned Mickey Mantle. "Mantle-*san*," he said, "liked the Ginza very much, we think. He and Mr. Billy Martin went to the Ginza and they stayed in Ginza all night, and the next day, Mantle-*san* struck out three times. A real Ginza swing."

At the ball park, Smith and Cruz seemed distinctly apart from their teammates. They stayed, after all, at different hotels and they did different pregame drills. The Japanese were deadly serious about their practices; they ran hard and exercised hard, and a good practice was considered important, a sign that a player was ready to have a good game. The *gaijins* didn't work that way; by nature, they coasted through practice, assuming that what they were capable of doing was a given. It was part of the sticking point between the *gaijins* and the Japanese. The far larger roles of the manager and the coaches in the Japanese game irritated Smith. There were 13 coaches on the Giants and 14 on the Hanshin Tigers. To his mind, that was far too much meddling.

That evening during batting practice, for instance, an American player named Steve Stroughter was getting instruction from a Tiger coach. "Look at that!" Smith said. "Just look at that. That batting coach is full of shit. Doesn't know a damn thing about what he's saying, but he's going to tinker anyway. The kid has been swinging that way all his life, but he's going to play with him anyway. Just a coach anxious to screw someone up." He checked the coach's number. "Hey, Ichi," he called to the team interpreter, Ichiro Tanuma, "who's number 84?"

"Katsura Yokomizo," said Tanuma.

"He ever play Japanese baseball?" Smith asked. The distaste was palpable.

"He played outfield for Hiroshima," Tanuma answered.

"Sure he did," Smith said. "A great star there."

It was not a good game for Smith. In the fourth inning, with the bases loaded and one out, he was sent up to pinch-hit. He grabbed a bat, but first he told Sadaharu Oh, now a Giant coach, that it was too early in the game to use him. "It is never too early to hit a home run," Oh said.

The first pitch caught Smith by surprise. He had been expecting the Hanshin pitcher to waste two or three and, instead, it was the best pitch he had seen in two weeks, right over the plate. He hit a soft pop-up to shortstop. He was not pleased with himself. The game, which did not have a lot of hits, took more than four hours and ended with Yomiuri's winning 5–4. To the Americans, the Japanese game seemed interminable; by contrast, the Japanese do not like telecasts of American games, which they find far too short.

SMITH HAD HOPED to be playing regularly by early June, but when he finally tried, his knee buckled completely. He would be a pinch hitter, it appeared, for quite a while, if not the entire season. Now the Japanese press was riding him hard. One paper thought he did not smile enough. Another quoted the Giants' general manager about how fortunate it was that Smith had only a one-year contract.

"That's mild," Bob Whiting remarked, like a veteran family counselor, involuntarily expert at watching the breakup of Japanese-American baseball marriages. "It won't get really good for another two weeks," he said. Two weeks later to the day, Whiting phoned. "It's begun," he said. "You have to know how to look for it. The tip-off came all last week. The camera on the televised games kept showing Smith and Cruz in the dugout. No one ever said anything, but the implication was always that they weren't paying attention and that they didn't care about the team. What they really feel is that Smith should be more contrite, that his face and manner should show more obligation—that he should be more Japanese. So today it's finally hit one of the tabloids."

"FIRE SMITH" was the headline. "The Japanese have a *gaijin* complex," the story said, "and it is being taken advantage of. The *gaijins* come here and don't do anything and Japan has become the laughing-stock of the world because of it. What is a powerful economic giant like Japan doing hiring someone like Reggie Smith? We're one of the seven advanced nations of the world. Occasionally, he'll come to bat and get a hit as a pinch hitter and management will say thank you, and he'll answer with a superior smile. 'I'm a major-leaguer.'"

Only if the Giants fired Smith and sent him home to America, the paper said, would the rest of the world respect Japan.

By late June, after a month of that sort of thing, Smith would sometimes wait in the locker room for more than an hour after the game, until everyone else was gone. This particular night, the Giants had taken an early lead, and so he did not even have to pinch-hit, and now, as he got on the subway with some friends, he said, "You know, it looks like baseball, it smells like baseball, but it isn't baseball at all."

SLOWLY, HE BEGAN TO HEAL. In July, he returned to the line-up full-time. He was pressing, and he struck out often and complained angrily about what he called the *gaijin* strike zone, a pitcher's delight. In Hiroshima, after being called out on strikes, he smashed up a couple of lockers. The Japanese were not amused. Nor was he; he was convinced that the Giant coaches not only did not back him up but rooted against him. Then, a little later, Oh benched him because he was "too nervous." The Japanese press loved it. It looked more and more as if he would not last the season.

Shortly after that, he tried to reverse the tide of his fortunes by having a "backward day," putting his entire uniform on backward, from underwear to shoes. The Giant players loved it, but the coaches were angry. He thought he was mocking himself, but they thought he was mocking something almost sacred. Japanese baseball. They ordered him to go in and change for batting practice. He refused. "I'll take batting practice in my mind," he said. Perhaps the Zen b.p. helped, for he hit a home run and a double that night. But overall, things were not going well for him, nor for the Giants, who were in the process of blowing a ten-game lead to the Hiroshima Carp.

A few days later, he was involved in a major incident in a game against the Carp. The Hiroshima bench began to get on him in a way that he could only partly understand: "*Gaijin, gaijin!*" they shouted, and then added some incomprehensible words in Japanese. Of the words in Japanese, he imagined the worst. To him, that was insulting. In his mind, they were all double-A ballplayers. Double-A players did not have the right to ride someone from the bigs. He started yelling "Fuck you" at them. The Carp pitcher retaliated with a brush-back pitch. The umpire did nothing. The Carp pitcher threw another. Smith used his bat to flip some dirt in the catcher's face. "If you want to fight," the umpire said, pointing his finger at Smith, "do it outside the stadium."

"If I wanted to fight," Smith answered, "he'd be lying on his ass on the ground right now."

The next night, before the game, he went over to the Carp bench and told them in a very cool and lightly ominous way to lay off the razzing and lay off the bean balls. Otherwise, he would pro-tect himself. He suddenly looked very much bigger than they did. Late in the game, with two men on, the Carp catcher called for a brush-back pitch: the pitcher refused and threw it on the outside corner. Smith reached out and hit a three-run homer that won the game and also ended a run the Carp had been making at the pen-nant.

Some of his friends had thought that he'd come to the end of the road, but after that night, things began to change for the better. He and Oh, whom he respected, had a long dinner that helped clear the air, and the umpires seemed to ease up and give him more of a strike zone (there were quite reliable reports that the sainted Oh had talked to them). He began to get better pitches and he began to hit. He shortened his swing to match the style of Japanese baseball—hands right in front of his face. Suddenly, he was not just hitting, he was carrying the team. That was important: earlier, when the Gi-ants seemed to have the pennant locked up, they had not needed him. Now, when they were making a run, he was dominating the game, going in the process from bad *gaijin* to good *gaijin*. By the end of the season, he had 28 homers and 72 R.B.I.s in only 261 at bats. (Tatsunori Hara, the team's star, who benefited from having Smith hit behind him, had 31 homers and 103 R.B.I.s in almost twice as many at bats.)

Soon after Smith got hot, the Japanese press was writing posi-tively about him. The Giants clinched the pennant on a day in which he hit three home runs. A series of articles in a Japanese sports pa-per featured his tips on hitting and referred to him as Professor Smith. There were even some commercial endorsements, which was unheard of for an American player. He finished second in the most-valuable-player voting, behind Hara. The owner of the team, Shoriki, referred to Smith's salary as a bargain. Smith himself began to talk of what he would do when he came back in 1984 and about the advice he would give a new *gaijin* player ("Forget everything you thought you knew about baseball and strike zones and strategy . . ."). Appreciated by the Japanese, he in turn became more appreciative of them, of how much they had created out of so little. Everyone seemed to relax a bit more. Acceptance bred acceptance. For the first time, there was on their part a recognition of how passionately he had wanted to excel.

In the end, some of the Giants' front-office people spoke of the fact that the team could not have won the pennant without him. Newspapers said that Smith was not like the other *gaijins*, who had come over only for the money. Instead, he had played hard and well under difficult conditions. Even a *gaijin*, it seemed, could learn something new about an old game.

The Fan Divided

From the *Boston Globe,* October 6, 1986

I GREW UP WITH MY SOUL DIVIDED. FOR I AM BOTH A MAN
of New York and of New England. Things as critical as this, the selection of a favored baseball team, are not, as some suspect, a matter
of choice; one does not choose a team as one does not select his
own genes. They are confirmed upon you, more than we know an
act of heredity. By an odd blend of fates and geography, I am somewhat schizophrenic in my baseball loyalties; I think of baseball, and
I think American League, and then New York and Boston. The National League has always been a distant shadowy place. I was born
in New York in the very borough where the Yankees play; my father,
a small-town boy with a small-town obsession about baseball, took
me to the Stadium in 1939 when I was 5, having in the previous two
years talked almost exclusively about the great DiMaggio. So I began not just with loyalty to a locale, but to a mythic figure, a man
worthy of his myth and who did not disappoint. He was to the little
boy sitting there that day, pleasure of pleasures excused early from
school, every bit as dazzling and graceful as my father had claimed
he would be. The Stadium seemed not so much a sports coliseum as
a cathedral; never had grass seemed so green, never had any group of
men caught my attention; this, unlike the world of elementary
school I had just left behind, was real. I departed that day a confirmed Yankee fan. Soon the war came, my father went back in the
service, and we moved to Winsted, in northwest Connecticut, which
serves as the selected site of my otherwise dislocated childhood.

Winsted then was the classic New England mill town of about 8,000, a serious baseball town, its own loyalties somewhat divided between Boston and New York. But it is about 20 miles nearer New York and the magnetic pull of the Yankees was somewhat more powerful then, in large part I suspect because the reception for the Yankee games, WINS-1010 on your dial, Ballantine Blasts and White Owl Wallops with Mel Allen, was stronger than that of the Red Sox.

But we were a divided family; my mother's family had grown up in Boston, and my Uncle Harry, her oldest brother, had become successful in the wholesale paint business. He occasionally visited us in Winsted and was intrigued by the idea of a young nephew whose knowledge of batting averages was so encyclopedic, and who could repeat so faithfully the wisdom of that era's sportcasters. He also had, it turned out, season tickets to the Red Sox games. That seemed almost beyond comprehension to me; it was not that we were so poor, but we were, in those immediate post-Depression years, most assuredly frugal. We lived on a World War II officer's allowance, and something like going to a baseball game was at best a pleasure permitted once a season. Uncle Harry was said within family circles to be something of a dandy; that is, he not only made a lot of money but he was quite willing to spend it. That he could go to all 77 home games, and sit in the very same seats, seemed both miraculous and quite possibly frivolous. We simply did not know people who did grand things like this. It seemed to mark him not so much as a relative, but as someone from another family who had mistakenly wandered into our lives. His seats, he said, were right behind the first base dugout, and he loved them because he could see the ballplayers' faces up close. They were such clean-looking young men, he said. Could this really be true? Did he have seats this good? If it were, then it struck me that Uncle Harry, if not actually on speaking terms with these distant and vaunted celebrities, was at least on *seeing* terms with them. He seemed to know a great deal about them—Pesky, Doerr, York, the mighty Williams. Pesky's

name, he confided, was not really Pesky. It was Paveskovich. Mel
Allen, to my knowledge, had never mentioned this. Could I doubt
Uncle Harry and his inside knowledge anymore? But it was true; in
time the war was over and we were allowed to travel again and we
visited Boston and Uncle Harry made good his pledge. He *did* have
wonderful seats and I could see in the players' faces up close the disappointment after they had grounded out, and turned back toward
the dugout. They seemed quite wonderful, so large and powerful,
and on that day, against Detroit, with Hal Newhouser (Ron Guidry
before Guidry) pitching, I found myself rooting for them.

So it was that my childhood concluded with two conflicting loyalties. The first was one to the Yankees, and most of all DiMaggio.
When I think of DiMaggio, I see him, not so much at bat, though
the stance was classic, but of him going back on a fly ball, or of running the bases, particularly going around second on his way to third;
I have never seen a tall man run with more grace. He was the first of
my heroes; my true (and pure) loyalty to the Yankees ends with his
retirement. Never in the age of Mantle was I able to summon the
commitment and obligation innocence that I had brought to the age
of DiMaggio. I was growing older. By the time DiMaggio retired in
1951, I was 17, and it was time to go on to other things.

But even as a young man, the vision and the loyalty were
clouded. For there was the other vision, that of the Red Sox, and
most of all, of Williams. As DiMaggio seemed so natural in the
field, so Williams seemed equally natural at the plate, first seemingly loose, and gangly, and then suddenly bound tightly and perfectly together, the swing at once so smooth and yet so powerful, all
of it so completely focused—as if he was destined to do this one
thing, hit a baseball and nothing else. Of his talents, there was no
lack of admiration among Yankee fans: When I was a boy, there was
a constant schoolboy debate not just about the respective merits of
DiMaggio or Williams, but of what would happen if each had
played in the other's park, DiMaggio with the Green Monster,

Williams with the short Stadium right-field porch. It was the ultimate tribute to Williams that had the trade been made, it would
have been accepted without complaint by most Yankee fans.

In the summer of 1946, my father had come back from the war,
and he had taken my brother and me to the Stadium to see a Yankee–Red Sox game. That was a glorious year for the Red Sox, all
their players had come back from the war, and the Red Sox players
more than those of the Yankees were making a comfortable re-
adjustment to baseball. Their pitchers were healthy, and by midseason they held an immense lead over the Yankees. On that day,
Aug. 10, 1946 (you could look it up, as Casey Stengel said), Williams
hit two home runs, the first of them a truly massive three-run shot
off Tiny Bonham that went into the upper deck. The memory of
that drive, the hardest-hit ball I have ever seen, remains with me today; I still see the force of it, the unwavering majestic trajectory, the
ball climbing as it hit the seats, the silence of the fans, stunned not
just that the Red Sox had scored three runs, but that a ball had been
hit that hard. Williams seemed that day to a young boy a glorious
figure, a hero who did what heroes are supposed to do.

I went on to college in Boston a few years later. There I was, like
most visitors to the city, puzzled by the harshness with which the
Boston press treated him. He was clearly the greatest hitter of his
generation in baseball, he had just returned from his second tour of
duty as a combat pilot, he was, it seemed, defying baseball's actuar-
ial tables, and it was a pleasure to go out early to Fenway and watch
him taking batting practice, a game within a game. I did not know
as much about the media then as I do now, but I knew that the
Boston papers were by and large bad (in fact, they were probably
worse than that in the early Fifties), that he was personally victim-
ized by the most primitive kind of circulation wars, and that he,
proud, idiosyncratic and unbending, was red meat for newspapers
which were desperately trying to survive in a world which no longer
needed them. What they did to him seems in retrospect to border

on cruelty. It is probably true that he played into their hands, and was his own worst enemy, though his behavior, so much criticized then, seems by the modern Richter scale of athletic behavior mild enough. I did not share that view of the Boston writers that the problem with the Red Sox was Williams. (I suspect that this was why John Updike's piece, "Hub Fans Bid Kid Adieu," has itself taken on such singular importance. It is as if after hundreds of lower courts had ruled unfairly against Williams for all those years, Updike, a writer of skill and knowledge, taking time off from the chronicling of suburban infidelity, became in effect the Supreme Court ruling in favor of him, overturning the lesser judgments of lesser courts.) It was not the fault of Williams at all. Quite the reverse: It struck me that the late Forties was a time of marvelous matchups between two almost perfectly equal teams, that the advantage that the Yankees held was one of pitching and depth—the ability to trade for a particular player. For example, in 1946 the Yankees traded additional bench strength for Eddie Lopat. That gave the Yankees a pitching staff of Reynolds, Raschi and Lopat, the core of the strongest pitching staff in the league for the next six years.

The memory of Williams and that special grace lingers. I now think often of him; we live in a nation which seeks heroes and cites as its heroes the kings of celluloid like John Wayne and Sylvester Stallone, each of whom managed to stay out of his generation's war. I am wary of heroes in general, but as I grow older, I have become more and more intrigued by Williams, the man apart. Perhaps it is that wonderfully leathery face, for Ted Williams even looked like what he was and what he did with that William Holden cragginess. Perhaps it is the deeds, that prolonged exquisite career, the willingness to go for it on the last day of the .400 season. But finally it is as well the ability to stand apart, crusty, independent, outspoken, true to himself, living to his own specifications, and rules, the frontier man of the modern age. I have a sense of a life lived without regret and I hope that that is true. Grown now, I can still close my eyes and I can see DiMaggio going back on a ball, or kicking the dirt at second base after Gionfriddo had caught the ball in the 1947 World Series; I can as clearly still see these 40 years later Williams swinging, the ball heading for the third tier.

As I grew older, my loyalties softened, and my priorities changed. I went to school in Boston, and I soon was overseas as a foreign correspondent. Other issues clouded the purity of my baseball loyalties. I would root for certain teams based on their special character or my feeling about their cities (I root as a matter of course against all Texas and California teams, and I was deeply disappointed when Houston knocked off the Lakers this year, thus depriving the Celtics of the chance to do it). The real world began to interfere with the fantasy world of baseball; my pull to the Yankees weakened and that to the Red Sox began to grow, for I liked the Red Sox teams of the late Sixties, Yastrzemski-Smith-Conigliaro-Petrocelli. In 1964, just back from two years in Vietnam, I went to Opening Day at the Stadium with my editor and a few other writers, and I remember two things, Ann Mudge, the girlfriend of Philip Roth, refusing to stand for the National Anthem as an antiwar protest, the first I had ever seen, and the sweet swing of a young rookie named Tony Conigliaro. In 1967 I went to an early-season game at Yankee Stadium. On that day a Red Sox rookie pitcher named Billy Rohr was pitching. About the sixth innning, it was obvious that he had a no-hitter going. The fascination grew, the crowd inevitably rooting not so much for a team, but for the event. The seventh and eighth innings passed. Still a no-hitter. In the ninth inning, with one out, Tom Tresh hit a shot to left field. Yastrzemski was playing shallow, if memory serves, and went back, and dove just at the right moment, his body tumbling into a complete somersault as he made the catch. It ranks with the Gionfriddo catch as the greatest I have ever seen, made more remarkable by the fact that it saved a no-hitter. The next batter, Elston Howard, lined a hit into right-center. I thought, as I had of Conigliaro, that Rohr had a great career ahead of him. He was to win two more games in his major league career.

That summer and fall, I was back in Vietnam; it was a bad time for me. The American mission was optimistic (this was just before Tet) and I was pessimistic, convinced that 500,000 men had managed only to stalemate the other side. I hated the futile violence of the war. It was not a face of America I was comfortable with, and the combination of the flawed commitment—so many men and so much hardware to do a job which could not be done, and the self-deception which accompanied it had put me in a grim mood. That was also the season of Yastrzemski; that summer and fall when I was not out in the field, I would go over to the AP office. Saigon was 12 hours different from Boston and so the results of the night games would tend to come in about 11 A.M. There was also a man who hung around the AP office, for the same reason: Doc, as he was known. Doc was Dr. Tom Durant, a Boston doctor helping the Vietnamese with their medical training (he is now assistant director of Mass. General), and each morning I would meet him there, bonded by this need to escape, and this common passion, and we would follow the results of a wonderful pennant race and perhaps the greatest one-man pennant drive in modern baseball history by standing over the AP ticker. I felt very close to him; we never agreed in advance to meet at the office but indeed we always did. We would sit there in that small airless room, and we could almost see Yaz as he was in Fenway, the exaggerated stance; it was all oddly exhilarating. Each day the heroics seemed even more remarkable, the box score would come clicking over the printer—Yaz, 2 for 4 with two RBIs—and then, more often than not, the mention of some extraordinary catch as well. In what was for me a bad season, his was a marvelous season and it reminded me of the America I loved, and which otherwise seemed quite distant. I have felt fondly of him ever since, and my affection has weathered even the current hokey hot dog commercials.

That next year I became a citizen of New England again, buying a home in Nantucket, connecting myself once again to Boston sports coverage, which now in modern times seemed to make the Red Sox players larger than life (Williams had played 25 years too soon, I suspected; he should have played in an era of semi-monopoly journalism) and returning to Fenway once again. I had remembered it as a small shabby park, an embarrassment after the grandeur of the Stadium, but now I saw it differently; in an age of antiseptic ballparks, gimmicky electronic scoreboards, fans who cheered every pop fly, it was a real ballpark. Going there was like going back in time, stepping into a Hopper painting. It must have been like this, I thought, when Smoky Joe Wood was ready to pitch. I had rooted for the 1975 team, a glorious and exciting team in a wonderful Series, wondering what might have happened if there had been two Luis Tiants instead of one. Then in 1978, for the last time, I faced the question of divided loyalties, the human heart in conflict with itself, to use Faulkner's phrase. I was no longer an automatic Yankee fan, but that was a good and gritty Yankee team, Munson-Nettles-Chambliss-Piniella-Jackson-Hunter, a Gabe Paul rather than a Steinbrenner team, not yet contaminated by the worst of all baseball owners. I like the chase as much as anything else, and that summer I found myself cheering the late-season New York surge. It was also a very good Red Sox team as well, Rice-Lynn-Yastrzemski-Evans-Fisk, weaker as usual in pitching. The season was as good as any I have ever seen, the early, seemingly insurmountable Boston lead, the feral, almost ruthless late Yankee surge to reclaim part of first place. One hundred sixty-two games played and both teams dead even—that was not a flawed season, that was an almost perfect season. Of that in the bitterness of postmortem charges and countercharges, there was much talk about a Red Sox collapse. I never believed it. The Yankees, as usual, had a demonstrably better pitching staff. Perhaps, I thought, the key moment took place six years earlier when the Red Sox made one of the worst trades of modern times, swapping Sparky Lyle for Danny Cater. Lyle was then young, a proven lefthanded reliever, 53 saves in his last three seasons; Cater was a good, albeit limited, pinch hitter. Lyle was the perfect relief pitcher for the Stadium and he gave an improving Yankees team exactly what it needed, a kind of instant late-inning legitimacy. In seven years as a Yankee, he had 141 saves, and in that year, 1978, when his star was already in descent in New York (Goose Gossage had arrived and Lyle went, said Nettles, from Cy Young to Sayonara in one season), he nonetheless had nine saves and a 9-3 record. In a season where two teams end up with the same record, that was all the difference the Yankees needed.

That team is gone: Piniella as manager and Randolph and Guidry are the only survivors. In the age of narcissus, Steinbrenner is the perfect modern baseball owner now, the bully as owner (if Tom Yawkey was flawed because he loved his players too much, Steinbrenner is flawed because he envies them their talent and youth and fame too much). He has won the tabloids, and lost the team. The 1978 team struck me as one which was bonded together by a mutual dislike of him; now, eight years later, his act has played too long, he is the national bore, and contempt has replaced dislike. It's not easy, in an age of free agency, to screw up owning a baseball team in the media capital of the world, but he has done it. The team is a wonderful extension of him, overpaid, surly, disconnected; the quintessential Steinbrenner player is Rickey Henderson. I do not doubt his talent, indeed his brilliance, but he seems, whenever I watch, in a perpetual sulk, entirely within himself, and watching him is almost as much fun as watching Carl Lewis during the 1984 Olympics. In this year I wish the Red Sox well, I did not think it was a good race, there was too much stumbling around. In a personal sense, if I am pleased for anyone, it is Don Baylor; trashed by Steinbrenner, he gained the sweetest kind of revenge, hitting against righthanders. His trade subtracted character from the Yankees and added it to the Red Sox. And I rooted as well for Tom Seaver, carried in this season as much by a feral instinct to compete as by natural skill, awesome if not in talent anymore then in toughness of mind.

If the Red Sox stumble through, however imperfectly, then I am pleased, for there have been enough very good Boston teams which, playing far better baseball, had their pennants denied. If they win, so be it: The gods owe them one.

Renewed Spirits at Fenway Opener

From the *Boston Globe*, April 11, 1989

ON THIS SEMI-BEAUTIFUL DAY, WITH THE SUN MAKING A mere cameo appearance, spring finally arrived in Boston. The Red Sox opened in Fenway, limping in slightly, and none too soon, since their record was 1-4.

In a nation with so little ritual that our morning television shows search desperately for any vestige of it and will cover almost anything—the wedding of minor British princes who are commercial representatives of the crown, and the death and funeral of a Japanese emperor whom they never covered in life—Opening Day is one of our few ceremonial moments.

It marks, particularly in a city like this where the winter is so harsh, not merely the opening of an athletic season, but a benchmark on the calendar. What precedes is winter. What follows is spring. On Opening Day, Lou Boudreau once noted, there is no past, all is future and hope.

I think he is both right and wrong: I think the attraction, particularly in a ballpark like this, is that it blends both future and past as almost nothing else in our lives. We celebrate not just the beginning of something new, but the remembrances of the past when we were younger. It is an occasion both regenerative and filled with nostalgia, filled with the fragments of a child's memories. It is for many males of my generation the place where we were first brought by our fathers, and where we first shared their world.

Lou Gorman was discoursing on this before the game when, surrounded by reporters, he was allowed to speak on subjects other than the future of Wade Boggs. Gorman is 59 now, and he first came here 50 years ago when he was 9.

"It was Ted Williams' first season, but I didn't know that, although he became my favorite player," said Gorman. "My father took me. We lived in Providence then and we drove up, and the trip up seemed to last forever, you know what a kid's impatience is like. We got here, and the park seemed so large. Every Opening Day still reminds me of it. I was hooked."

That same season, I told him, I was 5 and my father took me to Yankee Stadium and he had pointed out the great Joe DiMaggio in center field and told me to watch him go from first to third on a single, which I did, though in truth I had no idea what he was talking about.

Gorman and I, who had never met before, were now joined by this connecting link of our first seasons half a century ago. "Remember the marvelous color of the grass," I suggested. "The grass was never so green," he said.

It is true that the ritual seems to mean more in Fenway, a surviving park from the pre-modern age. Its very imperfections in an age of perfect dimensions and grassless grass are comforting to me. When I enter the park, I now have a feeling that I am walking into a Hopper painting, and that Smokey Joe Wood will be pitching. The only thing that at first seems to have changed from those wondrous photos of 60 and 70 years ago is that the men no longer wear hats and ties.

That sense of the past is emphasized by the players themselves, who seem more than in any other sport to be part of a direct genetic line with their athletic forebears. They are not the overwhelming new physical specimens that abound in other sports. Rather, they are, in height and weight, not that remarkable. What sets them apart is in the shoulders and chest. They are, by type, chunky compared to their fellow Americans, all the Red Sox, that is except Oil

Can Boyd, who seems almost unbearably slim and frail looking, and with his glasses, looks like a slightly studious graduate student who has wandered into the wrong office.

On this day, the sense of excitement is palpable. Being a Red Sox fan is like having a calling: they are by breed and training hardier and more loyal than fans elsewhere, at once shrewder, more tolerant and, yes, more loving than most of their counterparts elsewhere, and they are ready for the new season.

Everyone seems to be at the park earlier than usual. Wade Boggs, a man who ritualizes every part of his baseball endeavors, is the first to work out, and was throwing before anyone else was on the field. He is a man who comes to the ballpark at certain hours, throws at certain hours, takes grounders at certain hours. Mr. Boggs is not just a marvelous hitter with a remarkable capacity to concentrate and focus on baseball in the midst of what would be at the very least distracting to most of his teammates and fellow countrymen, but he has become now a celebrity of the first magnitude. In recent weeks, he was featured on *20/20* with Barbara Walters, the equivalent of what the *Time* magazine cover used to be, and confirmation that his celebrityhood, hard won though it may be, is now complete and is no longer confined to mere athletics. The preoccupation with Boggs, the endless stream of journalists gathering to chronicle him and ask about him, is a reminder that the society changes, and the game changes.

Boston has changed and so has Fenway. The skyline of the city behind the right-field fence is noticeably different, markedly grander, and on this day it was the coach of the Harvard hockey team who was chosen to throw out the first ball, his entire team stationed behind him, all of them warmly cheered. Town has become gown and gown has become town, although the Clearys are more of the new Harvard than the old. (Years ago, when I was still an undergraduate at Harvard, Cooney Weiland was the hockey coach, and Mr. Cleary's father was a prominent referee. On one occasion, Weiland was berating the elder Cleary on a tough call, until finally someone from the athletic director's office came down and told Weiland to shut up, and to remind him that Harvard was in the complicated process of trying to recruit the referee's two sons.)

Nor is Fenway completely immune to change. The mutations within the park itself are relatively minor. There are some advertising signs and, yes, there is an electronic scoreboard. (Can it be that the Yuppie generation, with its profound sense of entitlement, began in those cities with electric scoreboards where it was deemed that the game itself was not enough to amuse the faithful and that new forms of entertainment must be added?)

I first came to this park in 1946 when I was 12. The Red Sox of my childhood were every bit as heroic as the Yankees, and their names were Williams, Doerr, Pesky and DiMaggio. The numbers of both Williams and Doerr have been retired and now adorn the right-field fence, and Mr. Pesky still dresses regularly for the games. He is an assistant to the general manager and, by his reckoning, this is his 46th Opening Day at Fenway. As such, he admitted, he woke up nervous today.

The fact that Boston had gotten off to a bad start, 1-4, did not bother him that much since he had seen a good many other bad starts in what is truly a long season, and he could remember a good many comebacks. He had told Bob Stanley before the game not to worry, that in 1948 Boston had gotten off to an even worse start.

"I think we were fifth or sixth," said Pesky. "We were terrible. Then we began to come back. On the last day we tied Cleveland and we had the one-game playoff."

There would not have been a tie, I suggested, if Charley Berry, the umpire, had not blown the call on a ball that Lou Boudreau lined foul to right field off Mel Parnell.

"You're right," he said. "Everyone in the park knew it was foul. Berry blew it. It gave them two runs and those were the only runs they got off Parnell that day. He calls it right and maybe there's no need for a playoff."

So it is, despite the weather, an almost perfect day. Mr. Rice seems to be swinging like he did a few years ago, and the Red Sox win, and for me the past and the future blend. I am both boy and man. I have gone to Opening Day, written sports for the *Globe* for the first time since I was their Harvard stringer in 1952 when I was 18 and was paid on the average $35 a week. Then I rush for the shuttle, because I plan to take my young daughter to a party for the 1969 Mets. And then, having disguised myself successfully as a boy all day, we'll go out and celebrate my 55th birthday.

WHY MEN LOVE BASEBALL

From *Parade Magazine*, May 14, 1989

MY WIFE LOOKS AT ME AT THE END OF THE EVENING, AND I understand her look. "You are all still boys," she is thinking. "Will you ever grow up?" We have been at an elegant dinner party in New York where, midway through the dinner, I name-dropped. I just returned from interviewing Ted Williams for 12 hours, and I have let this be known before an assemblage of talented and accomplished men and women—writers, Wall Street financiers, renowned television journalists. All other topics are dropped by the men. The dinner focuses now on only one subject, Ted Williams: What is he really like? Did I have fun? Was he *nice* to me? I watch all the attention shift to me. I drink in the pleasure of the palpable envy of my peers. This is how I make my living—interviewing people, writing books—but for the first time in my life I have a sense that I could, like Tom Sawyer, sublet my interviews and charge these grown men great sums of money for the right to do my work for me.

Men of my age are still bonded by baseball. I cannot vouch for young men who grew up in subsequent generations in greater affluence with greater stimuli at their disposal, but for the generation I know best—men in their late 40s and in their 50s—baseball still turns us into boys again. I think I know some of the reasons now. I am bonded to my father through baseball, because he took me to Yankee Stadium when I was 5 and pointed out the great DiMaggio, and from then on we often went to Yankee Stadium together. It might have been the first thing from his world that he shared with me. I saw this game through his eyes.

In addition, I know now that I felt more comfortable as an on-looker in the semi-fantasy universe of baseball than I did as a partic-ipant in my real life as I grew up, awkward and uncertain of myself in those years. The Yankees, whom I then favored, always won, while more often than not, in things which mattered to me, I always seemed to fail. Boys, when they are young and troubled, do not talk to each other about what bothers them, no matter how close the friendship. There is no real intimacy among us. We talk about things of the exterior, about sports. Baseball was not merely a subject for us, it provided us a social form as well.

It was also, as Bart Giamatti told me, a world with less stimuli. A. Bartlett Giamatti is now the commissioner of baseball, coming to his place after a rich life in academe, where he served first as a pro-fessor and then as president of Yale. In the town of South Hadley, Mass., when he was growing up in the late '40s, there was no movie theater, no computer games, no VCR, no television to speak of. There was baseball. He played every day with his friends; and then, when they were no longer playing, they talked about it. Living in the radio range of Boston, Bart Giamatti was a Red Sox fan, and his favorite player was Bobby Doerr. He played second base because Doerr played it. His room was nothing less than a small baseball museum, a little Cooperstown.

He had made his room into a baseball sanctuary, and he faith-fully listened to every game he could. Years later, when I talked with him, he tried to analyze why baseball meant so much for him and others like him at that moment. Baseball, he said, was the first ap-prehensible myth for a young boy of that generation, the first uni-verse he can comprehend. Sex is still beyond him, God is beyond him, war and politics can be discussed but in any real sense are dis-tant and cannot be comprehended. Baseball is within reach. A boy could read the newspapers and listen to the radio and know that this game was important and that these men were great men, and then he could go out in the afternoon and emulate their acts. Bart Giamatti could be Bobby Doerr. Years later, one of the happiest days of his life came when he met Doerr at a Hall of Fame ceremony. Awkwardly (once again a little boy, although the ex-president of Yale University) he told Doerr that he was his hero. It was Mrs. Doerr who did the better job of putting the moment in perspective. "Mr. Giamatti," she said, "you're the former president of Yale—you're a hero to people like us."

If Bart Giamatti was a fanatic Red Sox fan, then Joe Lelyveld was an equally obsessed Yankee fan. Joe Lelyveld is one of the most distinguished journalists in the country, a veteran *New York Times* reporter who has reported from all over the world and who recently won a Pulitzer Prize for his book on South Africa. But in 1949 he was a sixth-grader, newly arrived in New York, somewhat lonely in his new environs. At that moment he became, in his own words, a scholar of baseball and the New York Yankees. He owned some 30 books on baseball, all of which adorned his room. His allowance went for *The Sporting News* and assorted baseball magazines. He collected cards. He played baseball every day that he could. In his room on his bulletin board were the autographed photos of the Yankee team that you could buy at the stadium.

Tommy Henrich was his favorite player. Henrich was a wonderful player, an exceptional clutch hitter who made the most of his skills. Lelyveld was an expert on the life of Tommy Henrich. The articles about him in *Sport Magazine* were always complimentary. They told how good a family man he was and how respected he was by his teammates. The admiration of Mel Allen, the Yankee broadcaster, who called Henrich "Old Reliable" for his ability to hit in the clutch, was obvious. Henrich was a worthy role model. That spring, with Joe DiMaggio ailing, Henrich had to carry the team, and Lelyveld decided to come to his assistance. He did it by creating a ritual in which he could, through the skillful use of his own mental powers and by fierce concentration, aid Henrich in hitting the home runs required at critical moments. It was nothing less than youthful American voodoo.

He would sit by himself in his room on the West Side of Manhattan, listening to Mel Allen. When Henrich came up in a clutch situation, he would sit there in an armchair with his glove on, and he would bounce a ball off the wall. Then he would look out the window at the New Jersey side: There, right across the river, was a huge Spry factory with a flashing light with the company's name. It was mandatory for him, at precisely the moment that Henrich was hitting, to look at that sign. In his ritual, his role was clear: If Henrich came up and Lelyveld did not play his part perfectly, if he dropped the ball or if his eye wandered from the Spry sign, his powers—considerable though they might be—became useless.

Lelyveld used his powers carefully, and he was not promiscuous with them. He did not seek unnecessary home runs that merely added to Henrich's statistical prowess. But when Henrich came up in the late innings with the game tied or the Yankees a run or two behind, Lelyveld turned on his full powers. His eye did not wander from the sign. He did not drop the ball. His powers were nothing less than phenomenonal in the early part of the season. It seemed that his voodoo worked effectively again. Time and time again, Tommy Henrich came up in clutch situations and hit home runs to win the game.

So it was that 40 years later I ran into Lelyveld, by now an executive of the *Times*, at a party. I mentioned to him that I was writing a book about baseball in the summer of 1949.

"Did you know," asked Lelyveld, "that in the final third of that season, Tommy Henrich hit something like 16 home runs, and 12 of them were game winners?"

"I knew that, Joe," I answered, "because I'm immersed in the season. But how did *you* know it?"

"Because I helped him do it," said Joe Lelyveld.

THE GOOD OLD DAYS—
FOR BASEBALL OWNERS

From the *New York Times*, May 29, 1989

ROGER CLEMENS OF THE BOSTON RED SOX, DOC GOODEN OF the Mets, Orel Hershiser of the Los Angeles Dodgers and Frank Viola of the Minnesota Twins are all part of the newest club in baseball—the $10,000 an inning club. Assuming they stay healthy and pitch around 200 innings a season, that will be their piece rate. (Mr. Viola, the newest and best paid member, is actually closer to the $15,000 club—or $5,000 an out.)

When I read of today's salary negotiations, I think of the very different age in baseball 40 years ago, and I think of George and Vic.

George was George Weiss, general manager and skillful architect of great Yankee teams, and Vic Raschi, who died last fall, was one of his great pitchers. They hated each other, and their annual salary struggles were landmarks of an era when management dealt all the cards in salary negotiations, and a player's recourse was to retire.

If there was a comparable price-per-inning club for pitchers, it was $150, and Raschi constantly struggled with Weiss for the right to be a member of it.

Weiss, almost completely devoid of charm, was ruthless and cold-blooded in contract negotiations; he had a God-given knack at contract time, one Yankee said, to turn what was a positive, healthy relationship into a cold, bitter one. He did not mind that at all. It did not occur to him that it was important for ballplayers to like him: That was not part of his job. He firmly believed that a well-paid ballplayer was a lazy one and that a hungry player, even one who resented management, was a winning one.

That attitude had helped create an important part of the ethos on those Yankee teams. The players, badly underpaid, needing their World Series checks, became the enforcers on the team. That gave Weiss the philosophical basis to be penurious, but he had a more basic one as well: The lower the sum of all the players' salaries, the greater the additional bonus he received from the owners.

The owners gave Weiss a budget, say, of $1 million a year. Weiss worked to keep the salaries down, say, to a total of $600,000 a year. Of that remaining $400,000, Weiss, by agreement, took 10 percent.

He had no illusion that sports was fun. Baseball, to him, was a business, and he never lost sight of this. Typically, at the team party celebrating the Yankees' four-game sweep of the Phillies in the '50 Series, a joyous occasion, he dampened the occasion for almost everyone by making a speech.

He reminded the players that because the Series had lasted only four games, the owners had not made as much money as they should have and therefore salaries would have to be held down in the coming year.

Weiss was so cold in his professional dealings that for a time Jimmy Cannon, the talented *New York Post* sportswriter, wrote columns referring to him as Lonesome George. One day, Weiss went to Toots Shor's restaurant, threw down a couple of columns, complained about Cannon and then said, "But what the hell, Toots, who reads that guy anyway?"

"You do, George," Shor answered.

Vic Raschi became one of the great stars of the Yankee teams that won five pennants and five World Series in a row from 1949 through 1953. In those five years, he won 92 and lost only 40. He was, his teammates thought, possibly the fiercest competitor on the team. He was like a bulldog, tenacious, almost violent about losing a game, particularly after he had been given a lead.

Once during a game with the Red Sox in which Raschi had the lead, he seemed in the seventh inning to be struggling. With Walt Dropo up, Casey Stengel sent Jim Turner, the pitching coach, out to talk to Raschi. Turner ambled out and spoke a few words. The resentment in Raschi's face was visible from the dugout and Turner quickly returned to the bench.

"What did you say?" asked Stengel. "I asked him how he was going to pitch to Dropo," answered Turner. "And what did he answer?" Stengel asked. "Hard," said Turner.

In those five years, Raschi started 160 games and completed 73. He did this despite terrible physical pain. He hurt his knee in 1950 when Luke Easter of the Indians lined a ball off his leg. But he did not have an operation for two years because he was afraid it might cost him part of a season. That meant he played in almost unbearable pain and could barely run and hardly field his position.

His teammates were duly careful around him on the days he pitched. He snapped if they even offered him pleasantries. If they did not pick up on that signal, he would tell them to get away from him.

He did not want photographers to take his picture on a game day: They still used flash attachments, and Raschi hated the fact that for five or six minutes after each pop he could not see properly. He tried to warn them off, but if they did not listen to him, he would spray their shoes with tobacco juice.

Because Raschi gave everything of himself as a player, he expected nothing less than complete respect for his accomplishments.

Weiss seemed to want him to be a strong, forceful man as a pitcher—and a passive man as a negotiator. When Raschi went to negotiate with Weiss, it was as if he was a different pitcher, one who had won 10 games for a seventh-place team. Weiss came armed, not with the latest success of the Yankees and Raschi's integral part in that success but rather with what he had not accomplished—games he had not finished, games against lesser teams he had lost.

It was as if Weiss was trying to withhold not merely Raschi's money but his dignity as well. Weiss had the real leverage, and that made their struggles all the more unfair. Weiss never looked him in the eye but, instead, he looked down on the floor or out the window or off to the side, and he would say after an exceptionally successful season, "Prove to me why you deserve a raise."

Raschi, more than almost anyone else on those teams, stood his ground. After all, he was a winning, starting dependable pitcher for a great team, and starting pitchers were always hard to come by. His only alternative would be a decision to retire, and in this case it was a real possibility. He was just proud enough to do that.

At the end of the negotiations, when Weiss magnanimously agreed to grant a $5,000 raise as a reward for a 19- or 20-game season, he would close the meeting by turning to Raschi and saying his last words of the afternoon: "Don't have a losing season." Those words would hang in the air for weeks and months for what they were: a threat.

Weiss seemed to Raschi and his teammates like a man with a very long memory for slights, and Raschi had a feeling that the moment he showed any sign of slipping as a player, Weiss would turn the screws on him, and he would be gone. The top salary he made after all those great seasons and those five pennants was $40,000, and it had been a war to get even that much.

In 1953, still bothered by injuries, he slipped slightly, winning 13 and losing 6 and starting only 26 games instead of his usual 33 or 34. Raschi, who was 34, had a sense that the end was near.

When he received his contract from Weiss, it called for a 25 percent pay cut. He sent it back, unsigned, with a note to Weiss, saying he had made a cripple of himself in the Yankees' cause. That winter, the Yankees sold him to the Cardinals. They did not notify him personally, and he learned of the deal only though newsmen. One called Raschi at his home. Raschi, proud to the end, said in what was a virtual epitaph for baseball management of that entire era, "Mr. George Weiss has a very short memory."

My Dinner with Theodore

From *Ted Williams: A Portrait in Words and Pictures*, 1990

MY APPOINTMENT WITH MR. THEODORE WILLIAMS OF THE Islamorada, Fla., Williams family had been agreed on well in advance, though we had not yet talked to each other. That is normal in matters of this gravity, and our earlier arrangements had been conducted through intermediaries.

My representative had been Mr. Robert M. Knight of Bloomington, Ind., who, in addition to being my occasional appointments secretary, is coach to the Indiana University basketball team. Mr. Knight, on occasion, has had troubles with members of the press himself, and was almost as celebrated as Mr. Williams in this regard.

It had taken no small amount of time to win over Mr. Knight's good opinion, for somewhat early in our relationship I had failed him on a serious literary point. Mr. Knight, unbeknown to many, is a literary man and I would not be amiss if I referred to him as a kind of literary executor for Mr. Williams. On that earlier occasion, he had quizzed me on my qualifications to write about Mr. Williams.

I had done reasonably well until the final question. Mr. Knight had asked me to quote the best-known sentence of John Updike's famous *New Yorker* piece on Mr. Williams. I had not known, and Mr. Knight had, with no small measure of disdain, pointed out that it said, "Gods do not answer letters."

Still, I had gradually managed to win my way back into Mr. Knight's good favor, and the fact that someone such as Mr. Knight recommended me as a worthy reporter-historian to Mr. Williams had weighed heavily in my favor.

Mr. Williams was reported to have said that if Mr. Knight gave his goddamn approval, why that was goddamn good enough for Mr. Williams.

I arrived well in advance at the motel where Mr. Williams would call on me, and I was told he would come by at eight the next morning to summon me to our meeting. The motel itself was not exactly memorable. Simpler America, vintage 1950s southern Florida, I would say, if architecture were my specialty, which it is not. But I do remember that the cost of it for the night was roughly what the cost of orange juice is at a hotel in the city in which I live, New York.

At exactly 8 o'clock in the morning there was an extremely loud knock on my door. I answered it, and there was Mr. Williams, and he looked me over critically and then announced, "You look just like your goddamn pictures." So, I might add, does Mr. Williams. He has reached his 70s, admirably tanned and handsome and boyish. He seems not to have aged, though he no longer, as he did in his playing days, looks undernourished.

Mr. Williams took me to his house and granted me that agreed-upon interview. The interview with Mr. Williams, who is enthusiastic about whatever he undertakes, was exceptional. Not only did he answer my questions with great candor, but he also managed to give me several demonstrations of correct batting procedures.

He emphasized that I should goddamn well swing slightly up since the mound was higher than the plate. Referring to his close friend Mr. Robert Doerr, of the Junction City, Ore., Doerrs, with whom he has been negotiating on this point for 50 years, he said, "I still can't get that goddamn Bobby Doerr to understand it."

His advice was helpful, particularly since I, like him, bat left-handed, and for a moment I wondered whether with coaching like this, I might make a belated attempt at a career as a designated hitter. I was a mere 54 at the time.

I found Mr. Williams on the whole to be joyous and warm-hearted. He had opinions on almost everything, and it was clear that he had loved playing professional baseball and had stayed in touch with a large number of his teammates, which is unusual for a professional player, 30 or 40 years after his career is over.

Mr. Williams also sought to advise me about political developments in Salvador and Nicaragua. There seemed to be a considerable difference in our opinions on how best to bring a measure of happiness to those two countries, but Mr. Williams did not hold against me my lack of enthusiasm for greater military involvement.

Late in our meeting, Mr. Williams found out that I was a fisherman. It was not information I had volunteered readily since I was afraid that if he found me inadequately skilled with a fly rod, his judgment of me as a writer and interviewer would decline accordingly and he might even report back unfavorably to Mr. Knight.

The interview took up most of the day, and that night Mr. Williams and his lady friend Lou took me to dinner. It was a wonderful dinner, and Mr. Williams paid for us. We had been together 12 hours and he was everything I had always hoped he would be. I considered it to be one of the happiest days in my life.

History's Man

From *Jackie Robinson: Between the Baselines*, 1995

HE WAS HISTORY'S MAN. NOTHING LESS. THOUGH HE CAME to the nation disguised as a mere baseball player, he was, arguably, the single most important American of that first post-war decade. It was not just that he was the first black to play our one showcased national sport, nor that he did it with so dazzling a combination of fire and ice, that he was in truth the black Cobb. What made him so important was the particular moment when he arrived and the fact that he stood at the exact intersection of two powerful and completely contradictory American impulses, one the impulse of darkness and prejudice, the other the impulse of idealism and optimism, the belief in the possibility of true advancement for all Americans in this democratic and meritocratic society.

It is easy now, a half century after Jackie Robinson first played for the Dodgers, when we live in an age of Michael Jordan and Scottie Pippen, and Jerry Rice and Emmitt Smith and Frank Thomas and Bobby Bonds and countless other brilliant black athletes to forget the ethos which existed in America of the 1940s, just before Robinson broke in with the Dodgers. There was a special cruelty to it: for this society not only blocked black athletes from competing on a level playing field, and it did not merely prevent them from gaining their rightful and just rewards from their God-given athletic talents. We as a country were worse than that: we discriminated against blacks, prevented them from playing, and having done that, we denigrated them and said that the reason that they could not play in our great arenas with our best whites athletes, was because they were not good enough.

We defined elemental fairness. We denied them entry to our greatest and most revered arenas, and having done that, we said that the fault was theirs, that they, the they being Negroes (though that was not the word which was used, of course), did not deserve to play with our great whites because they were not good enough. They were, we said, too lazy. We also said of them that they were gutless, and would not in critical situations show the requisite grittiness and toughness demanded of big league ball players. And having said both those things, and having denied almost all blacks in the country any kind of parity of education in those years, we also said that they were not smart enough to play our big-time sports. The only thing they could do—this was self-evident from track meets—was run fast. The issue of courage was particularly pernicious: even if they seemed to have enough natural talent, we said, they would fold under the pressure of big games. Having said this, and it was, I assure you, passed on as a kind of folk gospel at the bar of a thousand saloons, and on the sandlots of a thousand small towns and cities, we denied them any chance to give the lie to words so uniquely ugly, and indeed un-American. Their athletic bell curve was, so to speak, not as good as ours. This, by the way, was not just said in the South, where the reasons for blocking any progress by black people was obvious; rather it was said all over the country. That was one part of the ethos of the time.

The other completely contradictory impulse was that of elemental American fairness. It is critical to our national sense of self-identity that we believe that we are above all, a fair and just society where every child has as much right to prosper as any other child. The greatest and most obvious arena where this could be proved was, of course, sports. We had as a nation always thought of sports as a place where American democracy proved its own validity and where generation after generation of new immigrants showed their worthiness as Americans by prospering first here before they went on to excel in other fields. We as a nation had, for example, on the eve of World War II, taken special pride in the success of the DiMaggio family of San Francisco, that the three children of the immigrant fishermen had made it to the big leagues, and that one of them, Joseph, was the greatest player of his era. That proved that American democracy worked. There was, sadly, only one ethnic group excluded from that exclusionary vision right up until 1947.

Therefore Jackie Robinson's timing in 1947 was impeccable. It was the perfect moment to create a broader, more inclusive definition of American democracy. For it took place right after the victory over Nazi Germany and authoritarian Japan in a great war which was viewed in this country because of the intensity of our domestic propaganda, as nothing less than a victory of democracies over totalitarian states, of good over evil. It had been a war about elemental justice. A generation of young Americans who had gone off to fight in that war returned more determined than ever to make this country whole in terms of justice and fairness. The kind of discrimination which had been practiced against native-born black Americans up until then was no longer feasible. At stake was the most elementary American concept of fairness, in this most democratic of venues, sports. In American folk mythology, a rich kid who had a fancy uniform and an expensive glove still had to prove, when he tried out for a team, that he was a better player than some poor kid from the wrong side of town who did not even own a glove. Now that basic concept of fairness was about to be applied along a racial divide as it never had been before.

It was the conflict between these two conflicting concepts of which Jackie Robinson became the sole arbiter. To most citizens of the country, particularly younger Americans, anxious that their country be as fair and just as it claimed it was, Robinson's debut was more than an athletic performance; rather it was like a political work in progress, an ongoing exercise in the possibilities of American democracy. When he finally arrived in this most open and public of arenas, not only was the whole country watching, but Robinson was performing in an area where success was stunningly easy to calibrate—every school boy could if he wanted, measure the ability of this man. Nothing could be hidden. We are not talking about some great medical school accepting one black student covertly and the rest of the country thereupon not being able to chart that student's progress. Rather we are talking about the perfect arena for so great an experiment. Rarely therefore has one good man given the lie to so much historic ugliness. Branch Rickey had picked well: Robinson was not just a gifted athlete, he was a gifted human being, proud, strong, disciplined, courageous. Robinson did not merely integrate baseball, he did not merely show that blacks could play baseball, and football and basketball, as well as whites could, he helped put the end to arguments in other fields. When the Supreme Court ruled on Brown seven years later, and when Martin Luther King came along in Montgomery eight years later (and when Lt. Colin Luther Powell entered the United States Army eleven years later), the deed was essentially already done. Most of the country was ready in no small part to give blacks a chance in other venues, because Robinson and those who had come immediately after him, like Mays and Aaron, had shown in the most final and compelling way, that if blacks were given an equal opportunity, they were more than worthy of it. The argument was over. One vision of America, a cruel and self evidently crippling one, had mercifully come to an end in 1947, and another, infinitely more optimistic, had been greatly strengthened.

Maybe I Remember DiMaggio's Kick

From the *New York Times*, October 21, 2000

LET ME BEGIN WITH A MEMORY. IT WAS OCT. 5, 1947, AND I was in the Yankee Stadium bleachers, with the Yankees trailing 8–5 in the sixth. With two men on and two men out, Joe DiMaggio hit a tremendous drive to the deepest part of center field. A huge roar went up from the Yankee partisans in the bleachers, and then, as Al Gionfriddo made his celebrated catch, it seemed to ebb and turn into a gasp, while from the same section a second roar of approval exploded from the Dodger fans seated right there with us. Did I actually see the catch? I think I did. Did I see DiMaggio famously kick the dirt as he reached second, a moment replayed on countless television biographies of him because it was the rarest display of public emotion on his part? Again, I think I did. Who knows? Memory is often less about truth than about what we want it to be.

I think memories like this are critical to the current excitement in the city—baseball remains the most rooted of our sports and connects us to generations before, so that at a moment like this past and present merge. When I was young there were three teams in the city and all three were good. Since there were only 16 teams in both leagues and only about four or five of them were actually competitive, a Subway Series for a time seemed something of a New Yorker's birthright.

The last time two New York teams played in a Series, Dwight Eisenhower was running against Adlai Stevenson, the subway token was 15 cents and the door was just beginning to open for black and

Hispanic players. In 1956 the Yankees, not exactly an affirmative action employer, were ever so timidly making their first accommodations to a more diverse sports world. Elston Howard had joined the club the year before. These days, on the occasion that El Duque pitches, the current Yankees will start as many as six players of black and Hispanic origin.

There was in those Octobers now past a great sense of celebration. A Subway Series helped New Yorkers do one of their favorite things—think about themselves. You could, in some of those years before television and air conditioning made their great strides forward, walk down the street in one of the boroughs, hear radios blasting out through open windows and never miss a play.

It's all different now. If you get in a cab these days the odds are slim (it must be those foreigners that John Rocker was complaining about) that the driver will care about baseball. Today's players are bigger, stronger, faster and much, much richer. Ballantine beer is gone, as are Old Gold cigarettes. Baseball no longer dominates the landscape of sports as it did. Because of television, by the late '50s and early '60s pro football was beginning to reach parity with pro baseball. But it's going to be fun here for about two weeks, and it's going to flood many of us with memories of what we will choose to think of as a simpler era and where we were on a given day when baseball ruled the city.

Normally getting just one team into a championship event serves to bring a community together, and people talk to each other about sports across the normal barriers of class, age, and ethnicity. A Subway Series is slightly different; it both unites and divides. Right now the city seems quite pleasantly wired for the event: after all, there's nothing more exciting than a war within a family, which in a way this is.

On a brief poll on our block, I find a doorman and a super who are for the Yankees, and a doorman and a super who are for the Mets. In our building, Ralph Thomas, who runs the elevator, is, I think, covertly for the Mets, but he's quite low-key about it because he knows that Jeff and Linda Drogin and I are Yankee fans.

The crowds will be noisier than in the past—there's less civility at the ballpark because there's less civility in the society. The networks may be worried about the lack of geographic diversity and its effect on ratings. The rest of the nation will probably be underwhelmed. After all, much of America, for reasons that continually perplex most New Yorkers, sees us as loud, noisy, and aggressive, above all insensitive to the nuances and pleasures and culture of other places. That is, the rest of the country sees New York much the way the rest of the world sees America.

Both teams seem to me very good, well balanced with good pitching. If anything, the Mets have been playing better all-around baseball for the last six weeks. But I'll go with my roots. The first game I remember hearing was in 1941, when Mickey Owen dropped Strike Three on Tommy Henrich and we still lived in the Bronx at the Grand Concourse and 174th Street. Rooting for the Yankees, it seems, is in my gene pool. Besides, I like Joe Torre. He's as decent and wise a man as I've met in professional sports. The Yankees in six or seven.

THE ULTIMATE GAMER

From ESPN.com, August 3, 2001

WHEN IT WAS TIME TO ARRANGE OUR SCHEDULE FOR NANtucket this summer—a watering hole that I have gone to for 32 straight years since I bought a house there as a young man—I was aware that we would have a shorter season than most because of various impending deadlines. But, year-round resident of Manhattan that I am, I was buoyed nonetheless by the fact that in addition to my other pleasures, if I skillfully bent my schedule to his, I would get to watch Pedro pitch three or four times, not in person, of course, but on television.

Pedro, naturally, is Pedro Martinez, and he is, to my mind, not merely the best pitcher in baseball today, but something rarer still— a genuine artist.

I say artist, because of the level of craftsmanship involved, the assortment of pitches, the variety of speeds, the perfection of location. Pedro Martinez is not only ahead of the hitters, he is ahead of the fans, the announcers, and most likely his own catcher.

Roger Clemens is having a great year, and his work ethic is admirable; he is still something of a power pitcher at 39 because of his remarkable offseason workout schedule. But though he has evolved from a power pitcher to a more complete pitcher, he is not an artist—what carries him is talent and willpower, and a true predator's desire to triumph. Pedro is an artisan; for the true fan, watching him pitch is like getting a lesson in the infinite possibilities of the game.

(If I refer to him as Pedro in this piece instead of Martinez, it is not that we are intimate pals; it is because that is the way the Boston fans—who feel they are intimate with him—refer to him.)

Therefore the chance to watch him work—or operate—was something I greatly looked forward to. Alas for me, and for millions of others, and especially for Boston fans and his teammates, Pedro has been suffering from an inflammation of his pitching shoulder since late June. So I am undergoing, like so many others, Pedro deprivation. His absence has surely cost the Red Sox five or six wins, but for me it was more personal; I now had something of a hole in my vacation schedule, and would have to be able to find other less leisurely sources of entertainment. Might I, in order to fill the void, have to learn to be a bird watcher, or take up tennis again or go on long bike rides or learn to play golf?

Still, that the Sox have stayed so close to the Yankees without Pedro and Nomar Garciaparra means that we will surely have something of a pennant race, even if the drama doesn't heat up until after my vacation. That the Red Sox have two great players like Martinez and Garciaparra strikes me as showing the hands of the gods at work, not unlike coming across for a long overdue bill—say, in return for Bill Buckner's misplay and Bucky Dent's home run. (I think the gods also had a hand in deciding that Nomar would play in Boston where his name could always be "Nomah.")

And Martinez and Garciaparra are not just two of the very best in the game, but also two of the most likeable—players who self-evidently love the game and whose every move reflects it.

I have watched the Red Sox closely since the pennant-winning team of 1946, when I saw my first game at Fenway. That was the season that Dave Ferriss of Shaw, Miss., won 25 and lost six. Years later he told me that the crowds were so large and noisy that he would on occasion step off the mound and look around him, in order to take note that it was real, and that there were so many people out there cheering for him and who cared that much about what he was doing. I do not know if I have ever seen a more popular player there than Garciaparra (he seems to have played with Ty Cobb, his manager Jimy Williams once noted, describing his love of the game).

I do not want to get into some kind of competition here about which team in sport has the best or the most long-suffering fans, but from my own distinctly nonscientific survey, it strikes me that there is a commitment and a passion—and, finally, a loyalty—in New England for the Red Sox that is different and greater than that of all other sports fans. And so, I believe, New England fans deserve them both.

I have always suspected Red Sox fanaticism is the product of three exceptional confluences: the long, hard winter that makes ordinary fans long for the spring and the summer, with the symbol of it being baseball; the distinct geographic formation of greater New England that makes the Sox a truly regional team, a region totally connected by radio and television coverage of the team's games; and, finally, the Red Sox are almost always very good—which is to say, just good enough to break your heart.

How fortunate then that someone who loves the game so much and plays it with such elegance and intelligence as Pedro Martinez performs before fans who know what baseball is about and are able to appreciate and value his singular skills. He loves—and understands—the game, and it shows every time he pitches.

So I feel partially deprived this summer. I saw him in one game earlier in the year. I betook myself to Yankee Stadium with my friend Gay Talese, the writer, and we watched what was in effect a perfect game—not in the literal sense, but in the more figurative sense, in that it was baseball played in all ways to perfection. Martinez had hooked up with Mike Mussina, in what was simply one of those rare games when fans could understand that the teams were so evenly matched, that every pitch count mattered, and that every runner on base, even in the early innings, might be the deciding moment.

Mussina, for my money, though not really a power pitcher of Pedro's range, is also an artist, and great fun to watch. Though he can occasionally throw a fastball at 93 or 94, he does not live off his fastball. He is the ultimate pitcher's pitcher, he knows the craft, he lives off his intelligence, his sense of the hitters, a great instinct for location, and the ability to keep the hitters off-balance. Watching him pitch is like going back in time and watching Bob Feller hook up with a more powerful version Eddie Lopat—that is, a Lopat who in key moments could reach back and throw heat.

That day they both struck out 12. Mussina, remarkably, was the equal of Martinez. One of the great things about watching Pedro pitch is the pressure he puts on other teams—spot him a run, and it can seem like the biggest hole in the earth. The Red Sox took an early lead, but the Yankees scored twice, on a Bernie Williams home run and a run they scratched out. On this day, it was like watching two masters pitch. I did not keep a scorecard—I stopped scoring long ago—but if Mussina went to three balls on any batter, I have no memory of it. It was a very good pitcher rising to greatness, and exerting the maximum leverage on opposing hitters, because pitching against Martinez meant that he was allowed almost no mistakes.

Some colleagues of mine believe Pedro Martinez is the best pitcher ever. There are even statistics which point this way: He has the best winning percentage of any pitcher in baseball history; he is No. 2 in hits allowed per nine inning game, 6.73; he is No. 2 in strikeouts per nine innings, 10.36, right behind Randy Johnson; he has the lowest career ERA of any starting pitcher in the last 80 years—if you don't count Hoyt Wilhelm, who should not count because he was a knuckleballer, and there ought to be a separate category for them anyway; and, of course, about 10 other indices.

That seems a little heady, and it is very hard to compare different eras. Is he better than Koufax or Gibson or Carlton, or Feller, or Clemens, when they were in their prime? We might ponder that.

There are those great Koufax years: from 1961, when he finally discovered where the plate was and harnessed that great talent—up to then he seemed to be dangerously near being a reincarnation of Rex Barney, who it was said would have been a great pitcher if the plate had been high and outside—through 1966. In 1960, Koufax was just beginning to get there: He walked 100 and struck out 197. But the next year was the breakthrough one, an 18–13 record, 96 walks and 269 strikeouts, and it signaled the beginning of a great six-year run of almost complete domination, ending in 1966 with a 27–9, 317 strikeouts and only 77 walks, and an ERA of 1.73. Then, seemingly still in his prime, having pitched a total of 54 complete games in his last two season, he walked away from baseball at the age of 30.

Or Bob Gibson, in those marvelous mid-'60s and early-'70s years, when he was so dominating that they actually changed the level of the mound because of him. We can cite 1968, when he was 22–9, struck out 268 with only 62 walks, pitched 13 shutouts and 28 complete games—take that, Sandy!—had a season ERA of 1.12, and in one memorable game, a fierce and majestic prince on the mound, the drive and passion and ferocity clear for the entire nation to see, struck out 17 Tigers, a great fastball hitting team, in the World Series.

I was 34 years old that season, watched that game, understood, I thought, what drove Gibson, and some 25 years later, in part because of what I saw on television that day, I wrote a book that was in no small part about him.

Gibson, too, was a gamer. In the World Series, he was 7–2, with 92 strikeouts in 81 innings, and a cumulative Series ERA of 1.67 (Koufax in 57 World Series innings pitched, had an ERA of 0.97). A few years ago when I wrote a book on Michael Jordan, I sent a copy to Gibson, with an inscription: "The person he reminds me of is you."

So who knows who is the best? Only the hitters could really know, and who batted against Feller and Koufax, and Gibson and Martinez when all were in their prime? What we do know is that Pedro Martinez is the best in the game today, a nonpareil, that he almost always dominates, and perhaps most important, he is a true gamer. The bigger the game, the better he pitches.

Let us recount two great Pedro moments: One against the Yankees in September of 1999, the other against Cleveland in a 1999 playoff game.

Let us take the first one, against the Yankees, in what was a very tough pennant race, where he clearly has to carry the Red Sox—especially in big games, where his psychological presence can influence his teammates and affect more than the game he is pitching. I went back the other day to watch a replay of it. He was matched against Andy Pettitte, leading in the seventh, 2–1, on a two-run Mike Stanley home run. Bobby Murcer, calling the game for the Yankees, kept repeating, "One run for Pedro Martinez is like five runs for anyone else," while Tim McCarver kept saying, "What a great ballgame this is."

Late in the game, Boston had loaded the bases with no outs, but Jeff Nelson had come in and gotten the Yankees out of the jam, first with a force play at home, then a double play. That was a huge incentive for the Yankees to turn the momentum the other way. They had Jeter, O'Neill and Williams coming up. So, of course, here we have Pedro at his best. The count went to 3-2, and he got Jeter on a called third strike. The next hitter was O'Neill. Again a 3-2 count. Got him swinging, his 11th strikeout of the game. And then Bernie. The count was 0-2, and he decided not to waste any time. Got him on a breaking ball. He struck out 17 Yankees that night, a personal best. Excepting Don Larsen's perfect game in the World Series in 1956, this might have been the greatest game ever pitched in Yankee Stadium, and given a choice to be on hand at either, I would have taken the Martinez-Pettitte game.

The other great night for him as a gamer was the fifth game of the Divisional Series against Cleveland. By that point, it was clear that the pitching on both teams was gone, that the pitching staffs were exhausted. Martinez himself had been hurt, and had had to come out of an earlier game with a shoulder that was giving him pain. By the time he entered the fifth game, the score had begun to resemble a football score, 8–8 at the end of three innings. Ailing shoulder or not, he pitched six magical innings of no-hit baseball.

Here is what we know about him—and I am indebted here to my generous colleague Dan Shaughnessy, the immensely talented *Boston Globe* columnist. He has every pitch: fastball, slider, curve and change. The change, notes Shaughnessy, is remarkable—it starts with the same fierce motion, same delivery, same angle as the fastball, but with much less speed. In spring training, he will even tell batters that the change is coming, and they still can't hit it.

No small amount of Pedro's success, Shaughnessy believes, comes from his unusually long fingers. That allows him to do more things with the ball. "It's like Michael's big hands—the ball is smaller for Michael than it is for the other players, and he can do more things with it. That's true of Pedro, as well," Shaughnessy says.

The Red Sox paid handsomely for him when they got him from those poor folks up in Montreal, but it has turned out to be a bargain of the first order. It was Montreal which got him on the cheap. He was 22 years old at the time, clearly just coming of age; in 1993, his first full season with the Dodgers, he won 10 and lost 5, had an ERA of 2.61, and struck out 119. He appeared to be a pitcher just about to bloom. Then the Dodgers traded him, even up, for Delino DeShields. Pedro seems to get along with most people in baseball, but Lasorda is another story. The anger here is a blood thing, because the Dodgers never gave him a real chance and judged him on his size, not his talent and his heart.

So forget whether he's the best ever. Just accept the fact that he's an artist, and there are always too few of them and too many others who think they're artists, and flaunt their behavior as if they're artists, but aren't, legends only in their own minds. Settle for the idea that he's the best around these days, a Cy Young winner three times, and in both leagues, and that it is a pure pleasure to watch him, a craftsman at work, all those tools, and all that intelligence and that self-evident love of the game.

So I've missed him this summer. Last Saturday there was a series against Chicago, and it was a beautiful day, just that kind of day when you're supposed to be outside, but I figured, if he had been pitching, I somehow would have cheated on the weather—maybe told my wife that I was working on a book—and stayed inside and watched the game.

But Pedro wasn't there, so I was forced to be something of a grown-up. I went fishing with my pal Allan LaFrance, who is a builder on this island and a friend for 20 years, and his friend Pat Taaffee, a carpenter. We went off the Great Point Rip on a gorgeous day and the water was alive with fish, bait fish everywhere, and the big fish trying to nail them. When we caught a blue, the baitfish and the miniature sand eels they had already hit, still undigested, would come out immediately. I've fished here for more than 30 years, and I don't think I've ever seen so many fish in the water. We had a strike or a follow on almost every cast. We caught and released more than a dozen blues and even took two good-size stripers. If you can't watch Pedro pitch on a perfect day in July, this was not half bad as a substitute.

Torre Makes a Good Boss

From ESPN.com, December 5, 2001

THIS IS IN PRAISE OF JOE TORRE. WHAT A PLEASURE IT HAS been to watch the Yankees during the years he has managed in New York. May I also suggest that this year he had what was probably his best of year of managing, this being a Yankee team that was aging and somewhat vulnerable, and seemed, especially in the beginning of the season, better on paper than it was on the field.

It is in praise of him not merely as a baseball man, but in the more complete sense as a man, for the two are not always the same. To understand the difference, all you have to do is think back to the appalling turmoil that surrounded the cartoon-like Billy Martin era in the Bronx years before Torre arrived.

Torre is as complete a person as high-level professional sports can produce, especially in this hyped-up era with its higher visibility, where the rewards are greater than ever, and where therefore the shelf life of a coach or manager tends to be briefer—you go up higher and faster than in the past, and you can descend even more quickly. The role of the media, after all, is greater than ever, which imposes an immense temptation to take care of yourself at the expense of your players, to indulge in me-first leadership.

Torre has been successful in New York for any number of reasons: He has had very good players, by dint of George Steinbrenner's passion to win, and his players are by and large, mature, unusually self-reliant men (especially when calibrated on the Richter Scale of contemporary athletic maturity, where sheer ability and the willingness to accept responsibility for your actions are not necessarily on the same team).

But I think it is important not to underestimate how well Torre's own exceptional human qualities have served him, his honesty and sense of humor, and his instinct, despite all the media pressures on him, to be exceptionally straight in his dealings. This has helped shape the clubhouse and made these Yankees a team that sportswriters coming from venues that are nominally violently anti-Yankee have come to respect, if not actually like.

So, in one of the three or four most heavily scrutinized institutions in the country (perhaps less scrutinized than the Pentagon, but more scrutinized than the Department of the Interior) and with an exceptionally demanding and highly volatile owner, he has managed to be true to himself, and his players know it. If they are straight with him, he will play it straight and protect them—if need be, even from the owner.

Somehow, when I think of Torre, I conjure up the opposite vision of Steve Spurrier, the immensely successful coach of Florida who (a) always seems to be running up the score, but more importantly (b) seems to give out the impression by body language and facial expression that when things go wrong, it is not that he coached poorly, but because his players did not execute his game plan as well as they should.

I do not know Torre very well personally, but even my limited dealings with him gave me added respect for him. We met about eight years ago, when I was working on a book about the 1964 World Series between the Yankees and Cardinals. Torre had not played in that Series—he joined the Cardinals a few years later—but he was a great friend and admirer of Bob Gibson, who was the star of the Series and a central figure in my book. He was obviously intrigued that someone who is not nominally a sportswriter was going to write about one of the great athletes and fiercest competitors he knew.

Therefore, he went out of his way to be helpful. There was nothing in it for him, which for most readers probably does not mean much. But for anyone writing about sports it means a great deal—by and large, when you deal with an athlete or an ex-athlete, one of the things that hangs quite heavily in the air is one of the oldest questions of all time—what's in it for me?

It struck me that Torre went out of his way to be generous, not because he cared that much who I was, or wanted to ingratiate himself with me, for there was no way I could help his career or get him back into baseball at that time, but because he thought I was serious, and—most of all—because he loved Bob Gibson and he wanted to be sure I got him right. Torre's generosity was about something very old-fashioned, loyalty to a magnificent teammate, years after they had played their last game together.

I remember leaving the interview that day, impressed not merely by the wonderful quality of Torre's stories about Gibson, but about the nature of the man I had just finished interviewing. He had an old-fashioned sense of honor and loyalty to a teammate. It told me a good deal about two men, Gibson, the man who inspired that loyalty, and Torre, the man who, in such an egocentric line of work, still possessed it.

I was impressed at the time, and had made it a point in the years after to pay attention to Torre, and he has not disappointed me. He always seems to be in character, very much the man I dealt with then, albeit in ever more explosive and pressurized circumstances.

I am always a little wary of journalistic psychological assumptions, but I have come to believe that Torre behaves this way because it is who he is, and the way he was raised, his home, his religion, the nurturing of an admired older brother, and that he was taught to deal with people in a certain way, the way he would like to be treated by them. He seems to be a man secure in his knowledge of who he is, and secure in his faith. Equally important, though he would obviously prefer to win rather than to lose, how he behaves as a man and how he sees himself is not based on his career winning percentage.

It is a rare quality these days, and it extends far beyond sports. My wife, who is not a devoted baseball fan, has watched him over the years, in all kinds of difficult situations, especially in this year when the Yankees made their great postseason run, with the shadow of the New York tragedy hanging over them, and she was stunned by Torre's constant grace under pressure, the test Hemingway set up for men years ago—he is, she says, the most elegant of men; he always seems to get the situation he is in right and to say the right thing.

She is right. The key to Torre is that he is a good baseball man, but he also knows there is much more to life than baseball, and that, finally, it is how you behave, most obviously when things are not going on well, that defines you.

If Torre is a man who has come to peace with himself, George Steinbrenner has seemed, at many times in his career (less so now than in the past), a man far from comfortable with himself, often given to bullying those around him and denigrating his players during losing streaks. Some of his pettier qualities have been reined in recently, and I suspect part of the change is simply a factor of age. He was 71 this year, and most of us become less volatile as we get older.

But one of Torre's great successes has been to serve as an insulator to protect his players from the owner and, whenever possible, to take the heat himself. Another has been to be able to change the ambiance at the Stadium from the time, just a decade ago, when the Yankees could not get the free agents they wanted, and were being used by shrewd agents to bid the price up for other teams. Does anyone think Mike Mussina would have come to the Yankees in the Billy Martin era?

The Steinbrenner-Torre relationship is a fascinating, constantly shifting one of balances and counterbalances. Torre serves, as all managers do, at the owner's whim, and Steinbrenner has more whims than most people, and they come to him more quickly. If he knows he needs this manager, there is also no doubt that he has no small amount of envy for Torre's larger public and media popularity and, as such, we get the occasional reminders of his irritation, the long delay in re-signing Torre, and the occasional throwaway lines that Torre never won until he came to the Yankees, and thus managed the players Steinbrenner signed. There is a good deal of truth to that, but it is also true that the clubhouse ambiance has changed dramatically in the Torre years, making the Yankees more attractive to the free agents Steinbrenner wants to sign.

One of the things that has always fascinated me when looking at men who are engaged in fierce pursuits, in the military or sports, for example, is the difference between being strong and being tough. Steinbrenner, for whatever insecurities, has always struck me as someone who wants to be tough (there was an unusually stupid Howard Cosell piece about him years ago which called him the George Patton of the Yankees—though, of course, Steinbrenner had never heard a shot fired in anger), but does not know the difference between being tough and strong. From his own background, and from his own self-doubt, I suspect, come a certain amount of swaggering, bullying and tough guy talk, as if that is the way real tough guys talk.

Torre is, very quietly, something quite different. He is quietly strong—a strength that comes from a healthy sense of accurately appraised self-value, and a willingness, if need be, to walk away from any situation which might be unacceptably difficult or abusive. As such, there has been an invisible line drawn in the sand at the Stadium without him ever having to draw it. Because of that, he has not only done an exceptional job managing the Yankees, but has also helped do something that a number of us thought once could not have been done—he has helped turn George Steinbrenner, though still a work in progress, into a good owner.

THE PERFECTIONIST AT THE PLATE

From the *New York Times*, July 9, 2002

IN LATE AUGUST OF 1946, WHEN I WAS 12, I WATCHED TED
Williams hit the most vicious drive I have ever seen. The ball, in my
memory at least, was still soaring majestically when it hit the seats
in the third tier in Yankee Stadium. Forty-two years later, when I
was 54 and he was nearly 70, I spoke with Williams about the drive,
both of us magically still boys on this date because of the subject
matter. As I did, and as the details of that game all came back, I
watched a smile spread over his face. "Tiny Bonham," he said at the
end, naming the Yankee pitcher. I am sure he remembered the exact
quality of the light and what Bonham threw as well.

He remembered because he was highly intelligent and he employed the full force of that ferocious, aggressive intelligence in the
pursuit of only one objective: being the greatest hitter who ever
lived, which he might well have been. Pitchers, in his words, were
dumb by breed, and he studied them constantly looking for, and
usually finding, their weaknesses.

He transcended baseball. He was a link not just to one of baseball's golden eras, the last man to bat over .400. He also had served
during two wars that have long since passed into history and was
someone our parents and grandparents had seen play, and about
whom they surely had strong opinions. He leaves men of my generation still debating the same questions we argued about when we were
boys: What he might have done had he played in Yankee Stadium,

with its more accessible right-field seats; and what his statistics might have been had he not had to give up nearly five full seasons to military service.

Difficult and cantankerous when he was young, and easily wounded, he had been the victim of some of the sleaziest journalism of modern times, particularly on the part of the Boston sportswriters whose tabloid papers were struggling to survive in a too crowded field. But he always held true to his own beliefs; reporters were, in his phrase, "knights of the keyboard." How amused he might have been with the coverage of his death. He led the evening news on ABC and the two surviving Boston papers treated his passing as a virtual state event.

Relatively late in life, considerably mellowed, he let the world in to see him. What we saw was a surprisingly warm and generous man, someone rich within himself, who had always lived by his own codes and to his own specifications when it was immensely costly to him. The things he did, both good and bad, he did because he could never do otherwise.

The defining Ted Williams moment came on the last day of the 1941 season. He was hitting .39955 that morning, which in baseball statistical terms rounds off to .400. Joe Cronin, the Boston manager, offered to let him sit—the .400 would be his. No way that Ted Williams was going to sit that out: he played both games of a doubleheader, went 6 for 8, and finished with a .406 average, well outside the reach of purists. We can only imagine the pressure that, in today's society, agents and advertisers would use in begging a lineal successor not to go out and risk so much for so little.

He was a completely authentic man and he never bent to fashion; he remained to his final days the unvarnished man. His failure to wear a tie in an era when ballplayers were supposed to wear ties, particularly at events in their honor, was more than a fashion statement, it was a statement of personal freedom: if he showed, he showed as Ted Williams. It also reflected the fact that he was completely comfortable in the universe of baseball but quite uncomfortable in the larger universe around it. He had great status in the former and was completely uncomfortable with status as granted in the latter. When he retired from baseball, he moved to Islamorada, Fla., where in lieu of his former teammates, his pals became the local fishing guides—grizzled, rough men with much the same earthy view of life. Nor did he doubt that as one of the most passionate fishermen of our time, he could fly-cast better than they could.

He was politically conservative but in his core the most democratic of men. Few players of his generation championed the rise of black athletes as he did. His speech at his induction into the Hall of Fame in 1966 is notable for its generosity to Willie Mays: "The other day Willie Mays hit his 522nd home run. He has gone past me and he's pushing, and I say to him, 'Go get 'em, Willie.'" Baseball gives every American boy a chance to excel. Not just to be as good as anyone else, but to be better. That is the nature of man and the name of the game.

What he loved most of all was hitting. No one ever did it better. He was among the first of the great power hitters to go to a much lighter bat because bat speed was of the essence, and whippier was better. He even noticed that in the summer, on moist muggy days, bats picked up extra weight from the grass, perhaps a critical half ounce, which would be 1.5 percent of the total weight. Some teammates argued with him. Off they all went to the post office to weigh the bats. Williams was right, of course.

Once when he was younger he was called out on strikes at Fenway. He came back to the dugout ranting and raving about the injustice of the call, and more, the fact that home plate was out of line—that, he said, was why the umpire had blown the call. Some of the Boston pitchers teased him about it, a serious mistake on their part. So the next day Joe Cronin went out and measured the lines and as ever Williams was right—it was out of line.

So here is our chance to make one last correction. Keep all the other records, the career .344, the 521 home runs and the career on-base percentage of .482. But change the career strikeout number from 709 to 708. It's the least we can do.

If They Strike, I'm Going Fishin'

From ESPN.com, July 26, 2002

MY FRIEND RICHARD BERLIN AND I HAD SPENT FOUR DAYS up on the Tabusintac River in New Brunswick, happily fishing for giant brook trout, and now we were on our way back to the United States. About 50 miles from Presque Isle, Maine, where we would board our plane back to Boston, we finally picked up the Red Sox–Yankees game on the radio, the last of a three-game series.

By the time we could hear it, the Yankees were leading 7–6, and Jeff Weaver, whose arrival in New York from Detroit had seemingly threatened to throw baseball permanently out of kilter, was pitching. At that moment, Weaver, in the words of one of the Boston announcers, could smell the end of his day's work, and his seemingly sure victory. Then Nomar Garciaparra hit a two-run homer to put the Red Sox ahead, the fifth of the day off Weaver, a man who had only a few weeks ago seemed to have ended competitive baseball.

Berlin, a man of Boston, was thrilled. I—who was born in the Bronx, grew up in New England, live in New York but have a summer house in Massachusetts, and loved the older Red Sox players I met when I did a book on the 1949 Yankees–Red Sox pennant race—had mixed feelings.

I feel a certain orbital pull to the Yankees, by dint of living in the same city and the inevitable emotional pull toward players you watch almost every day on television, but I feel a different kind of emotional pull to the Red Sox, particularly because they have over the years seemed overwhelmed by their fates (or by their DNA). My good friend Marty Nolan, the distinguished and now retired *Boston Globe* editor, once summed up the frustrations of being a lifelong Red Sox fan by saying, "They killed my father, and now they're coming after me."

In theory, a Red Sox victory fits in with my greater code of fairness, and yet because I'm a New Yorker, there is a sense of having more complicated feelings. I can be as nostalgic about Williams, Doerr, Pesky and DiMaggio, as I can about Keller, Henrich and DiMaggio.

I told Berlin simply that I did not think this one was over yet and that the Yankees' strength was their bullpen. Radio remains a marvelous instrument by which to pick up and enjoy baseball, and in the ninth inning with Ugie Urbina pitching, and Jason Giambi batting, our rented SUV was as good as being in the ballpark. Giambi is a very good hitter, one of those rare players who, inflationary salary or not, is worth almost what he is paid. He has an uncommon eye, he picks the ball up very quickly, and he knows his job, which means that he knows it is as important in certain situations to get on base as it is to hit a home run.

Urbina had Giambi 0-2, starting him out, joy of joys, with a change. And then Giambi using all his skills, hung in, and worked the count, fouling off good pitches, until he finally hit a dribbler against the Boston shift, and started what would be the winning rally. All in all, it was a great at-bat. And then the Red Sox fell apart. It had been, though we had missed the first two games, baseball at its very best, two very good teams representing two heralded franchises, playing at almost exactly even levels. Giambi vs. Urbina had showcased one of the very best hitters in baseball working against a tough, nasty reliever.

There had been little more any serious fan could ask for in terms of confrontation—if the Yankees won, they would go up four games, if Boston won, it would be behind only two and would continue to show that it could outplay the Yankees in head-to-head competition. Both now had ownerships that seemed to reflect the passion of their fans. The Yankees had improved themselves over the offseason, but the Red Sox had improved themselves perhaps even more, and they might have, unlikely though it might have seemed before the season started, better starting pitching than the Yankees, and they seemed to have the most un–Red Sox–like of attributes, considerable team speed, and better fielding than in the past. They did something that few Red Sox teams have ever done— they fielded better than their Yankee rivals.

I mention all this because we are being told that a strike is imminent—that the date has even been picked out, Sept. 16; the people who make these decisions do not, after all, for reasons of good manners want it to be before Sept. 11 because they do not want to look petulant and spoiled on the anniversary of the terrorist bombings. That might not be good public relations, and good public relations are very important these days.

Perhaps sometime after that special date the players will walk out. So be it. If they walk, they walk. We have been told for more than a year and a half that a strike (or a lockout) is in the cards, that the differences between the sides are irreconcilable, and that if the players don't walk at a certain point the owners will lock them out.

The truth is, that in all that time as far as I can tell, there has not been the slightest serious movement on either side for any kind of settlement. No give at all. A commissioner, whose own baseball team seems to be the prototype for a kind of perennial loser, runs the show. (As I write, Milwaukee is a mere 22 games below .500, and a mere 22½ games behind St. Louis. Only Tampa Bay, that most storied franchise of franchises, has lost more games in all of major league baseball. Is there anyone connected to baseball who does not think that if Peter Gammons was given this same franchise with the same budget, and had two years to move players around, he would not have somehow come up with a much better, younger, more interesting team?)

What we have is a world of greed and arrogance and some measure of stupidity: arrogant owners, arrogant players, and arrogant agents. No one willing to work on (or even try to come up with) any kind of formula that would give even the semblance of negotiation. The idea—I suppose this is the genius of it—is to wait until the very moment when fan interest should be at its peak, when the pennant races are in full bloom, and then turn it all off. The fans will be angry, it is presumed, and will demand some kind of action. I'm not so sure.

I have no strong feelings at all on this one because I gave up thinking long ago that the conflicting sides care very much. I see no point in caring more about baseball than the chief operators and chief beneficiaries do; that is, the people who are ostensibly in charge of its health and who make their living off the game.

So if they want to walk, it's all right with me. If they can't find an equitable formula for revenue sharing, to give the game some measure of economic balance, they don't deserve to be in charge of, or profit from the game. The players have turned out to be capitalists, very shrewd ones at that, and the owners are caught between being capitalists and hobbyists, and have lost control of their own domain over a period of years.

When the world was changing on them in terms of free agency and the owners could have worked out a good deal with the players, they were too full of themselves, and too arrogant to see what the new structure of baseball was going to mean. Later, when they still had a chance to work out some kind of deal, they were too divided among themselves to be strong. Which is where we pick them up today—not that smart, and not that visionary, and not that unified.

The owners went from an age of authoritarian power—the players were in a condition of complete economic servitude—to a new age that demanded nuance, wisdom, economic self-control, and respect for their employees. Not surprisingly, they have been floundering ever since. They have lacked at the very core, vision, a sense of how to measure their pie honestly among themselves, and then how to seek a means of sharing that pie with the players.

What the NFL and NBA have figured out in very different ways is how to balance the interests of the players with the interests of the owners. Baseball owners for a variety of reasons have failed at this. They cannot deal equitably with the players because they have not figured out how to deal equitably with each other.

It's not the Yankees who are ruining baseball—it's other owners who bought in and thought they could run the game to their own specifications, and found, once in the game, that they were wrong, that the old authoritarian era had changed, and that it cost more than they thought to be a member of this particular rich man's club. They don't like the price of poker now that they're in the game. (Remember Wayne Huizenga, one of my all-time favorite owners—he came in, bought a pennant and a World Series championship and then, not liking the balance sheet, completely dismantled his team. Now there's a franchise rich in history for you—a modern dynasty so to speak—one more likely to be studied at Harvard Business School than by baseball historians.)

The truth about George Steinbrenner is that for all his flaws and his bombast, he has become a rather smart owner in recent years, and he has maximized the rules for his own best interest and that of a team in the media capital of the world. He finally has learned about the importance of pitching, he has not traded his young talent away, and he has left a gifted manager alone.

Unlike his counterpart in Texas, Steinbrenner did not spend $252 million on one position player, however talented, without upgrading his pitching staff. And as for the position player in question, he gives us a certain insight into the mentality of the players—maybe he's a great person and a great young man, and certainly everyone seems to like him, but the truth is, facing a very short career like any athlete, he has severely limited his chance to test his real greatness because he has truncated the chance to play at moments of maximum competition when greatness truly matters, in postseason. He left a wonderful team with great fans in a city where he was immensely popular, to play for a team that is at the moment only 19½ games out of first place with almost no prospects for an improved pitching staff and a disillusioned owner who is talking about pulling back from high salaries.

(At the very least what A-Rod has done is to give a warning to any broadcaster who's inclined to say what a great competitor he is—maybe he is, and maybe he isn't but he's voluntarily taken himself out of the highest level of competition for some time.) Maybe A-Rod should be the chief negotiator for the players' union. Mike Hampton, coming off a marvelous year with the Mets two years ago and choosing to go with free agency to Colorado, yes Colorado (I'm not talking about it as a state for the young at heart who love the outdoors, I'm talking about it as a state for baseball pitchers), can be his deputy.

As for Steinbrenner, he's hardly the richest owner in baseball. And he's right when he points out that when they've taxed the more successful owners on behalf of the smaller markets in the past, the smaller-market owners have not been very quick to put that money back into players' salaries.

In the past when there was a strike, my sympathies were fairly clear. I tended to side with the players. So in a way this is more of a warning to Donald Fehr and the players, because I'm never on the side of the owners. But Fehr should know that in this economy and in this country right now, almost no one is on his side. They might not be against him, but they sure as hell are not for him.

This time, like most fans I know, I have a plague-on-both-your-houses attitude. If they strike, I'll do other things. The morning paper will be a little less interesting—like many males of my generation, I read it back to front, starting with the sports page. But the world will go on without baseball. I'll definitely miss it in October. I like the game, and maybe, slowly warily (very warily) I'll come back if they ever see fit to play again. But I've invested a lot in caring about both New York and Boston this year, and I don't like investing my emotions and not getting something back, and being cheated when it finally matters, at playoff time. If they can walk it or shut it down, I can walk it and shut it down, too.

Sure, I've enjoyed watching this season. I've enjoyed watching Pedro Martinez come back from his arm troubles, and Nomar come back from his terrible season, and I've enjoyed watching Alfonso Soriano, with the great elasticity in his muscles, explode into greatness. I've been impressed by the graceful way Giambi has handled a double whammy, a huge contract and move to the center of the New York spotlight and never flinched.

One of my great pleasures has been a surprising one—the simple delight I take in listening to Jim Kaat, as he broadcasts the Yankee games. Quietly with no blather and bombast, he gives what is one of the most enjoyable and thoughtful ongoing seminars on pitching I've ever heard. Jim Kaat, you're right up there for my MVP.

There are, remarkably enough, and hard for all of the people who dominate baseball to believe, other things for us to do in the summer—movies to go to and books to read. Me, I like to fish.

My friend Richard Berlin and I had just spent four marvelous days on the Tabusintac in New Brunswick, fishing for large ocean-going brook trout. The lodge where we stayed was beautiful, the fish were, if not plentiful, certainly abundant and very tenacious, and on the last day there, I had caught a 6-pounder and a 5-pounder, and Berlin, a vastly superior fisherman, had done even better. Those are, by the way, given the species, very nice-sized fish. The truth about fishing is that there are good days and bad days, but even the bad days are almost always good days, and while I have had days when I did not catch a single fish, I have never known the fish to go out on strike.

AND SO IT HAPPENED

From the *Boston Globe*, December 19, 2004

I SAT THERE IN MY MANHATTAN APARTMENT, WATCHING THE parade with great pleasure. In some ways, not altogether surprising, Manny Ramirez was the hero of the parade, MVP on a team that did not have an MVP (unless it was that famous and extremely popular and ever-versatile first baseman-DH-left fielder Manny Ortiz). In the parade, Manny was holding up a sign making fun of Derek Jeter, Jeter the golfer, and on this day everyone loved both the holder and the sign. How hard it has been all these years to mock Jeter, the otherwise unmockable. It was the best sign in the parade—and Manny had it. Manny, of course, reflected the season: Manny the unwanted at the beginning, Manny the MVP at the end. Again, that is not so surprising: When I think of him, I think of him as a double-edged Manny, as in Live-by-the-Manny, Die-by-the-Manny.

That was a quality brought home most painfully in the first game of the World Series, when in a space of two innings he got a critical hit, applauded himself so enthusiastically that he did not turn it into a double, and then belatedly tried for second. Only Cardinal fielding even worse than his base running kept him from being thrown out. That in turn was followed by two unforgivable fielding errors in two innings. But he kept getting hits and he kept on being Manny, and his lapses, such as they are, were forgiven; to love Manny is to forgive the unforgivable. In the end we all loved him and his Mannyisms; and he, wonderfully happy on the day of the celebration, was the star of the parade.

Is this the beginning of a great and most unlikely cultural accommodation between player and fan base, the Mannyization of New England, or will it be (a bit less likely) the New Englandization of Manny? Will it last a long time? How deep goes this love affair? Stay tuned.

The great curse of the gods of baseball is gone. With all respect to my great pal Dan Shaughnessy, I never thought it was a curse. Not even a milder hex. A shadow maybe, but not that of the Babe. The shadow of Willie Mays, when the Sox did not sign him back in 1949 when they had first shot at the then-18-year-old Mays because he played in Alabama for the Birmingham Black Barons in the park of the Birmingham (white) Barons, a Sox farm club, and they had been tipped by the (white) Barons owner to Mays's greatness. The Sox' talented regional scout George Digby told me that he was possibly the best player he had ever scouted, but the Red Sox management wanted no part of him.

A shadow like that can last a long time, and the damage it can do is immense, especially at a time when the great new talent bank was first black, and then black and Hispanic.

But I thought it was a good—and on occasion a great—team, a franchise that all too often had an ownership that was never quite as good as it should have been, and as such the team came up just a bit short. The teams were almost always competitive and fun to watch, and those great World Series expeditions are worth pondering: four trips, 1946, 1967, 1975, and 1986, 28 games played, further than that you cannot push it. Teams that are cursed do not go to seven games in October. Teams that are cursed disappear in October.

Everything about them was attractive: the ballpark with its sense of living history; the deeply knowledgeable fans, singularly loyal if a bit wary; the sportswriters, who were, for a long time, possibly the best in the country. Thus there might be a shortfall in pitching, but there would never be a shortfall in critics. And, of course, the harsh winter, so much time to talk about so little else. All these things mean that they matter.

In the past, the ownership tended to come up just a bit short, usually in pitching. In 1949, in that extraordinary pennant race that went down to the last game of the season, it was Raschi, Reynolds, and Lopat for New York, soon to be joined by Whitey Ford (and with, of course, Joe Page, the rare great reliever of that era), against Parnell and Kinder. That has been true right up to this season, when it has become ever clearer that George Steinbrenner, his team less and less a product of his farm system, has involuntarily come up with a new philosophy of putting together a pitching staff: Buy old, and buy high. In recent years the teams have been almost exactly even, with the Yankees commanding a slight edge in starting pitching and having the one player who was critical to the franchise's success, Mariano Rivera.

The new Red Sox ownership seems to be the smartest the city has ever had: John Henry may not be from New England, but he strikes me as someone who is acutely aware that in baseball terms he owns one of the jewels in the crown, and that though it is a private company, the Red Sox are, in all real ways, public property, that his accountability, in this case an almost mystical thing, is to something larger than baseball, to an institution that, as much as anything, encompasses an entire region and, more than anything, binds it together.

As such, the owners responded to last year's shortfall in precisely the ways that their predecessors rarely did. They added a desperately needed starter in Curt Schilling; they junked the bizarre closer-by-committee and got Keith Foulke as their closer. They were in a difficult position on the Nomar front, but they handled a complex and painful situation with considerable skill.

And so it happened. They finally won. And they won in a marvelous way: Three down to the Yankees, they then went on to win eight in a row against two of the best teams in baseball. It was like putting an exclamation point at the end of the last sentence about the season. And that brings us to the final, haunting question. Will success spoil Red Sox Nation? Will the magic be gone? Was the real bond a sure sense of eventual failure?

I don't think so. As someone who has traveled the country and has heard a great many confessions from fans all over the map, stories of love and disappointment, but above all stories of faith, I think it is important that there are two quite separate parts of Red Sox Nation: There are the Category One, faith-based people, the home-grown fans, the children of New England, the most rooted of fans, no matter where they live today, whose loyalties go back generations—weaned on stories of the young Ted and the aging Jimmie Foxx and Lefty Grove (fans for whom Yaz, at 65, remains something of a newcomer); and there are the Category Two fans, the people out there who root for the Red Sox because they are the main obstacle to the success of the dreaded Yankees. I should point out that on occasion Category Two fans become Category One fans, but the process is by no means automatic.

I have no doubt of the durability of the Category One fans. That's because it's in the DNA, much, much deeper than with most fan bases, built on the resonance of the game in the region and an unusual living connection to the past, on memories passed on lovingly, generation to generation. I never thought these fans rooted to be disappointed. Instead, they rooted in a very personal way, as if by proxy for those who had gone before them in their own families, and who had always been disappointed. Theirs was a special connection, one of enduring love mixed with a profound foreboding.

And the pleasure of it all, the sweetness of this particular fall, will that last as well? That, of course, is a very different question. It's a lovely feeling right now, but things like this do not last a long time.

If you need a victory by your favorite sports team to give you some kind of enduring emotional upgrade, then you are, I suspect, in real trouble. It's a pleasant fix, this winning, and in this case it's long overdue and a lot better than losing. But the American League East is a competitive, expensive battleground, and no one has enough pitching and everyone's pitchers are too old. This is the time for happiness, for an amnesty on Red Sox villains of the past, a time to forget all the things that went wrong at all the last moments, and to look forward to the coming season. All good things happen in the spring, we all know that, and besides, Bronson Arroyo looks as if he's about ready to break out as a big-time major-league pitcher.

Play it (again), Theo.

BASKETBALL

I write as someone who has been able to enjoy my
own profession for 46 years now, and I realize that
life is crueler for athletes, taking away from them at a
young age what they do best, love best, finally what
defines them. I realize as well that with someone as
driven and passionate as Michael, that playing is like
life itself, that there is, in a benign sense, an addiction
here, and that it is harder to walk away from his sport
than almost any of the rest of us can imagine.

SAY IT AIN'T SO, MIKE

ESPN.com,
May 2, 2001

THE BASKET-CASE STATE

From *Esquire*, June 1985

BOBBY KNIGHT AND I ARE HAVING LUNCH AT ANDY'S COUNTRY Kitchen, which is some ten miles out of Bloomington. We are friends, unlikely as that may sometimes seem to him, to me, and to anyone who knows either of us, and he has volunteered to help me on my tour of Indiana. It is critical, he feels, that I dine at Andy's. The sign outside, slightly intimidating, says NO PUBLIC RESTROOMS. Andy's special for this day is either the salmon patties or the chicken dumplings. Each comes with two vegetables. The price is $2.50. Bobby is delighted. "Better than the Carnegie Deli in New York," he says. "What does a sandwich cost there—nine dollars? Maybe ten dollars, am I right?" He competes, I think, even at lunch; Bobby wants to *win* lunch. Right now in his mind he is ahead at least $6.50.

The only other people at Andy's are three hunters, and they catch my eye as we catch theirs. They are not pleased to have people here as well dressed, as *alien*, as we are—sweaters, slacks, semi-expensive clothes. They eye us with palpable suspicion. Then they see Bobby. "Bobby Knight . . ." one of them says, ". . . okay." They are hard-looking men, more than just rural—settlers, really. For a moment I cannot think of precisely the right word, and only later does it strike me that these men are *untamed*. I see them and I think of men from those Civil War photos, severe and unbending, expecting little out of life, and rarely, therefore, disappointed by it. Slowly they begin a cross-table conversation with Bobby about hunting. The grouse hunting has not been particularly good, the weather has been too warm. Gradually they are relenting, and accepting him. As they leave, one of them comes over and asks for his autograph. I am stunned; they did not seem your typical autograph hunters. But then, given the culture of Indiana, which is the culture of small towns, and the importance of Bobby Knight in Indiana, for he is easily the most recognizable person in the state, the dominant figure in the world of Indiana basketball, it is not altogether surprising.

He and I are fascinated by the degree to which the sport has become the connecting tissue of the state. The feeling of the state, the nuance of it, he says, remains rural even now, although Indiana is a great deal less rural than it was twenty-five or thirty years ago, and the small towns are drying up. But, he notes, if people do not live exactly as they did thirty years ago, they still *think* as they did then. Even the city kids at Indiana University, he says, are not like city kids from other states. They are different—simpler, less spoiled, probably less sophisticated. There is no brittleness to them. It is as if they are closer to their past. Which is just as well for him, he suggests. The fans do not want their players to be too sophisticated. They want them to be like the kids they knew in high school. They want the kids to show that the game matters.

INDIANA IS NOT the only place where basketball has such a powerful hold: there is an area that runs like a belt through parts of Appalachia and into the South; it includes parts of West Virginia, Kentucky, Illinois, Ohio, and Tennessee. This is a section of the country that the American industrial surge never reached, and where the small towns, villages often, neither grew nor died; they just stayed there suspended between life and death. In an atmosphere like that, where so little meant so much, there was only one thing that male (and often female) children did, and they did it every day and every night, and that was play basketball. It was a sport for the lonely. A kid did not need five or six other friends; he did not need even one. There was nothing else to do, and because this was Indiana, there was nothing else anyone even wanted to do. Their fathers nailed backboards and rims to the sides of garages or to nearby trees. The nets were waxed to make them last longer, and the kids spent their days shooting baskets in all kinds of weather. This was the land of great pure shooters, and the true mark of an Indiana high school basketball player was hitting the open shot.

If a small town had a good player, the aficionados would start watching him play when he was in junior high school, and if, blessed event, the miracle had happened and there seemed to be more than one gifted player in the same grade, then the crowds for the junior high school games might be even larger than those for the high school. The anticipation of what might happen in three or four years was almost unbearable (although sometimes it petered out into bitter disappointment when a talented young player failed to grow physically). It was, said Bob Hammel, the sports editor at the *Bloomington Herald-Telephone* and a particular connoisseur of the sport and the state, like a basketball-crazed NBA city about to get the number-one pick in the draft. Friday night was almost a ceremonial event: it was high school basketball night. People did not go anywhere else; about the night there was a ritual observance. College and professional teams learned quickly to schedule their games on Thursdays and Saturdays.

A community's identity came as much as anything else from its high school basketball team. These were towns too small and often too poor to field football teams. (In the Fifties, before a major statewide program of consolidation, there were some nine hundred high schools playing basketball and perhaps two hundred playing football.) Basketball became critical in determining a town's identity. It was what the state needed, for there was so little else to do in these small towns. In the days when all this took place, when the idea of basketball was bred into the culture, there was neither radio nor television; it became in those bleak years the best way of fending off the otherwise almost unbearable loneliness of the long and hard winters. There were few ways for ordinary people to meet with one another. The lights in a house went on very early in the morning, and they were turned off very early in the evening. Guests and visitors were rare. There was church, and there was basketball, gyms filled with hundreds, indeed thousands of people, all excited, all passionate. In a dark and lonely winter, the gym was a warm, noisy, and well-lit place.

Basketball worked in Indiana not just because kids wanted to play it but because adults needed to see it, needed to get into a car at night and drive to another place and hear other voices. So it began, and so it was ingrained in the customs of the state. What helped fan the flame was the instant sense of rivalry, the desire to beat the next village, particularly if it was a little larger. The town of five hundred longed to beat the metropolis of one thousand, and that metropolis ached to beat the city of three thousand, and the city of three thousand dreamed of beating the big city of six thousand. If it happened once every twenty years, said Hammel, that was good enough. The memory *lasted*, and the photograph of the team members, their hair all slicked down, stayed in the local barbershop a very long time.

That helped create the importance of basketball in Indiana, but what crystallized and perpetuated it was the state tournament. It helps explain why this sport dominated the theology of Indiana as it failed to do in similar states. Outside of Indiana there were state tournaments, but they were divided into classes, usually A, B, and C—A for the large metropolitan high schools, B for the medium-size schools, and then the C for the small country high schools. Indiana was, and is, different. There is only one tournament. Big schools play against little schools. This not only focuses all the attention on a single competition, which strengthens the sense of unity within the state, but also allows the dream to live. In a thousand hamlets in an essentially rural state, the dream is that a tiny school with a handful of boys will go to the state finals and fulfill the ultimate fantasy—beating one of the big city schools, Muncie Central or Indianapolis's Crispus Attucks.

The entire state roots for this to happen again, as it happened once before, in 1954, when little Milan beat Muncie Central as Bobby Plump took the winning shot with three seconds on the clock. In an odd way the tournament summons the dream, and the dream unifies the state; when the dream happens, or at least almost happens, the state rests again comfortably in its myth, that this is still a simple and quiet rural life.

In truth, Bobby Plump and several of the key players on that team did not come from Milan: they were even more countrified than that. They came from Pierceville, about three miles away, a village that consisted of about forty-five people, and to them Milan was the big city, the place they went to if they were lucky and their parents went shopping on Saturday. Milan had a population of one thousand people, and sometimes on Saturday Plump's father would say that they would go to town and do their trading. Mr. Plump would shop and go to the Odd Fellows, and then Bobby would be able to take in a movie and have something to drink at the soda fountain. Plump remembered feeling bashful and awkward every time he went to Milan, because it seemed so big.

Pierceville, by contrast, had only a grocery store, a service station, and a post office. There was one church, but no resident minister; instead, preachers came on loan from surrounding churches, or local laymen conducted the service. There was no such thing as a fast-food franchise or a movie theater. Gene White, who played on that team, didn't eat in a restaurant until he was thirteen years old, and the restaurant, naturally enough, was in Milan. Cities had restaurants. The Milan kids, White remembered, seemed snobbish at first, and better dressed with more expensive clothes, which probably meant that they bought a better brand of overalls.

This was southeast Indiana. It was all farm country, but the farms were small and the farmers scratched out a marginal living. No one owned very much land and no one ever had very much money; there weren't many people to make money from. In the Plump family, with six children, there was neither indoor plumbing nor a telephone. These were not lives of poverty, as an outsider might have thought; instead, they were lives of simplicity. They had all the basics but precious few luxuries. Growing up, Bobby Plump remembered, there was an unwritten rule that there were a lot of things you just did not ask for, because they could never be attained—like telephones. Bobby Plump wanted one so that when he called a girl he didn't have to walk over to his neighbor Glen Butte's house. Some of the boys' fathers had to travel a considerable distance to hold jobs. It was, in fact, a classic slice of small-town rural life. None of these boys owned a car; their mobility limited, the one thing they could do was play basketball each day.

Of the fathers of the boys who grew up in Pierceville, Plump's worked at the small pump factory in Lawrenceburg, Gene White's father drove a school bus and ran a feed mill, Glen Butte's father drove a truck and farmed, and Roger Schroder's father ran the family general store. It sold groceries, canned goods, clothes, and indeed became the first store in the area to carry television sets. It was also the place where everyone hung out. Mr. Schroder had put two benches in the front of the store, and that was where people came and sat and talked. The store took the place of a local paper, serving as the community's source of information. That made the Schroders the most prosperous of the Pierceville families. The other boys assumed that though they would not go to college, Roger would, because his older sister was already in college. Plump once asked his father if he could have gone to the university without the championship season, which brought a scholarship. "You're the youngest of six kids," his father reminded him, "and I couldn't afford it for them, and I don't see how I could have afforded it for you."

Even by Pierceville standards Plump, whose mother had died when he was five, was painfully quiet. "Bobby's so shy," Gene White's mother once said, "that he won't even ask for a second piece of cake when he wants one." It was as if he could only express himself through playing basketball. They all had baskets in back of their houses. Plump's was somewhat under ten feet, and the court was limited by a concrete back porch that extended into the court and cut down the potential range of their shots. Schroder's was better, ten feet even, with a level court, albeit filled with gravel, which made ball handling hard (though by working on gravel, they were better ball handlers when they finally put the ball on wood). They played every afternoon, and then at night they strung a 300-watt bulb on an extension cord along the house above the basket, tied it to a shovel handle, and used tin sheets to reflect the light down on the court. That allowed them to play until 10:00 during the fall and winter, and until midnight during the summer.

They had grown up together, playing basketball every day. When they were in junior high school they had a good team, and in the eighth grade they lost only one game. After that, people in the Milan coffee shops began to pay attention to them, asking questions about how the team was doing. They had arrived. In their sophomore year in high school they began to sense just how good they were. That year Herman "Snort" (so named for his temper) Grinstead was still coach. There was a moment that season when, angry over their indifferent play and an embarrassing 85–40 loss to neighboring Osgood, Snort kicked seven players off the team and played his sophomores. Eventually he would allow two of the best players back. With the sophomores playing, Milan had beaten some of its toughest rivals. Because of that, there was a sense in the town that they had something. All the players were good, they could all shoot, they could all handle the ball, and they were all unselfish with it. Everyone, particularly Plump, had exceptional speed.

It was becoming increasingly clear that their success was not a fluke. None of them was big: Gene White played center at five feet eleven, but he was smart and had the knack of making opposing centers do exactly what he wanted them to. In their junior year they were even better. In a typical small-town power struggle, Snort Grinstead had been fired. He had bought new uniforms without authorization; there was no money in the athletic budget for them. Snort offered to pay for the uniforms himself, but it was too late. He was let go, and Marvin Wood was hired.

Wood was twenty-four, by his own description an Indiana farm boy who had grown up in a town of seven hundred, his background remarkably similar to that of his team. He had gone to Butler University and played there, and since high school he had known he wanted to teach and coach. Growing up in so small a town, he had few other role models. When he first came to Milan, he made $4,000 a year coaching and teaching; one summer he augmented that by $1,000, working as a night guard in the Seagram building in Lawrenceburg. He was a serious, religious man; if he suggested on occasion that his players go to church on Sunday, he meant it. The only time any of his players ever saw him lose his temper was when one of them cursed during a baseball game. That was the unpardonable sin. He had been told by his own high school coach that Milan had plenty of talent, and he was quickly impressed by his team's ability. What struck him beyond their athletic skills, though, was their rare cohesiveness as a group. They were unusually close even for country boys. They seemed not so much teammates as brothers.

Wood immediately installed the "Hinkle system," developed by Tony Hinkle at Butler, a patterned, deliberate offense that suited the talents of these young, tough, disciplined players. The Hinkle system gave the team the ability to control the ball and thus the tempo of the game; it meant that a team of uniformly good shooters would always be able to get a good shot. This was critical, because playing against bigger, stronger players, they would almost surely be out-rebounded. In their junior year, wanting to slow down the pace of a game, Marvin Wood invented what he called his cat-and-mouse game (years later Dean Smith would name it the four-corner offense). Wood used it to bring other teams out of a zone; it fit his team perfectly.

Wood thought he was lucky to be coaching in an environment like this. He had almost no disciplinary problems. He set curfews during the season, 10:00 P.M. during the week, midnight on the weekends. On New Year's Eve he told them they could stay out until 1:00 A.M. He intended to check up on them. They had better, he added, set their watches to his. That night Bobby Plump and a friend went out on a double date, and on the way back to Plump's house the car broke down with a flat tire. Nevertheless, Plump and his girl made it back to his house by 12:55. They were sitting in the car, in front of the house, when a car pulled up. In it was Marvin Wood. Plump's watch showed 1:00. Wood's watch showed 1:05. Wood's watch won, and Plump did not dress for the next game. It all seemed, Plump thought thirty-two years later, much simpler then.

In their junior year, the dream began. When Milan went to the sectional tournament, a local GM dealer named Chris Volz had the entire team driven there in Chevrolets. He had them driven to the regionals in Pontiacs; to the semifinals in Buicks; and to the finals in Cadillacs. When they won the first game of the regional tournament, that was important, for a Milan team had never before won in the regionals. It made them the best Milan team of all time. That year they lost in the semifinal round of the final tournament to South Bend Central, 56–37. Bobby Plump had nineteen points. That evening South Bend won the state title. Wood was so depressed by the defeat that he thought of leaving coaching, going back to graduate school because he wasn't adequately prepared to coach his team. Instead he decided to stay on. The dream was in motion.

As their senior season unfolded, the whole state began to watch, then hope, then finally believe. The turnouts were so big that Milan's home games were moved to neighboring Versailles, where the gym could seat two thousand, twice as many as in Milan. Milan lost two games in the regular season. Everyone was confident now. Once again Volz supplied them with ascendingly expensive cars to drive to the tournaments. The critical game of the play-offs came in the regional final in Butler Fieldhouse against Crispus Attucks, an all-black school that had a very good team built around a young sophomore named Oscar Robertson.

Wood, watching the sheer power of Attucks and the innate grace and skill of Robertson, hoped that the experience of his own seniors would be enough. Robertson was simply so beautiful a player and so extraordinary an athlete that in a year it would be too late. Oscar as a junior would be too strong for these country boys. Yet Wood was intrigued by the confidence of his team; though other teams were reluctant to play Attucks—a certain apprehension about playing bigger, stronger blacks—his own squad had no such fears. If anything, he sensed, the Attucks players were a little nervous about playing these country boys about whom so much had been written. The Milan dressing room was right next to the drinking fountain in Butler Fieldhouse, and before the game, one by one, the Attucks players all came by for a drink of water, but mostly, Wood thought, to stare and try to figure out who these boys were and what the source of their magic was. Wood told his team to get ahead, try to get a ten-point lead in the second half and then sit on the ball. Milan was able to do exactly that, largely by some very good and very patient shooting. As the game progressed, his team remained absolutely confident, and in the second half Attucks began to make mistakes under the pressure. Milan beat Attucks 65–52. (In that sense, Wood knew they were lucky in their timing. If these same teams met a year later, he was sure, there would be no doubt about the outcome.) Then Milan beat Terre Haute Gerstmeyer 60–48.

That brought them to the final against Muncie Central. Central was the traditional state basketball power in those days. Milan went ahead early and took a 15–7 lead. It was awesome, Wood thought, to be in a field house that held almost fifteen thousand people, all of them, it seemed, cheering for his team. At the first time-out, Gene White, giving away six inches at center but still the smartest high school player Wood had ever seen, came over to the huddle. He was sure he could handle Muncie's John Casterlow. "Coach," he asked, "what do you want me to do with him? I can move him anywhere you want. I can take him in, I can take him out, or I can put him in the bleachers." Confidence, Wood decided, was not going to be a problem that night.

Then Wood sent his team into his cat-and-mouse offense. Usually that was designed not so much to slow the game down as to control its tempo. This time it backfired. Muncie used the delay to creep back into the game and tie the score, but Milan still took a 23–17 half-time lead. In the second half, though, Milan went dry and did not score a field goal; at the end of the third quarter the score was tied at 26. Wood then decided to stop the flow of the game completely. He would hold the ball until the very end, and only then in the closing minutes would he put it back in play. In those closing minutes, he was sure Milan's experience and smarts would pay off. So at the beginning of the fourth quarter, his team now two points behind, Bobby Plump just stood at half court, holding the ball under one arm. He held it there for four minutes thirteen seconds. At one point in the middle of the stall Plump looked over at Wood. Wood was just looking down at his shoes. Then Milan put it in play, quickly tied the game at 28, and then again at 30. Then, with eighteen seconds left, Milan had the ball and a chance for the last shot. Marvin Wood called time out.

It became the most famous shot in the history of Indiana basketball. There was no doubt who Milan wanted to take the last shot. It was Plump. He was their best player and particularly good under pressure. Plump, knowing that defenses were keying on him, would spend the early part of a game making sure that the other players got the ball and got it where they wanted it. Late in the game it was different. His quickness—that marvelous first step—put extra pressure on the defense. Gene White suggested that the other players clear out an area for Plump to drive in. Everyone else would move to one side. The ball would go to Plump. He would hold it until there were five or six seconds left, and then he would drive for the basket. Depending on how tightly he was covered, he would either pull up and take a jumper or go all the way to the basket. In a one-on-one situation he was very good at driving around people. (He had, he later reminisced, been doing it all his life at Pierceville. Nobody was quick enough to stop him there, so nobody was quick enough to stop him here.) That meant a defensive man had to give him room.

During the time out, Plump, sensing the crowd, and the noise and the tension, almost fifteen thousand people engulfed in their own madness, felt nervous for the first time. But the moment he stepped back on the court and the ball came to him, he felt oddly calm; all he had to do was play. Jimmy Barnes of Muncie Central was covering him, but Barnes had to play off him a bit because Plump was such a good foul shooter. With five seconds left, Plump started his drive, realized that Barnes was not going to let him go to the basket, pulled up, and with three seconds left took a fifteen-foot jumper. He knew instantly that the shot was true. The ball went in. Little Milan, with a total enrollment of 161, and only seventy-three boys in the entire school, had just lived the dream. People in Indiana had been waiting for it to happen for years, and they have been waiting for it to happen again ever since.

With that, the madness erupted. No one, as Wilt Chamberlain once noted, roots for Goliath. This was David's day. The parade route through Indianapolis was jammed. The crowd for the ceremonies back home in Milan was so great that the police and firemen from all the surrounding towns had to be summoned to help keep order. As many as thirty thousand people showed up. Some had to park nineteen miles away and walk to the town because the traffic jams were so great. For years to come, people would drive thirty, forty, and fifty miles out of their way to go through Milan, like pilgrims to Lourdes, to see if they could figure out what had occurred and why it had happened, and what had made this town different.

For the players, the season changed all of their lives. Where before very few people from Milan went on to college, the entire team now had a chance, and almost all of them went. As going to college, once unthinkable, became possible for them, so it became a possibility for other Milan kids as well. The team became famous, particularly Plump, who received letters addressed simply "Plump, Indiana." Plump went to Butler, where he had a very successful career, setting single-game and career scoring records before going on to play with the Phillips 66 Oilers of the National Industrial Basketball League.

Bobby Plump is forty-eight years old now, and it is thirty-one years since he took the ball with five seconds left and drove to the basket. But that season and that shot still mark him. It is a basic part of his identity. People still think of it (and where they were when he made it) when they see him. When his children, who are grown now, are in distant cities, someone will on occasion recognize the name and ask if they are by chance related to the boy who made the shot that won the state title for that little school back in Indiana. Thrust into the limelight, Plump learned over a long, painful period how to deal with it, how to give a short speech at a banquet. This most rural of boys who had always been so quiet, in part because he felt a little poorer than everyone else, grew in confidence; there was nothing they had, he gradually learned, that he did not have, and indeed he had something they did not have. Eventually he became a very successful insurance agent.

OVER THE YEARS people have waited for it to happen again. It is harder now. The world has changed. The state has undergone a major reorganization and consolidation of its school districts (there was fierce opposition to the consolidation, not because it meant lesser education for the young people of Indiana but because it diluted precisely the kind of loyalties and identities that Milan represented). Some of the consolidated schools now have names like Southeast Central. The kids do not know one another as the kids in Milan once did; they are not as likely, in Marvin Wood's phrase, to be like brothers. The game has changed as well. The next year Oscar Robertson took his Attucks team to the championship. His team beat an all-black team from Gary. "Watch our colored boys beat the hell out of those Gary niggers," went the joke in white Indianapolis. Robertson's team repeated in 1956. Gradually, with the coming of teams like Attucks, the nature of the game had changed. The players were bigger, stronger, and faster, and they played above the rim. In the past, when the Milans of the world had conjured up big city schools, they had thought of schools with larger enrollments but the same kinds of kids. Now they had to envision bigger schools with bigger, stronger players.

It was harder now for the rural game to beat the city game. One moment brings it home: In the 1956 championship game, the second one for Robertson's team, Attucks played Lafayette Jefferson. Lafayette was a very good team of the old order, not unlike Milan; it played intelligent, controlled, careful basketball. Its players were good shooters. They shot their free throws underhand. In the championship game they did everything right. But it made no difference. Attucks was playing in the air. Blacks, according to the myth then, were supposed to come apart under pressure, but Robertson played like a professional—cool, methodical, almost flawless. If he was double-teamed, he always found an open man. If he was played tightly on defense, he deftly faked and drove to the basket. All that raw talent at Attucks had suddenly been disciplined. It was like having an old man in a young body running a team. That night Robertson scored thirty-nine points. The old order had ended.

For Attucks, the hardest thing at first had been getting games. Until 1943, when the black schools were allowed into the Indiana High School Athletic Association, Attucks's teams could play only other black schools and had to go out of state to get enough games. Even when Attucks was finally a member of the association, the big powerhouse schools were wary of playing them, for there was nothing to be gained and a great deal to be lost. So in the beginning only smaller schools anxious to fill their gyms had been willing to schedule them. Nothing had been easy.

If Attucks played on the road, the team had a hard time finding places to eat. Attucks was so poor a school that it did not have a real gym; in desperation, it played most of its home games at Butler Fieldhouse. In those early days, as the team traveled through rural Indiana, the crowds were often hostile. The opposing players themselves were fairly well behaved; an odd kind of basketball etiquette raised sport above native prejudice. If anything, the bias showed more in the referees. It may not have been deliberate, but it was there. Close calls always went the other way, particularly if Attucks was ahead, which it usually was. Coach Ray Crowe told his players that the referees were worth ten points for the other teams, therefore they had to be that much more disciplined and had to work to get a sizable lead. Otherwise, the game would go the other way in the last few minutes. "If you have a big enough lead," he would tell them, "they'll leave you alone. Otherwise they'll referee the score and you won't win." He drilled them, as Branch Rickey had drilled Jackie Robinson, to be disciplined, not to respond to provocation, not to hear racial epithets, of which he thought there were surprisingly few. Talent was not a problem. All the Attucks players came from the "Dust Bowl," the playground nearby, where black kids played day and night, staying on the court only if they won. Years later, Robertson said that playing against white teams had not been particularly hard; what had been *hard* was making the Attucks team. Basketball was already a focal point of black talent, the one thing that all black kids wanted to do, and the competition within the school to make the team was fierce.

In a sense, Robertson thought, he was lucky in the way he grew up. His family was very stable. His father was a butcher. It was a disciplined life. The teachers at Attucks were first-rate. If anything, because there were so few outlets for educated middle-class blacks, they were overqualified. They were strong and sensitive men and women who in many ways could open doors for the children that the parents themselves could not. Crowe was shrewd and strong, Robertson thought. He emphasized to the players that in every game they would be on exhibit. At the same time he kept the dope dealers and the numbers men away from the school; his kids were going to have a chance to go to college if they could possibly make it. Some of them tended to slide away from classes; Crowe would have none of that. He was the homeroom teacher for most of them, and he posted their grades so that everyone could see who was not working. He also allowed Robertson to grow to stardom without feeling too much pressure. Robertson himself was beginning to realize that, in some way he had never understood before, he was special at this sport. He was growing taller, from six two to six four, and he could do things that other players could not. His game was never fancy. In fact, some people complained that it was almost machinelike, as free of mistakes as it was of excess. It was as if Oscar had taken the game and reduced it to its fundamentals. Slowly that came through to the fans.

If any one player changed how basketball was perceived in Indiana, it was Oscar Robertson. Attucks's winning a title might have meant a lot of talented but faceless black kids, but Oscar somehow stood out; he was doing what they had always done and admired, and doing it better. It was not possible to love basketball and not appreciate him. Where there might have been deep resentment, there was finally acceptance and admiration, and there was acceptance because there was not the possibility of denial. The Indiana fans were hip and they could understand, long before he went on to excel in both college and the pros, Oscar's true greatness. When Attucks won their first championship, Robertson thought thirty years later, he had been too young to understand it. He had thought it was a game at first. Later he realized it was a piece of history. He remembered there was to be a parade through the downtown, and that thousands of people—black and white—turned out. The route was prescribed, and the officials had been very careful about seeing that it ended up in the northwest section of Indianapolis for the bonfire there; they did not want blacks getting out of control in other white sections of town.

There was one other upshot of the game. In the past, even though there were certain school-district lines that ran throughout the city, blacks, no matter where they lived, were allowed to go to Attucks. After that championship the various coaches had stopped the blacks in their areas from going to Attucks. Robertson, in more ways than he had realized, had helped integrate Indianapolis.

This season, though, for the first time in years, going into the regional finals there was the chance of another tiny rural school winning the championship. A small consolidated school named L&M, or officially Lyons and Marco, with a total enrollment of 132 students in the top four grades and seventy-two boys, fielded a very good team (not lightly put together, either—a good deal of political engineering went into it). Lyons, which is listed on the road map of Indiana (population: 782), is larger than Marco, which is not listed at all and now has a population of about three hundred.

On this night in December, Bobby Knight is driving down to Elnora to recruit Jeff Oliphant, a top player for the L&M team, which is coached by his father, Tom. Actually, the recruitment is more or less completed. Knight absolutely dominates this territory, and there are very few kids whom he wants who do not want to go to Indiana (he lost a young black center from an Indiana parochial school to Notre Dame a few years ago, in part because, as one friend said later, he failed to understand that in conflicts in modern America between church and state, state does not always win). They are playing at a neutral gym in Elnora, partially to accommodate the overflow crowd and partially because the L&M coach wants to get his team ready for bigger tournament games and hostile crowds; this gym is said to seat 4,200, while the L&M gym seats only 1,250. L&M is playing Terre Haute North, which in the glory days used to be known as Terre Haute Gerstmeyer.

Bobby is here scouting. His team is playing better, he has won a couple of close games, but it has been a hard season. He is exhausted from the Olympic Games, embittered by the recruiting violations he feels exist in the Big Ten, and his team is almost always less athletically skilled than its opponents. We enter at Elnora. He looks around the gym and nudges me. "Harley and Arley are here," he says. He is exultant. I have not seen him so pleased since he won the battle of restaurant prices several days ago. "Who are Arley and Harley?" I ask. He points to two middle-aged men sitting together on the other side of the court. He is delighted: Indiana basketball history is with us tonight, and he is about to give me a further indoctrination into schoolboy legends. Harley and Arley Andrews are identical twins, and in the early Fifties, rural families being larger than most city ones, they played on the same Gerstmeyer team as their uncle Harold Andrews. The team was known, naturally enough, as "Harley, Arley, and Uncle Harold." In order to confuse referees further as to which Andrews had committed a foul, Howard Sharpe, their coach, made one wear "43" and the other "34." People claimed that at half time, Sharpe would have them trade jerseys if one of them was in foul trouble. (Often they'd switch jerseys from game to game to confuse other teams' scouts as well.) If that worked for Sharpe most of the time, it went against him in the championship game in 1953. "They called a foul that Harley committed and marked it against Arley," says Bobby. "The coach protested, but they wouldn't change it. Arley was their best shooter, and he fouled out in the fourth quarter. Terre Haute lost." He looks at me with slight condescension because I need a fill-in on something so basic as this. "Everyone in Indiana knows that," he says. Someone adds that Harley and Arley turned fifty the day before. People in Indiana *know* things like this; they can mark their own ages and their own expanding waistlines by those of the Andrews twins.

The L&M team is deftly put together. Lyons, undergoing something of a revitalization, may now have as many as one thousand people, although it was down to five hundred fifteen years ago. It is hardly an affluent area; there was some marginal coal mining, some small farming, and a little bit of local commerce. Then Dr. Bill Powers, a hometown boy, and a few friends decided to start a clinic. Powers is what is called an activist in big cities, and a doer in small towns. Gradually the clinic has grown, and so has the town: the clinic has three doctors, two dentists, an optometrist, an audiologist, and several other professionals, plus a nursing staff. It serves not just the town but a region with a radius of fifty miles. In a way, its presence is like having a small industry in a town largely neglected by the industrial revolution. Because of the clinic, other stores opened.

Dr. Powers also cares about the identity of Lyons, and about basketball. In a town this size, he says, the priorities are different from those elsewhere. A crisis is someone getting sick with a lingering illness such as lung cancer; it is hard on the community, because everyone here knows everyone else. Powers played at Lyons years ago, and though the teams were all right back then, they were nothing special. Powers was also the family doctor to both the Oliphant and the Patterson families. The Oliphant family is headed by Tom Oliphant, a Lyons boy who ended up coaching at nearby Worthington. Jeff, in the American tradition of coaches' sons, is a very good prospect, albeit most likely for the dread Worthington High. Meanwhile, Tony Patterson, also an excellent prospect, attended L&M. Patterson was as good a player as the town had boasted in years. Mrs. Oliphant, by even greater chance, worked as a receptionist at Powers's clinic. Gradually Powers began to talk up the idea that

Tom might want to come over to coach at L&M and bring Jeff with him. Jeff could play for L&M in his junior and senior years. That meant the Oliphant boy could play with the Patterson boy. Jeff knew about Tony Patterson and Patterson knew of Jeff; the idea of playing together was a powerful magnet.

By coincidence, one of the nurses in Powers's clinic was on the Lyons school board and was amenable to a change in coaches; it was not hard to find others who were sympathetic to the idea, including Robert Patterson, Tony's father, who was also on the board. It was well within the established priority of small Indiana towns, where the requirements were first for a good doctor and second (though the order *could* be reversed) for a good high school basketball coach. Soon the deal was done; the old coach was let go, and Tom was hired to replace him. Someone said, however, that the Oliphants were having trouble finding a house in Lyons. "Hell, in that case we'll build them one," a local banker was reported to have said.

On this night it is like going back in time. Every seat in the Elnora gym is taken. Terre Haute is the much-feared big city to these fans. The crowd is certifiably rural. It is a surprisingly old crowd, not just high school kids. Terre Haute is bigger and faster. There are three black starters, and the center looks a good six feet nine. L&M is much shorter—Oliphant is six six and a half, Patterson six five and a half. But slowly L&M pulls away, more by not making mistakes than by anything else. Bobby is studying Oliphant, who moves nicely around the basket and always seems to be in position.

We leave early. Knight always leaves a game early, because he wants to beat the traffic. He is pleased with what he's seen of Oliphant. Good passer, good hands, already well coached and disciplined, will fit nicely into the Indiana program. An agreement with both coach and son has already been worked out that will work to everyone's benefit: because IU is short of scholarships this year, Oliphant will come as a walk-on in his first year, probably red shirt, and then get a scholarship for four years. As a five-year student, he can pick up a master's degree if he so chooses.

"What do you project him as?" I ask Knight. "Small forward?"

But Knight insists he doesn't project such particulars. "I may be ten years behind the times," he says.

WE DRIVE THROUGH THE NIGHT, a few friends of his, two assistant coaches, and two writers. They are talking basketball and I am thinking that with the exception of a rare team like L&M, Indiana high school basketball has changed because the state has changed. Rural communities were losing their identity anyway; small farmers were finally giving up and moving to the city, and as farms were being consolidated so were schools. Besides, the lives of the people who stayed behind have changed. They know what goes on not just in the next town but in Washington and in foreign countries. There are more stimuli now, more alternatives in life, more things to occupy their time. Even people in the smallest hamlets have color television sets, and that means that they are no longer alone, they are able to bring the world into their living rooms, whether it is news, sports, movies, or even wars.

High school basketball is simply less important. The state tournament still matters, but there is less magic to it. There are other distractions: one can watch the NFL and major-league baseball and the Olympics. There is a professional football team in Indianapolis. Mostly there is Bobby Knight's team in Bloomington, which is carried on a statewide network and has become the focal point of the fever. The state, because of television, has replaced the village as the operative community. The nature of the culture has not changed; the size of the community has. The new village is now the state of Indiana. Ohio State and Illinois have replaced the neighboring village as the community to war against. But sports here and elsewhere still mean as much, probably too much. It was, I thought, easy to measure the popularity of the sport in the old days as a safeguard against an unrelenting loneliness. Now it's different; people live in modern instant subdivisions and have neighbors only a few feet away, and they have their television sets connecting them to the world. In some ways they care as much or more about sports than ever. The hardest thing to measure here or anywhere else is the new loneliness.

The Stuff Dreams Are Made Of

From *Sports Illustrated*, June 29, 1987

GREAT NBA FINALS ARE SUPPOSED TO LAST SEVEN GAMES, of which at least six should be close; this year's series lasted only six, of which 3½ were close. Even so, because of the nature of the matchups—the difference in the styles of the two teams—this series was in no way disappointing. The good games were so very good, and even the runaway games so resembled a clinic, that it was nothing less than the best against the best. A fan can ask no more.

Using only five men to any significant extent, exhausted and physically worn down as the series began, the Celtics had to play almost perfect basketball in every area to win, and they did that twice and almost a third time. For the younger, deeper, faster Lakers, the challenge was comparable: The Celtics are so tough and resilient that if the Lakers lapsed even a small degree, particularly on defense, the Celtics might capitalize and win. The Lakers were the better team, but only if they played their absolute best. Any lowering of their level and the Celtics would break through and win.

It was the kind of playoff series that showcases great athletes at the top of their game.

The Lakers were and are that good. They are a team of such speed and power that when they are playing their game, it seems almost not to matter who their opponents are. With the Lakers at their best, one has a sense of watching basketball as it will be played in the next century.

During one stretch of Game 1, Larry Bird hit 11 shots in a row.

Normally that kind of shooting from an established superstar can crush the opposition; in this case it did not even dent the Lakers.

They have become one of the most exciting teams in NBA history, one that can take control of a game in a matter of minutes. In the past it was the hallmark of the Celtics to drive through the opposition when it began to wilt and break a game open. In this series the Lakers returned the favor.

In the eight years since Magic Johnson joined them, the Lakers have won four championships and have been a powerful if somewhat schizophrenic team. They were, in most matters of critical importance, a Kareem team, bringing the ball upcourt at a steady pace and then setting Abdul-Jabbar up for a skyhook (a style perilously close to one which, were they the Celtics, would be called white basketball). But they were also a Magic team, one that showcased the latest in American athletic advancement, the 6 ft. 9 in. point guard who grabs the rebound himself and pushes it relentlessly upcourt, on occasion sacrificing control for tempo. Until this year that conflict between the two faces of the Lakers had never been entirely reconciled. It cost one coach, Paul Westhead (who had too clearly sided with Kareem), his job, and it reflected Pat Riley's skill as a coach that he was able to balance the two forces, paying homage to the Kareem team, while expediting the emergence of the Magic team.

This year the Lakers finally were Magic's team: Speed is power, power is speed. Slowly the cast had changed. Michael Cooper had emerged; A. C. Green and James Worthy had been added. Even Mychal Thompson, the most important pickup by either team this year, once was strong enough to play center yet was fast enough to play small forward at times. One had, at certain moments, a sense of watching a prototype of a different breed of athlete—strong, fast, disciplined—playing at a level of stunning intensity, with surprisingly few turnovers. If the Knicks of the late '60s could be described as four guards and one forward (Willis Reed), then this was often a team of four forwards led by a point guard who could, in a very recent era, have played power forward.

What made the series so special was the sharp contrast in the styles of Los Angeles and Boston and the knowledge that these two teams, with cameo appearances by Philadelphia and Houston, have essentially dominated the championships since Bird and Johnson entered the league in 1979. That and, of course, the fact that both teams have gradually been shaped to the styles and contours of their superstars, one white and one black.

The Celtics, this year's defending champions, play half-court basketball, and they play it better than any team in the league. That they had even made it to the finals was remarkable, given the death of Len Bias, the infirmities of Bill Walton and the fact that Kevin McHale and Robert Parish were both playing with injuries. But Boston finally lacked the bench mandatory for a tough playoff final and the speed to stay with L.A. in a running game. The Celtic front line, after all, was composed of three exceptional basketball players, while the first seven players for the Lakers seemed to be both exceptional basketball players and exceptional athletes.

One had to look no further than the contrast between McHale and Worthy to understand the classic matchup displayed in this series. If the Lakers controlled the tempo, it would mean that Worthy—possibly the fastest big man going to the basket in the league—would be a dominant player; if the Celtics controlled the pace, it meant they would be able to get the ball to McHale, surprisingly nimble and deft, uncommonly skilled at using his body and arms for maximum leverage. Each was an extension of the best of his team. For Worthy to be Worthy, Magic had to be Magic; for McHale to get the ball where he wanted it, Larry Bird and the Celtic offense had to move in proper mesh. If one was having a good game, the other probably was not.

Because the styles and the racial composition of each team were so strikingly different, race was very much at issue during the series (and indeed was covertly at issue even when it was not overtly so).

It was always there, as race is always there in American life, even when it seemingly is not.

One enters the subject of race and basketball as one enters a minefield: American blacks are clearly faster than American whites; in addition, they are now generally perceived as better natural athletes; and Los Angeles is a significantly blacker team than Boston. The first seven Los Angeles players are black; Boston, which was the first integrated team and the first team to start five blacks, has been for almost a decade one of the whitest teams in the league, and it starts three whites and often plays four at a time.

Even before the finals started, Dennis Rodman and Isiah Thomas of the Pistons had raised the question of race, both suggesting that Larry Bird was overrated and had become a superstar not so much because of the excellence of his game as because he was white and because white fans and media seized on and magnified his value. At the same time, the *Boston Globe* ran a story quoting some local black youths at a playground saying they favored the Lakers because the Celtics were so white. That story reverberated throughout the paper for the next few days.

Racism is about stereotypes on both sides, and like most stereotypes, racial ones can be both true and untrue. One can imagine, for example, the young and still healthy Walton as an ideal center for the current Laker team. Comparably, one can easily imagine the mid-career Abdul-Jabbar playing for the Celtics and fitting in perfectly well with their style. Yet, as the current Laker offense springs from Magic, so the current Celtic team is an extension of Bird. The Boston offense is built around a forward with great vision and great hands who moves well without the ball and who will, against an exceptional defense, come off a series of picks, ready to shoot or pass. It is critical on this team that everyone be able to shoot well from within a specified range. This is, for better or worse, defined as white basketball. That Bird would be an equally wonderful forward on the current Laker team does not change the stereotype (in part because Johnson would have difficulty on the Celtics as currently constituted; he would probably be too fast for them, and it is possible that an adjustment in his game might cost him what is best in his game).

The two men are now inextricably linked. They played against each other in the NCAA championship game of 1979, the year they both came into the league. Each has improved his game significantly every season since. Each has the rare gift of the truly great basketball player—the ability to make other players better—and each has played a crucial role in making his team a perennial contender (one or both of them has made the finals every year since they joined the league; Magic has been playoff MVP three times, Bird twice). The era of the '80s has been theirs.

During Bird's rookie year, one NBA general manager was asked what he thought of him. The G.M. was wary—yes, Bird was a good shooter and probably an even better passer than people thought. But even though his skills were obvious, the G.M. did not think that Bird was mentally tough enough for the long NBA season. Of all the predictions heard in professional sports, that one is among the least fortunate.

What was known about Bird was how good a shooter and passer he was. What was not known was how good a teammate he would be, how exceptional a rebounder he was, and most of all how tough of mind he would be—able to impose his will not just upon his teammates but upon a given game itself. He has, over the years, proved to be the ultimate professional, working constantly on his shooting and developing remarkable proficiency with his left hand. He has always had an extraordinary sense of tempo and a fine sense of what his team needs from him at a given moment—passing, rebounding or shooting.

Magic Johnson, too, has gotten better every year. By and large he did exceptionally well in controlling his ego as he adjusted his play to accommodate Kareem's. He has refined his own game, improving his outside shot, and he won the critical fourth game of the finals with a moving hook shot over the entire Boston front line. It was an additional shot he knew he needed in his repertoire, and he had picked it up from Abdul-Jabbar, playing H-O-R-S-E with him. In the often dour world of professional sports he has made the game seem a pleasure. It is quite possible that until this year we had not seen the full range of what he could do and did not realize that he is the rarest of professional basketball players—someone who can dominate the game and lead his team in scoring while playing guard.

The other aspect of Magic and the entire Laker team was the brilliance and discipline with which they played, both on offense and, perhaps even more important, on defense, where they dominated Boston in the first two games and took away the essence of the Celtic game. It is one thing to have tremendous athletic ability and quite another to discipline it, master it and apply it with great skill in situations of constant and enormous pressure. That takes both intelligence and hard work. Yet, if there is one thing that enrages the better black athletes—and coaches—of this era, it is the contemporary white perception, both in the media and among fans, that black athletes are natural athletes, doing night after night what comes quite readily to them. This is, of course, an ironic update of an earlier myth, which was that blacks were faster than whites but could not play in difficult positions in competitive professional sports because they lacked both guts and talent. Whites, by contrast, are seen as less gifted but headier athletes who practice and perfect their skills better because they have, it is implied, better work habits.

The black athletes feel that while they may have an edge in natural athletic ability, the white fan and white journalist do not see the endless hours they spend working on playgrounds and in gyms, perfecting moves, improving, refining, adjusting their games, exploiting the natural God-given ability by dint of ambition and intelligence. These, they feel, are the qualities that set the playground player apart from the college player, the college player apart from the pro, and the great professional player apart from the journeyman. Bird, to them, is therefore an interesting example of what might be called the adjective phenomenon—whites are hard workers and intelligent; blacks, when described by announcers and writers, are gifted athletes who come naturally by their skills. Bird is perceived as the lunch-box player who only by dint of hard work and high intelligence has created himself as a great basketball player, whereas what is seen of Johnson or Worthy is simply his natural skills, not the endless hours spent honing those skills and the intelligence to employ them constantly in making split-second decisions.

Of the comments that Isiah Thomas made, some were silly, but one important point, obscured by all the furor, was stated with great eloquence: "When Bird makes a play, it's due to his thinking and his work habits. It's all planned out by him. It's not the case for blacks. All we do is run and jump. We never practice or give a thought to how we play. It's like I came dribbling out of my mother's womb."

That was what was so important about Magic Johnson in this series. This was a great player at the height of his game, forcing his skills and will upon a team that quite regularly rejects the imposition of alien tempo and alien style and prefers to set its own rhythm. He was able, for six games against an extremely tough team, to play at a remarkably furious level with very few mistakes. Statistics are often misleading, but Johnson's assist-to-turnover ratio (78 to 13) for the series and his 19 assists and 3 turnovers in the decisive sixth game tell their own truth. The intelligence is in those statistics.

Bill Walton has said that when he was injured and with the Clippers a few seasons ago, he decided to do nothing for one game except watch Magic. Johnson's ability and intelligence, he said, were absolutely remarkable. "I watched him all game, and he was on the fast break all night," Walton said. "Split-second decisions every time, and he never made a single wrong pass. Not once."

There is no small amount of irony in all this: The NBA, as American institutions go, may be the greatest showcase of black talent and intelligence. Unlike pro football, where the issue of the black quarterback is still unresolved and where there has been no black head coach, in the NBA most point guards—the quarterbacks of the teams—are black, and there have been a number of black head coaches. The NBA is, in fact, the league most capable of producing genuine equity and real friendship among its black and white players.

Yet for all the progress in the NBA, the racial tensions and racial byplay are at times strikingly visible there, simply because it is where black players have advanced the furthest. The fault is not the league's or the players'; it is simply that on both sides we bring more baggage to the arena from the exterior society than we are aware of. Professional basketball may be an essentially black game, but the owners are white, most of the general managers and referees are white, and the media—with their ability to define and their innate reflection of the norms of the white culture—are primarily white. The black crossover athlete, who not only excels in his sport but also gains enough public identification (and white goodwill) to achieve major endorsements and a prominent broadcasting job, is still relatively rare: One thinks of O.J. Simpson, Reggie Jackson, Julius Erving, Bill Russell, Ray Leonard and probably Magic Johnson now, as well. It is still a select crew.

Indeed one of the ironies about the resentment of Bird by some blacks is that it is about media attention. Yet, in truth, when Bird and Johnson entered the league as rookies, it was Magic who had an instinct—a virtual homing device—for the media, particularly television, and Bird who was warier and more suspicious and who rejected the media's glare. Johnson was about basketball and the media; Bird was about basketball. He largely regarded the media as an unwanted intrusion. That was a reversal of the normal racial order, in which white journalists are far more comfortable with white players than with black players, and white players are more comfortable with (or less suspicious of) the white media than are blacks. From the start, Magic seemed to love the hype, which came principally from network television. CBS, desperate to create rivalries in a league savaged by expansion, seized on both him and Bird from the very beginning.

After a dozen years in which black athletes had seemed alternately resentful and political, after endless dour interviews with Kareem, here was a charming, ebullient young black athlete who seemed to like the game, like the camera and even like white people. One's first sight of Magic Johnson was of a pleasant young man with television journalists fawning all over him.

The remaining impression of him from those early years is that he seemed to be teamed in the backcourt not so much with Norm Nixon as with Brent Musburger.

"The Magic Man Versus the Bird Man," went the hype for their early NBA games. Bird wanted none of it at the time. "Guards don't play forwards," he said. Over the years Bird slowly came out of his cocoon and became more confident of his place in the league and of his ability to deal with journalists, eventually becoming surprisingly deft with the media (and delighting, one suspects, in the use of double negatives, thereby getting back at a generation of Indiana English teachers).

Slowly, inevitably, as they raised their teams to the highest professional level, as their teams became perennial challengers for the title, the connection between them, which had once been hyped and artificial, gradually became real. In a league in which expansion had ruined traditional rivalries, their rivalry and that of their teams remained genuine, and they reached the rare point where rivalry turns into respect and even affection. Bird led the campaign for

Magic as MVP this year, and Magic talked during the playoffs about how playing against Bird raised his game, made him better, and how he thought that when Bird retired he, too, might retire, that the special challenge implicit in their careers and their mutual era would be over. It was the statement of an athlete thinking not so much of a given series as of the athletic history books.

So linked are the two that last week Leigh Montville in *The Boston Globe* had a lovely column entitled "Friends, Foes for Life." Set some 40 years in the future, it portrays Bird and Johnson together at a nursing home, all the celebrity softball games, the celebrity tennis, the celebrity bowling behind them. Their game now is checkers. Theirs is an endless series. Magic leads 2,993–2,992.

" 'Who's ahead anyway?' Magic Johnson asks. 'You know damn well who's ahead,' Larry Bird says. 'Just get playing. This thing will be even when I'm through with you today.' "

A Hero for the Wired World

From *Sports Illustrated*, December 23, 1991

IN SOME MYSTERIOUS WAY THE WORD HAS GOTTEN OUT. The Chicago Bulls bus, the bus that he rides on (which is as close as most of these fans will ever get to the street where he lives), is to leave the Westin Hotel in Seattle at 5 P.M., and by 4:20 the crowd has begun to gather in the lobby, concentric rings of fans or, more properly, worshipers: They are more white than black, more young than old, more male than female, but they cut across every ethnic and demographic line. It seems almost ceremonial, a certain hum of anticipation rising each time the elevator opens. Finally at 4:50—for he likes to be the last man on the bus—the door opens, and out he comes, in his Michael Mode: His smile-and-sign-and-move-and-smile-and-sign-and-keep-moving drill is flawless. He is the seigneur—swift, deft, graceful, never rude—in the splits of the second in which he at once enters and departs their lives. "I actually saw him live," a boy says. Fame is indeed fleeting for those whose closest connection to it is to stand and work the 60 yards from the Westin elevator to the team bus.

I have not seen fame like this in almost 30 years. I think of the time, in 1960, when I was the one reporter in the country allowed to ride the train bearing Elvis Presley back to Memphis from the Army, and I think of John Kennedy in that same year, when he campaigned in California, and I watched the teenyboppers and saw the first reflection that in a television age, politics had become theater. I do not cover rock concerts, but I presume Mick Jagger and others who play at his level deal with this all the time. In a pretelevision age, Joe DiMaggio had fame like this and was comparably imprisoned, though his fame was limited largely by the boundaries of the 48 contiguous states.

There is an even greater dimension to the fame of Michael Jordan. He is one of only two black American athletes who, almost 45 years after Jackie Robinson broke into baseball, have finally become true crossover heroes—that is, they receive more commercial endorsement deals from the predominantly white, middle-class purveyors of public taste than do white athletes (the other is the pre-HIV Magic Johnson; the jury is out on Bo Jackson now that he's a mere one-sport man). But unlike Johnson, Jordan has created a kind of fame that exceeds sports; he is both athlete and entertainer. He plays in the age of the satellite to an audience vastly larger than was possible in the past and is thus the first great athlete of the wired world.

His good looks—indeed his beauty, for that is the right word—are a surprise to older white Americans, who by cultural instinct grew up thinking that Gary Cooper and Gregory Peck and Robert Redford and Paul Newman were handsome but did not see beauty in a young black athlete with a shaved head. Jordan has given us, then, among other things, a new definition of American male beauty. Not surprisingly, in many households it has been the children who have taught the parents about him and about his fame, artistry and beauty. About a year ago New York Governor Mario Cuomo gave a speech bemoaning the disappearance of the athlete as hero in America. Where have you gone Ted Williams and Joe DiMaggio? he asked. A friend of mine named Dick Holbrooke, a former U.S. State Department official, wrote him that comparable heroes still existed, but that their names were Michael Jordan and Magic Johnson and that today's children were inspired by the grace and ease with which they carried their fame. Cuomo called back and said, I stand corrected.

Jordan, infinitely disciplined, product of a very strong, very ambitious family, knows innately how to handle this staggering role—to deal with the media, to know what to say and what not to say and when to hide and when to go public, and to smile always. He is the first new-age athlete. And he is the right athlete at the right time. He plays the right sport, for its purpose is easily comprehensible even in a country where basketball has not yet taken root. Had the satellite been pervasive 20 years later, Pelé, also playing an international sport—soccer—on a level above even the best players of his day and with a charm that radiated easily across national boundaries, might have been first. Perhaps Muhammad Ali might have been first, but he was politicized by his conversion to Islam and the Vietnam War. Besides, Ali's considerable charm notwithstanding, boxing was never the ideal sport for the young, with whom all idolatry of this kind must start. Ali, far more graceful than most boxers, conquered his opponents by stylishly punching them senseless; Jordan meets his opponents and conquers by gracefully soaring over them.

More, he does this for an audience that greatly exceeds that of the ballet. This is sports as ballet, something utterly new and modern, its roots African-American, ballet as a contested sport. No one, after all, ever guarded Baryshnikov. When we talk in Jordan's hotel room, I talk to him about Baryshnikov and Nureyev and their beauty and grace, and he listens, curious, patient, intrigued by these stories of potential rivals, and when I am through, he asks only one question about Baryshnikov: "How tall is he?" Short, I answer, quite short—low center of gravity. I detect a small smile, a category 4 smile, almost invisible, a smile of private victory: Michael's pleasure as he thinks about posting up Mischa.

Jordan's is the most original of performance. What thrills the fans—and the other players and his coaches—is that almost every night there is something unique in his moves. It is not, says Bulls coach Phil Jackson, that Jordan's hangtime is so great; there may well be others in the league with greater hangtime. What sets Jordan apart, Jackson says, is what he does in the air, the control, the vision, the ability to move his body after he has seemingly committed it. If Jordan, Jackson notes with a certain delight, is the lineal descendant of those great basketball innovators who went before—Elgin Baylor, Connie Hawkins and Julius Erving, each learning from and expanding upon the accomplishments of his predecessors—then the most exciting question is, What is the next great player going to be able to do?

Ever since the coming of the communications satellite, there has been an inevitability to all this—that there would be an athlete of Jordan's surpassing international fame, that he would most likely come from soccer or basketball, because they are the most readily understandable of international games, the games that essentially explain themselves. Since America is the home team in the wired world, it would likely be an American sport. But American football has too many rules and cloaks its players in uniforms that deny individuality. Baseball has complicated rules too and seems, in contrast with basketball, a languid sport to the uninitiated, building slowly over an entire season. That left basketball. It was therefore almost a given that the first athletic superstar of the wired world would be a black American basketball player who played above the rim.

The last great export of America in the postindustrial international economy may be entertainment and media. We as a country are now to the rest of the world what New York was to the rest of the nation when New York was merely a domestic media capital. (Consider the relative fame and success in endorsements of, say, Joe DiMaggio and Mickey Mantle of New York compared with Stan Musial of St. Louis and Hank Aaron of Milwaukee-Atlanta.) We do not, as a nation, merely reprocess the talents of others through our powerful communications system; like any good isolationist society, we tend to export, first and foremost, our own deeds, concerns and talents.

Jordan's fame is of a kind that builds on itself. Images in our world beget additional images. Having seen one dazzling image, we hunger for another. We fear only boredom. Because Jordan's athleti-cism is so great, the camera seeks him out every night. And because the camera singles him out, he in turn receives the endorsements, particularly the immensely skillful Nike commercials. What we fi-nally come to is not merely the sale of sneakers but the creation of a myth, a movie in continuum, made up of brief commercial bites— the Michael Jordan story: Chapter 1, Michael soaring into space; Chapter 2, his palship with Mars Blackmon (even mocking Jordan's own lack of hair). In the end, he is a film star as well as an athlete.

The decision to broaden the story, year by year, was made by Jim Riswold, who writes the Nike commercials. He had heard early in Jordan's career that Bill Russell, not a man lightly given to compli-ments about other players, had told James and Deloris Jordan that their son was an even better person than he was a basketball player. We will proceed, Riswold thought, to show that. And he has. The Michael Jordan story, as told by Nike, has become such a cultural event that the release of a new commercial is preceded by great se-crecy. We are allowed to know only that a new Michael commercial is soon to appear on a television channel near you. Then there is a screening for journalists. A screening of a commercial for journal-ists! Of the next episode, to be unveiled at the Super Bowl, all we are allowed to know is that it portrays Michael with another American icon, someone older from outside sports. (The smart money is on a carrot-eating wabbit of cartoon ancestry.)

Jordan is a reflection of what the world has become and of the in-visible wires that now bind it. CNN, the network of the satellite, has been in operation for little more than a decade; the rise of the NBA as an international sport has taken place largely in the past five years. Some 75 nations received some combination of regular-season and playoff games in 1990–91, and that figure is up to 88 this season. The internationalization of the sport, of course, has dovetailed almost per-fectly with Jordan's pro career. He had been half hidden in college in the controlled North Carolina offense. Nike had signed him in '84, thinking it was getting one of the better players of the year. It did not know that it was getting the greatest athlete in the world. He was immediately able to showcase his abilities at the Los Angeles Olympics, while the world watched. From then on, the legend built.

When Nike bid to represent Jordan, his agent, David Falk, insisted that he not sign on as just another basketball player endorsing a sneaker, but that he have his own line. In time Nike agreed, and Air Jordan was created. Nike, which had come upon stagnant times in the sneaker wars, thought the Air Jordan line might do about $10 million in business the first year. Instead, despite the attempts of the NBA commissioner to ban the Jordan shoe, Nike sold $130 million worth of Air Jordans.

Thus began the legend (and the dilemma) of the young man who is the most talented athlete in basketball but whose fame and income transcend the game, making him entertainer as well as player. For everything in a media age must entertain; that Jordan can do so is his great value. He is not just the ultimate player; he is the ultimate show.

It is about more, of course, than scoring and smiling. Being a Pied Piper is not enough. He is a warrior, a smiling warrior to be sure, and that too comes through to the fan. There is an intensity to his game, a feral quality, and an almost palpable desire to win. Great athletes are not necessarily nice people, in the traditional definition of nice, which implies a certain balanced, relaxed attitude toward life. They are, at least in their youth, obsessed by winning, by conquering others. Jordan is, for all the charm and the smiles, the athlete personified, egocentric and single-minded, tough and hard—hard on himself, on teammates, on opponents—fearless and unbending, never backing down, eager to put his signature on an opponent, looking for new worlds and teams to conquer.

There are endless testimonials to this intensity: Michael wanting and needing to win at everything he does—pool, cards, video games; Michael staring for hours at a blank television set late at night after missing a critical foul shot in the final seconds of a play-off game against Cleveland; Michael, in the Finals against the Lakers last spring, hurting his toe, which then swelled up badly, and trying to play in a special shoe that gave him more room but also limited his ability to cut, coming over to the Bulls bench early in the game and saying to the trainer, "Give me the pain," which translated meant give me my regular shoe, and I'll play in pain.

He had hated the reputation, which he bore in his early years in the NBA, that he was a great player, perhaps the greatest ever to play the game, but that he would never be able to win a championship ring. This was so, it was said, because the Bulls offense, like it or not, would revolve too much around him, and in the playoffs, at the highest level of the game, he would, in this most team-oriented of sports, subtract rather than add by playing into the hands of the defense. He became, year by year, a more complete player. But what also became clear about him—as it was clear about DiMaggio—was that he was the ultimate big-game player, the bigger the game, the better he played, and the better and tougher he played in the final quarter, and even more, in the last four minutes, when everyone else was exhausted. All of his skills came together last year in the Finals, giving him the championship some said he would never attain.

Now, with that championship under his belt, he pushes for a second and for wider victories. His teammates at Nike and Gatorade are thinking now of Europe. His teammate NBA commissioner David Stern is thinking of the rest of the planet. Their time is clearly coming. The phenomenon of the athlete as global figure grows at an accelerating rate. The Olympics loom ahead, and when Michael leads the U.S. team in the gold medal game just outside Barcelona on Aug. 8, some 2.5 billion viewers in 170 countries will likely tune in.

And this is just the beginning. The stadium is now the world. Sports, particularly soccer and basketball, are ever more international (in soccer, only America lags behind the world, and that is partly generational; younger Americans are already more connected to the game than their parents were). The commercial impulse for more international competition can only grow—the show companies and the soft drink companies are increasingly international, and they hunger for this limitless audience.

As for Michael, he is contemplating other fields. We are sitting in Jordan's hotel room, and he is talking about playing another sport. It is hard to tell when he is entirely serious and when he is daydreaming. Sometimes the daydreams sound very real. Bo Jackson, he is saying, made it possible to be a two-sport man, opened it up for me. He clearly would like to compete against Jackson's achievement. Besides, all that jumping is hard on the knees. Football, he says . . . I could be a wide receiver. Almost nothing I couldn't catch. "But I won't go over the middle."

Then he goes on to baseball. He ponders a career there, for the loves the game and would still like to give it a try. At 28, could he hit the curveball? The question is tantalizing.

In the meantime, as his fame grows, his right to privacy shrinks. Almost everywhere he goes in the world now, he draws large, demanding crowds. Paris, cool to basketball, disdainful of Americans, was a surviving safe haven, a place where he could walk around with ease and relative anonymity. But the next Olympics, he knows, may cost him even Paris.

Character Study: Pat Riley

From *New York Magazine*, December 21, 1992

PAT RILEY IS IN SEARCH OF CHARACTER AND EXCELLENCE.
Nothing less. He is convinced that they go hand in hand. Most people, he says, think they work hard, but in truth, they really don't.
They are not willing, once they achieve a level of success, to make
that constant extra effort to extend their abilities to the highest level.
This is true about almost every aspect of life, he thinks, and it is particularly true about professional basketball. He is not impressed by
talent without character. He read David McCullough's splendid biography of Truman and was impressed not just by the quality of
the book but by McCullough's work habits. Riley is always on the
lookout for the defining moment when character manifests itself;
with McCullough, that came when the biographer walked the same
steps that Truman had walked on the day he received the news of
Roosevelt's death. That, to his mind, was excellence.

Excellence, it should be noted, exists in things both great and
small. Thus, there was the cable he sent his former broadcast partner Bob Costas for the exceptional job Costas was doing as the anchorman of the Barcelona Olympics, a job worthy of Riley's
expectations. Still, there was a flaw in Costas's performance that
bothered Riley. So his cable arrived several days into the games, congratulating Costas for his work. Then came the zinger: "But the ties,
Bob, the ties!"

Riley has always driven himself to maximize his own talents.
The world of basketball was changing while he was still in college in

the mid-Sixties. It was clear to him early in his pro career that he would never be a star and that just staying in the game would be a challenge. After three years with the then–San Diego Rockets (and coming perilously close to the tail end of his own professional career), he had a chance to stay in the league by signing with the Lakers. His marching orders were very clear. "Do you want a job on this team?" Fred Schaus, the general manager, asked. "Your job is to keep Jerry West and Jimmy McMillian in shape—to push them very hard every day in practice. Don't back off them. Make them work hard." So he stayed in the league as practice fodder. He gladly took the job and the assignment that confirmed the most elemental lesson of life: that the great sin was to be outworked by someone else at anything. It kept him in the league for five more years, and it meant that he went against one of the great players of all time every day in practice, in itself an education.

When he became coach for the Lakers, his strengths were often lost amid the obvious talent of his players. The Lakers, after all, had Kareem, Worthy, and the remarkable Earvin Johnson, a player whose sense of achievement came only from the success of others. Certainly, coaching a team with Magic Johnson gave him an asset few others had. "Somehow, unbeknownst even to himself, he had already learned the most important thing in life: He had learned that to get out of the game what he wanted—which was to be a winner— he had to use his rare abilities to help his teammates get out of the game that which they wanted," Riley says admiringly of Johnson. Coaching the Lakers, therefore, always looked easier than it was: Just wear Armani suits, comb your hair back in a style straight out of *Gatsby*, give Magic the ball, coast through the season, hope to beat the Celtics or the Pistons in June, and then hand out the rings. Instead, the real challenge was keeping so much talent so finely tuned in a league where the young players are millionaires now before they hit their first shot: It was a constant challenge making sure that their rings were on their fingers and not in their heads.

The best thing about the extraordinary job Riley did with the Knicks last year—taking a seriously flawed group of overachievers, and guiding them to 51 wins—was that everyone who cared about basketball understood for the first time how good he was, and it cast his previous achievements with the Lakers in a different light; self-proclaimed connoisseurs of the sport began to reflect on the Laker years, on how easily that very same group of egocentric young millionaires might have unraveled even earlier. As it was, his tour there lasted nine years, and it ended only when it became clear that the demons that drove him for excellence were no longer matched by the demons that drove his players. It was time for him to go. He broadcast for one season and did it well and might, if he had wanted to, have done it even better; he worked hard in his new apprenticeship—Costas, his partner, was impressed not so much by Riley the broadcaster as by Riley the student of broadcasting, and by his hunger to learn. It was also true, however, that he never entirely committed himself to broadcasting, that he was careful never to say anything over the air that might be used against him if he ever decided to go back to coaching.

He studied Costas carefully, understanding that he was a consummate professional. He and Costas paired off well, and one day on the air, Costas suggested a competition to see who was the better foul shooter. "The loser has to wear his hair like the winner," Riley said. For Costas, that meant a gel and a swept-back look; for Riley, a blow-dried look. Costas, who is a very good shooter, won. Riley got out the blower and did his hair; even as he did it, with, as he said, 40 million people watching, "it occurred to me how much I missed coaching."

The Knicks got lucky when both Riley and David Checketts came here to run a once-proud franchise in a city that cares desperately about basketball. The Knicks team he took over was virtually an expansion franchise plus one great (but increasingly disenchanted) player. It was not an easy season—everything had to be relearned, most notably the concept of the team. At first, the players lacked unity; they had too many cliques, and they did not believe in one another. One day midway in the season, he broke them down and made them stand in the locker room, clique by clique. "This is what we are," he said. "Look at us, a bunch of cliques, not a team." They won seven of their next eight and began to come together more as a team. In addition, he gave them a signature: No team would play harder, and no team would be more physical. When they took out the Detroit Pistons in the season's most satisfying playoff series, they stole the Pistons' own trademark of tough play (so that the entire league could enjoy the pleasure of hearing the Pistons whine about how physical the Knicks were). They had no right to go to seven games against the Bulls, but they did. That will be their signature again. "Our culture will be physical," Riley says. They will act more professionally—he has already come down hard on some of the younger players for talking trash during games. Toughness in the world of Riley is playing hard, being in good condition, and being mentally strong, not swaggering or blustering on the court.

He is the right coach for New York: smart, tough, professional. His presence is exceptional, but his presence—the looks, the clothes, the cool, all of which seem to demand the attention of the camera—simply exists. There is no preening. If others take the look more seriously than the skills and the work habits and the character, then that is about the eye of the beholder. The look seems born in Hollywood, but it is a product of something much deeper: upstate New York, an essentially blue-collar life. Riley is the son of a minor-league baseball manager who never got the chance to manage in the majors and turned late in his life to alcohol. It is the son vindicating the father, quite possibly the most powerful drive of all. Lee Riley fought back from alcohol to take a job as a janitor at a parochial school. When he was asked to coach the school's baseball team, he agreed, on the condition that he be allowed to coach in his janitor's clothes. That was pride, thinks the son, that there be no dissembling. In the eyes of one of Pat Riley's friends, screenwriter Bob Towne, the man in the Armani and the parochial-school coach in his janitor's clothes are the same man; both exist only on their own terms.

This season, thanks to Checketts's acknowledged skill in dealing with the salary cap, the Knicks should be much better by midseason—certainly the talent level appears to be better. But it will not be easy. The changes in the team are considerable; there are seven new players, many of them still trying to adjust not only to new teammates but to their own new roles, and if they are to come together it will probably be later in the season. But they will play hard, and they will play unselfishly, for those are Riley trademarks. He will accept nothing less. Early in the season, in a game in which the Knicks rallied at the end to beat a weak Boston team in the Garden, they played poorly and shot under 33 percent. It was not an easy victory, and it was most demonstrably not an artistic one. But in Riley's world, everything begins with character. Thus, as he later told the beat reporters, his players could not hit lay-ups, they could not hit jumpers, and they could not make foul shots. "But to play hard . . . as a coach it is something to die for," he said.

SAY IT AIN'T SO, MIKE

From ESPN.com, May 2, 2001

MICHAEL JORDAN, THE MOST EXCITING BASKETBALL PLAYER I ever watched, is making serious noise about coming back. This is by way of a personal note to him saying, I hope he resists the temptation and leaves us with our memories of him as they now exist.

I realize, having watched him for many seasons from a distance, and up close in what was at the time his final season, that the most dangerous thing in the world is to tell Michael he can't do something—he almost surely will then go out and prove you wrong, just for the pleasure of that, of humiliating not merely opposing defenders, but writers as well. But it is extremely unlikely that any return will add to his legend. Almost surely, in fact, it will subtract. This is important because the last time he left the game, it was as perfect a departure as a screenwriter could script.

We are not friends, Michael and I. That is not the job of the reporter and biographer, but I think I know him reasonably well, and three years ago I wrote a book about him in that last season. When Dean Smith, his old Carolina coach, asked Michael what he thought about the book, he answered that he had started it, thought it quite good, but that reading it was like reading his obituary, and he would have to read it some other time.

Fair enough, and in fact a good answer: For a surpassing athlete like Michael, leaving the thing you love most and do best, and which defines you, is, in fact, like an early form of death.

This then is a personal plea to him to accept the fates and stay retired. If he comes back, he will be 38 when the season starts and 39 in the middle of it. In basketball terms, especially for a small man, that is senior-citizen status. Three years away from the game is a very long time in the life of a basketball player, even one who is something of an aerobic miracle.

Some of the young players out there are very good—they might not be as great as Michael was, or as complete—but they might be better than they seem when you watch them. (It is one of my beliefs that if players these days are not as complete as they used to be—in no small part because they come out too early and have not been coached enough in college—they are also physically more formidable and accomplished every year.)

Besides, it should be noted, the Wizards, the team he is paid so handsomely to run, are very bad. Even if Charles Barkley can get his weight down to that of say, Shaquille O'Neal, it will not be a very good team. Barkley, not exactly an aerobic miracle at any point in his career, and loathe to train very hard in the offseason when he was younger and it was easier, would start the season as 37, be 38 in the midst of it, and is now 50 pounds over his playing weight.

Michael, it should be noted, does not like to lose, and does not have much patience for players who are not good. He will be surrounded by a good many of them in Washington.

It is important at this point to recall the last moment when we all saw Michael play. That was in Salt Lake City in June 1998; he was in the process of breaking the hearts of thousands and thousands of Utah Jazz fans. It was Game 6 of the NBA Finals, and the Bulls had gone to Salt Lake City leading in games 3–2. But the home-court advantage rested with Utah. Worse, the Bulls were in trouble, because Scottie Pippen's back was killing him, and he could barely play. Michael had carried the Bulls that night, as he often had in the past.

Ron Harper was sick that night as well, and Pippen was used primarily as a decoy. By the second quarter, Phil Jackson was going with Bill Wennington, Steve Kerr, Toni Kukoc, Scott Burrell and Jud

Buechler, not the most imposing five players to play so early in so critical a game.

As best he could, Jackson was buying time for his starters. He knew Jordan was exhausted, and he told Michael it was all right to cheat some on defense. Amazingly, the Jazz failed to put Chicago away early on. The Bulls managed to stay close, and late in the game Jordan once again put the Bulls on his back and carried them to the point where they could win. But the small tell-tale signs Michael gave out when he was tired were not so small at that point. The fatigue was obvious: He was not elevating well on his jump shot, and even shooting free throws looked like an ordeal.

Given all that, the last two minutes were remarkable even for Jordan. His jump shot looked terrible. His elevation and follow through were poor, and he had missed four in a row near the end of the game. With about five minutes left, Phil Jackson told him to forget the jumper and drive to the basket. That he did.

With 37 seconds left, Utah had the ball, but Chicago had whittled the lead to 86–85. And then it happened. Utah ran a little clock and with 16 seconds left, Jordan, sensing the play which was developing, slipped in on the blind side of Karl Malone and made a clean steal, brought the ball up court, slowly, deliberately, master of the universe once again, almost as if taunting Bryon Russell, left out there alone with the melancholy task of guarding him. With a little more than seven seconds left, Michael began his move, going to his right. Suddenly he pulled up, faked Russell to the floor (aided by a little tap on Russell's butt with his left hand) and absolutely confident of his shot, and with exceptional form, elevation and follow-through almost perfect, hit the game-winning jumper.

Utah missed its last shot, and Chicago won—its sixth championship in the Jordan years. Afterward someone asked Jerry Sloan about Jordan. He should be remembered, Sloan said, "as the greatest player who ever played the game."

It was the perfect final moment to one of the most brilliant careers in team sports. Michael was 35 at the time, not so much showing his age—he was as good as ever—but working ever so much harder to compete at that level.

Lest we—and he—forget, in those final weeks there had been a number of signs of age. The series with Indiana had been very hard, and the Bulls had barely slipped by the Pacers. If anything, the Indiana series was tougher than the Finals against the Jazz. In particular, I remember matchups he had with Jalen Rose. Rose, just emerging as one of the premier players in the league after a spotty beginning to his career, had proved very frustrating to Michael: He was tall, strong, and he seemed to be quite rested in those moments in the game, late second half, late fourth quarter, when Michael was accustomed to putting (smaller) tired defenders away.

That Chicago team, for all of Dennis Rodman's wackiness, was a lot better than the Washington Wizards are likely to be next year. By the end of that season, Dennissimo was unraveling at an ever-faster rate, his drinking was getting worse, and even someone as nuanced with bad boys as Jackson was having trouble keeping him even partially focused. But still he averaged 15 rebounds a game.

Pippen, only 32 back then, was—once he recovered from a foot injury and accepted his unhappy relationship with the Chicago management—in peak condition and playing at the top of his game. Kukoc was both talented and erratic—one was never sure which Toni would show up on a given night. The other players had played together for some time, knew their roles and their limitations. But the number of Bulls' victories per season was on the way down, from 72 to 69 to 62 wins in what might be called Jordan II, his return after his quick baseball retirement.

It will not be like that in Washington. I am one of those people who thought taking the Washington job was a mistake in the first place—not that Michael can't be a fine basketball executive, if he wants. He's smart and shrewd, and if he can get away from David Falk, who is too smart by half, he'll probably be a successful manager in his life after basketball.

Becoming a part owner and perhaps eventually a principal owner at Charlotte, an opportunity offered to him earlier on, was a far better choice than Washington. Charlotte was a young team, was not capped out, and had vastly more upside. Washington was the worst of two worlds, an old team that was capped out. The sweetener in Washington was said to be a $30 million bonus in taking the job, a short-range plus and a long-range minus, if you're already rich and your most precious commodity is your reputation.

I can understand Michael's frustration and impatience—he's a very impatient young man—with his own team, and I can understand him looking out at the current NBA and thinking to himself that he can still do it, that his game is more complete than that of almost all these players. And he's both right in many ways—and, I suspect, wrong. That is, I think he can still come back and play if he's with a quite good team that is only one piece short and does not have to depend on him. The Wizards, even if both he and Barkley play, will not be a very good team, and it will be, I suspect, very frustrating for him.

I realize that there is something unfair in all this—I write as someone who has been able to enjoy my own profession for 46 years now, and I realize that life is crueler for athletes, taking away from them at a young age what they do best, love best, finally what defines them. I realize as well that with someone as driven and passionate as Michael, that playing is like life itself, that there is, in a benign sense, an addiction here, and that it is harder to walk away from his sport than almost any of the rest of us can imagine.

But Michael, when he played, was always aware of his special niche, and of not wanting to slip. Of not playing a moment in his career when he was less than his best. He knew too many stories of athletes who had stayed too long, and were on the way down and held on, of Willie Mays falling down in center field late in his career.

Michael would talk to his friend, Johnny Bach, the assistant coach, telling Bach to let him know when he began to slip.

But here is the real truth: The player he will really be competing against is not Latrell Sprewell or Vince Carter. The player he will be competing against will be Michael Jordan, the best ever at that position, the Michael Jordan who emerged those six wonderful years with an almost perfect complement of talent around him.

That will be the toughest matchup of his career, going against the myth of the most charismatic and exciting player most of us ever saw, and who again and again—in what was ostensibly a big man's game—lifted his team above the odds and the competition. Those are images most of us would prefer to leave as they are.

The temptation for him to come back must be immense: You go from a life of the ultimate highs when every camera is always aimed at you, and then when you are still a young man, you enter a far more mundane middle-class existence. You get all the privacy you once wanted—but at a terrible price, the loss of what was dearest to you.

I suspect if he comes back it will be fun again for him for a time—a brief time—playing the game he loves so much, and being on the road with his teammates; he and Charles will be quite a pair. He will love the excitement generated by the crowd and the thrill of the competition. The NBA's television ratings, now in a predictable post-Jordan depression, will probably bloom again. God knows, I'll watch again for a time.

And some of it might work. Michael might lift the Wizards to a higher level than they've played at—that would not be too hard. There might well be some wonderful nights when it all comes back, and he can score 40 or 50 points.

But I remember how hard those final weeks were in 1998, and I know how much he hates to lose and how much he hates to play with indifferent teammates, and if I were Michael, I would not take a chance on what was not only one of the most brilliant careers in modern sports, but as close to a perfect exit as I've ever seen.

In Admiration of Iverson

From ESPN.com, June 11, 2001

THE FIRST GAME OF THE 2001 NBA FINALS WAS ONE OF THE best basketball games I have seen in a very long time. There is just nothing like great talent fused with great passion in a big game.

It was not just that everyone, myself included, expected Goliath to coast to the title, and it was not just that David beat Goliath in Game 1, but it was the nature of the game, the pure ferocity with which David played, and in time the matching ferocity with which Goliath had to counter.

Even if the Lakers had won, which in the end they did not, it would have been a magnificent game, because the Sixers had pushed them so hard, pushed them to match Allen Iverson's level of passion. For it was obvious that Iverson controlled the pace of the game, not just by his own play but by his infectious effect on his teammates, and thus in turn his effect on the Lakers.

If that Game 1 assault upon the Laker journey to an unbeaten playoff record wasn't bad enough, the Sixers, in Games 2 and 3, again challenged the Lakers. In both games, they lost, but they also pushed L.A. very near the breaking point, leaving them confused and uncertain at critical moments in the fourth quarter. Game 1 clearly had not been a fluke, or a result of too long a layoff for the Lakers. Iverson has the rare capacity to bring a lesser team to parity with what was seemingly a far more powerful team.

I have been learning to admire Iverson this season, and it's turning out to be a good deal of fun. I don't know whether it matters if I like Iverson or not. We come from different worlds, and we are likely, once the Finals are over, to remain part of our different worlds. Just to admire him is good enough.

Iverson is very simply, no matter how well Shaq or Kobe or Tracy McGrady played, the great story of this basketball season, and if you think about it, I suspect, the single most interesting success story of the past basketball, baseball and football seasons. He has taken a team of players with a medium talent level and struck terror into the hearts of a team with vastly greater size and talent. He has commanded our interest and our own emotions in these Finals against great odds. He has Phil Jackson calling timeouts, and Lakers fans aware that a five- or six-point lead near the end of the game is not enough because Shaq can't shoot free throws. On the sidelines Jack Nicholson looks unnaturally tense.

We, the fans, are engaged in these Finals as we did not intend to be. He has made us look at the two previous challengers to the Lakers—teams from Sacramento and San Antonio that obviously had a great deal more natural talent—and made us think they did not play very hard on defense, and they could be intimidated by the Lakers. Because Iverson cannot be intimidated, and the Sixers, in turn, cannot be intimidated. This makes for very good basketball and a wonderful story.

Learning to admire Iverson took time. I am not a hip-hop kind of guy. I don't call people "Bro'," or talk of "The Hood." To me, Pearl Harbor—the news of which I remember all too well—is the beginning of a hard frightening four-year war (during which we moved some 10 times because my father went back in the service), not a bad, indeed almost a profane movie. However, Iverson, if he has seen it, might well think it's a good movie—after all, it's made for his generation with lots of video-game dogfight sequences.

I own no rap CDs, and by instinct when I hear the name Snoop Dogg, it sounds to me like that of someone who should be in a comic strip. So, we have our cultural differences, or perhaps more accurately our cultural divide. I think it's safe to assume that in my eyes he arrives with more cultural baggage than I like, and that if I were doing a piece on him, I would have more cultural baggage than he would prefer.

I, like many others of my generation, did not like what he seemed to represent. Nor was it just the surface manifestations of alienation, although in truth they matter, for we judge each other first on surfaces. ("I don't want," said a friend of mine who has Knicks season tickets, speaking of the old Iverson about three years ago, "to root for someone who looks like he might mug me.") And the surface manifestations are, in fact, very different, and to the white middle-aged fan, they are at first quite offputting: the cornrowed hair, the tattoos, the body piercing, the somewhat volatile relationship with the law.

But more important was his game. He was, I thought, like all too many young athletes in the NBA, disrespectful of opponents, disrespectful of teammates, disrespectful of his coaches, and in some way, I thought, disrespectful of the game. The transgressions in previous years were all too numerous, the fights with coaches, the deliberate tardiness to practices, the sulking when he was taken out of a game, the sense he gave out that his real team was his posse, who represented what he was and where he came from, and that it was to them that his true loyalty lay, not his Sixers teammates, who were involuntarily merely his business associates.

I saw all the talent, heard all the fuss, and thought that in the end the talent didn't really matter, because finally it was about self, and as much as he added to a team with his talent, he managed in other ways to subtract with his behavior.

In the past, I—and, I think, a great many sports fans of my general background, gender, class, race—have remained largely immune to his talents. Yes, he was very talented, exceptionally quick, and tough, and he could score and he could pass. No one, it seemed, could get a shot off that quickly. But 50-point games do not move me.

I saw the passion as I saw the talent, but I had a sense that the passion, like the talent, was primarily about self. In the end, there's nothing more boring than the rise of a talented, self-absorbed star in this modern entertainment society, whether it's on the part of movie stars, television stars, athletes, or for that matter, the self-inflated television personalities who cover them and are often equally as self-absorbed and who promote themselves instead of simply doing their job.

So, there was always a gulf between us. We come from not merely different, but really quite separate Americas. We only meet, in the sense that we meet at all—which we do mostly electronically—because of his superb athletic skills. Otherwise, we would be each other's invisible men, effectively vague, faceless shadows to each other in our daily lives, at best stereotypes.

I am white, a college graduate, old enough to be his grandfather. I was 26 when his mother was born. I belong to the generation which, when it was young, held its breath hoping that Jackie Robinson would succeed when he broke in back in 1947, and I have watched with pleasure the coming of the social revolution in American sports, the coming of the new immensely talented black athletes in all sports.

In my 20s and 30s I covered Civil Rights in the South. I take a certain degree of alienation on the part of black athletes for granted—I'm somewhat surprised when it isn't there. I'm not easily offended by manifestation of black dissent or separatism. The decision of Cassius Clay to become Muhammad Ali did not bother me. Nor did his decision not to serve in Vietnam—although it greatly offended many journalists from the generation older than me (even when their own sons were not going to Vietnam).

The early afros of the 1960s didn't bother me. Athletes at the 1968 Olympics raising their hands in black power didn't bother me. But I feel that whatever your beliefs, you have to prove yourself, first and foremost, by what you do, and how good you are at your profession, and your alienation better not interfere with your job.

Having said that, let me make a number of other points. We should, I think, before we continue, be aware of a number of things. One is that the media does not always get the business of who is a good guy and who is not a good guy exactly right, and that it tends to go softer on winners in these judgments because it wants, however unconsciously, access to winners.

The media wants good guys to win and the bad guys to lose, and tends almost without knowing it, to award an edge in being a good guy to the winner for merely winning. Inevitably, it thereupon tends to search harder for the warts of the losers than the warts of the winners.

Sometimes, because of this, it tends to blow the call.

Thus in the ongoing competition between Joe DiMaggio and Ted Williams back in the 1950s, the media—actually the press in those days—spent a good deal of time deciding who gets white hats and black hats. And they decided that DiMaggio was the good guy, and Williams the bad guy. That turned out to be a colossal mistake.

DiMaggio might have been the better all-around baseball player, but he was a deeply misanthropic man, surprisingly ungenerous and uncommunicative to all; even some of the same reporters who helped keep the flame of his alleged elegance burning, would, when speaking in private, talk about how unpleasant he had been with them, and how they had always been forced to adapt to his rather selfish treatment of them.

By contrast, Williams, tempestuous, systematically assaulted by a brutal Boston media, was by far the better, in all ways a more open and more interesting person. He was a beloved teammate. But the Yankees won regularly, and the Red Sox, much weaker in pitching, won only once. DiMaggio got the white hat, Williams the black.

Comparably in the Bill Russell–Wilt Chamberlain competition, Russell (surrounded generally by better teammates) almost always won on the court, and was in time awarded the white hat by the media. In truth, Russell has always been, except to a small handful of people who go back a long way with him, aloof and unacceptably difficult to deal with, whereas Chamberlain was by contrast open, generous and accommodating to all kinds of people.

So, it is important to remember that the media can get its images wrong: or as Danny Ainge once said about Charles Barkley, back before Barkley emerged as a national charmer (someone with far greater talent to host a nightly talk show than Jay Leno), I've known a lot of bad guys pretending to be good guys, but Charles is the only good guy pretending to be a bad guy I've ever known.

We ought to be aware that athletes, both white and black, who are often said to be religious, might in fact be narrow-minded and bigoted. We got a reminder of that this year with the Knicks. I am also aware that athletes who are presumed to be likeable, and are portrayed as likeable, are not in fact necessarily likeable, particularly as they have in recent years become ever bigger players in the sports–popular cultural scene, paid more and more, and, of course, coddled more and more, and, of course, shielded more and more from the rules and codes of the larger society.

We ought to remember that some of them have learned not merely the ability to spin beat reporters, but in the case of Dave Winfield, for instance, allegedly a good guy—who will ever really know?—there were virtually full-time public relations people working for him to create an aura that Winfield was a concerned citizen and a good guy. (I was once assigned a magazine piece by the *New York Times* on Winfield, but by the time I had dealt with all the People from Dave, Paid for by Dave—and not the Yankees—his lawyers and his own PR people—I decided he wasn't worth bothering with.)

"What kind of guy is X?" I once asked my friend Steve Kelley, a talented columnist for the *Seattle Times*, mentioning a player on the Lakers a decade ago who seemed to be unusually pleasant and personable. "He's athlete-nice," Kelley answered. That struck me as a shrewd assessment—and a new category. What it meant was that X was within reason amenable to dealing with the world around him, was not a raving egomaniac, and would on occasion talk with people with some degree of openness and candor, and did not expect to be catered to at all times. But it had to be done on his terms and when it suited him and that he would be open and amenable was hardly a given.

So, Kelley was offering me a different scale on which to judge athletes, one different from measuring other human beings, other than say stars of the movies and television. Everything tends to be done on their terms, and they expect everything to be done on their terms. We are grateful for their smaller attentions and we more readily forgive their medium-sized transgressions.

As one of Mickey Mantle's teammates once said of him, it was a function of his charm and his fame that he could play the worst practical jokes in the world on his teammates, and everyone would laugh because it was Mickey Mantle doing it.

So, the question about Iverson is not whether or not he is likeable. Let us assume that he is neither more or less likeable than most professional athletes, although perhaps slightly more alienated as noted by lifestyle, not surprising considering the raw nature of his childhood. Let us assume that he is as much culturally outside the reach of the average middle-class white fan as the normal son of the ghetto who never makes it to professional basketball is—that is, that there is a lot of stuff that festers there.

I suspect Iverson would not like the average person who roots for him very much, nor would, in fact, the average person who roots for him necessarily like him if they met in a neutral setting.

Let us assume as well, that a certain amount of raw sexist and homophobic language is not that unusual in the average locker room—although to make a CD that demeans women and mocks gays takes it a good deal further and means that we are well-advised to hold back a bit more in our enthusiasms as to who he really is.

But here is what we should remember, and it was something pointed out to me years ago by Roger Angell, the gifted *New Yorker* writer, when I asked him what a player on the Red Sox was really like. "They are what they do," he answered, wiser in the ways of being around big-time athletes than I.

That was it. They are what they do. Which strikes me as wise and as good a definition for measuring an athlete as we have. We do not, after all, have to buy the goods they flack for, the sneakers, and the soft drinks, the sunglasses, the telephone services. We do not have to hold them up to our children as role models. We are free to tell our children that John Lewis, the heroic Georgia congressman, or my friend Ron Ridenour, the grunt who blew the whistle on My Lai who died a few years ago, are better role models than any athlete.

But if they are what they do is the test, then Iverson passes it handsomely this year. In a nation where too many people have what is now called attitude without talent, or attitude without passion, he has, it seems to me, all three, and ironically the more passion he displays, miraculously the less attitude we see—as if he has forgotten that in addition to playing so hard he also has to stick his finger in the world's eye.

So, that is why I have come to admire Iverson so much this season. Having come perilously close to being exiled to Detroit (and being saved only by Matt Geiger's refusal to go along), he has shaped up.

All the talent and all the passion have finally been fused to something larger—team. He has gotten along with his coach. He no longer sulks when he comes out of games. He is no longer late to practice. He has not only made his teammates better, the prime test of any basketball player, but the ferocity and intensity of his game has been infectious, and his teammates seem to me to have become an extension of him.

Everyone on that team plays hard, and they play hard all the time. You cannot put the Sixers away. If the Lakers early in the fourth quarter make a major run of 10 or 12 points, enough for most teams to be a dagger in the heart, the Sixers are immune. They are not intimidated. Back they come. They never think they are going out of a game.

Much of this, I think, comes from the psyche of Iverson. He seems to me to be lionhearted. He is supremely talented as well. He has not just played hurt, he has played very hurt. So have his teammates.

He has been the invincible man, refusing again and again, when faced with opponents who have superior ability, to lose. He has driven himself and his teammates to a level where they normally would not be. He has helped take a team that is, in a technical sense, not necessarily that talented, and not only lifted it to the Finals, but he has made it competitive with an L.A. team that appeared ready to roll over it just as it had rolled over everyone else lately.

He has given us a competitive Finals. That's worth admiring.

FOOTBALL

It was football, but it was never about football. It was about belonging. On those fall Saturdays, we belonged for the first time.

THE GAMES HARVARD PLAYS

Inc.,
October 1990

SUNDAY, BORING SUNDAY:
A FAREWELL TO PRO FOOTBALL

From *New York Magazine*, December 16, 1974

I AM STILL YOUNG ENOUGH TO REMEMBER THE GOLDEN age of professional football, an era which preceded by a few short years the present decline and fall of professional football. Those were great years: Tittle, Graham, Motley, Casares, Ameche, Matson, Marchetti, Lipscomb, Unitas, Moore, Rote, Gifford, Huff. The coronation, of course, was the 1958 overtime Colts–Giants championship game. Who will ever forget those years, the epic struggles of the New York defense against Jimmy Brown, or the even more epic struggles to find a good working television set, one reasonably free from electronic snow?

They were years of twisting rabbit ears and trying to find friends who lived on the high ground. We began the era in neighborhood bars, which were the first to venture into large black-and-white sets; we moved into private homes only with the coming of mass ownership of sets. Then into bars again with the coming of color, and then, as the cable finally arrived in New York, back into the homes again. Gay Talese was the first on our block to own a color set, and many of the great Sundays were played in the immortal shadows of Talese Stadium (that is, once Nan Talese learned how to tune the set). Those were great years: it was a living part of our life, escapism at its high-quality best.

Though I worked in many different cities over those years, there was always a tacit agreement among friends about Sunday: yes, we cared about the game, we knew who had the best local reception, we knew who would play on Sunday, and we would all show up. More, we were the embodiment of the modern fan. We did not root for specific teams (though, of course, in the Super Bowl we rooted for the Jets against the Colts; regionalism had some uses, though given the excitement Namath generated, we would have rooted for him if we'd lived in L.A.). We did in a perverse way root *against* certain teams—Dallas in particular because of its sudden infamy, and because to me at least Tom Landry was the least sympathetic of coaches, looking more like a regional director of the F.B.I. than anything else. What we really rooted for was the game itself, or more specifically, for the two-minute drill. Thus we rooted for the spread to be under seven points midway through the fourth quarter so that we could see Tittle or Conerly, or Unitas or Starr at his best. We were football sybarites rather than loyalists. But we were also good fans: we knew the game, we knew the teams, we knew their idiosyncrasies (I don't think any of us ever lost any money betting on Roman Gabriel in a big game during his Rams years).

In those days football seemed the almost perfect sport and it seemed unlikely that we could ever get enough. Yet even the golden years finally reached their peak, the height of an era. My own instinct is to choose the latter part of the Lombardi Era, in particular the N.F.L. championship game of 1967 when Green Bay defeated Dallas 21–17. It was a lovely match-up: Green Bay was at the height of its fierce powers; Dallas, a pre-expansion expansion team, was probably more talented but also more mechanical. It was a climactic moment: the game was so fine, the sport so good, the technological coverage of it so superior, that an offensive lineman, one of the most obscure players on the field, was able to dictate (not write) his memoirs and thus produce a major national best seller. Significantly, his title, like the game itself, was an ode to technology—*Instant Replay*. Yet, at this very dizzying moment, the forces which would quickly undermine the game were already at work. The leagues were in the process of merging, there had already been a common draft of far too many teams, there were football doubleheaders on the way. There was, in fact, a football glut. Soon we would be served more and more of less and less. What television did in making pro football our national sport and thereupon what television and rank commercial greed did in destroying it is a parable for our time.

FROM THE BEGINNING television was crucial to the success of professional football, just as it has been crucial to its erosion (not unlike the role of television with the president: to slay the dragon we must first inflate him). The game itself had always been much better than its pretelevision status. It was, in fact, a brilliant national sport lacking only national exposure. It had been forced to compete with college football, with its great regional strengths, in a way that pro baseball, for example, had never had to compete with college baseball. It was for its loyalists (and those in many cities lucky enough to have tickets) an absolutely stunning sport. Television removed it from obscurity; its growth paralleled the growth of television in this country. Before 1956 there was only scattered hit-or-miss coverage; in 1956 CBS picked up the N.F.L. games regularly; the Colts–Giants game, which many use as a way of marking the coming of pro football, was in 1958. Now compare that with the coming of television: in 1951 there were only 10 million television sets in the country; the next year there were 15 million sets and 70 CBS affiliate stations; by 1958 there were an estimated 41 million sets and 189 CBS affiliates. We now had a truly national audience and a truly national sport.

FOOTBALL AND TELEVISION adapted extraordinarily well to each other. The camera has an almost whimsical ability to like or dislike people, institutions, and events. It had an instant love affair with football. Where the subtle and less violent skills of baseball were often minimized by the camera and where the geometric proportions of the game often escaped the camera's mastery, football was quite different. The ball was large enough to see, football action centered remarkably well for the camera, and indeed the camera found action where the naked eye, preoccupied with following the ball, had seen only vague blurs. There were, we discovered, plays within plays. Offensive linemen struggling with defensive giants became as absorbing as following the ball itself. In the Sixties, video tape came and allowed even more postplay action. The naked eye had clearly been outstripped by technology. And if baseball seemed by its very pace to be designed for a more leisurely America, an America where Lincoln and Douglas could debate for hours on the courthouse steps (in large part because the audience, having spent hours driving by wagon to hear them debate, wanted its time and money's worth), football was again different. Television had speeded up the pace of American life because it demanded action and because action could be filmed; football was part of a growing demand for action and confrontation—socially, politically, and athletically.

WHAT ALSO MADE THE GAME so good in those days was the quality of the teams and the sense of identity that they projected. There were only twelve teams and they were, by and large, good ones. They had character and identity and continuity. College football was limited by a lack of continuity; great players came to college, but quickly graduated. Now, with the coming of pro football, the continuity was prolonged. A player's cycle might last seven or eight years; a team's cycle—the coming together of seven or eight truly great players—might be four or five years. This continuity was crucial to fan commitment; the longer the duration of a team's character, the longer the fan was likely to be genuinely interested.

Teams coming together like that over a long period of time began to have genuine characters and identities which the fans could readily grasp. And here again was the essence of pro football at its best. It was not good players against other players, but identifiably great players against other great players. And as such the game transcended regionalism and became, in the best sense, a national sport. The perils and troubles of the regional team were secondary; even if the Giants were lagging, the interest in pro football continued—there were so many other good teams to watch. One reason that the sport was so good was that the mathematics of it was so good. By and large there are about ten or twelve blue-chip players a year coming into the pros and about 50 players worthy of pro selection. In a pre-expansion draft of twelve teams each club could draft four times within the first 50. A weak team could strengthen itself reasonably quickly; a strong team could nonetheless replenish some of its gaps. One of the agonies for a Jets fan for the last couple of years has been the knowledge that the weaknesses in the team are appearing much faster than the capacity to replenish them, that the team steadily gets older and has more weaknesses, while Namath, the superstar, also becomes older.

Obviously some sort of expansion was inevitable; in a country of 200 million, and given the talent bank in America, I suspect the ideal number would have been sixteen. But under the projected Rozelle expansion plans, the league will go to at least 32 teams; this means that the reward for being the best team in football will be to pick the thirty-second best college football player in the country; that is, a player two-thirds of the way down on the third round of what would have been the old draft. (For an even better example of how expansion can ruin a sport, I give you hockey, where in a decade the sport went from one league with six teams to two leagues of 28 teams, all of this from a talent bank of 21 million Canadians.)

CLEARLY THE VERY SUCCESS of pro football in the Sixties led to its undoing. It was an irresistible temptation: here, every Sunday, millions of the nation's most affluent citizens were locking themselves into rooms for three and six hours with television sets. Seventy-eight million Americans watching on a given day! Clearly anything as good as that could and should go on forever. Clearly also, the more teams, the more games, and the more games, the more commercial possibilities. If CBS could have its league, NBC would have a league too. Without NBC's television contract, the A.F.L. might well have failed, and, most likely, only two or three of its teams would have been incorporated into the old league. But television guaranteed survival of even the bad teams. Everyone got richer and richer. Greed was at the heart of it.

Instead of the controlled expansion of the past there was now a quantum jump in teams and in the number of games. Then a merger and a common draft. Which meant that overnight the quality of the N.F.L. roster was cut in half and the number of truly great players on any given team cut even more drastically: every great player lessens your chance of ever again drafting another great player. Where once there might have been six or eight great players on a team, now there will be two or three. The few interesting teams this year—Miami, New England, Buffalo—were, not surprisingly, the A.F.L. teams at the very bottom at the time of the combined draft.

I realize that I write this farewell to football as a resident of a city possessing two genuinely bad teams with little hope of any short-term improvement. But in the past that would not have mattered; the rest of the league would have been enticing. Now, by and large, the rest of the league is boring, more and more faceless, character-less teams with less and less identity; the chances of two interesting teams' playing on a given Sunday are very slim. The great strength of pro football a decade ago was that it was a national sport; now, with expansion, it has largely become a regional sport. Too many teams with too little talent, the quality eroding faster than the draft can replace it. There is a slow but inevitable convergence on competent, boring mediocrity. Eventually everyone will have a record of

7-5 except for a few teams which are 6-6 and a few more which are 5-7 (Curt Gowdy will just as inevitably hail this as a sign of improvement in the league, the fact that any team can beat any other team on a given Sunday).

It will get worse before it gets better. Two more teams are to be added this year: Tampa and Seattle. Which will dilute the excellence about 8 or 10 percent (if the W.F.L. functions next year, it will be equivalent to about two and a half to three N.F.L. teams and will dilute the talent another 10 percent). The people who run the N.F.L. are aware that what they are offering week by week is a diluted product—but they have a marvelous gimmick for getting around what might be a self-evidently boring schedule: increase the play-off schedule. A marvelous artificial hype. Two full seasons. The first one a boring season to eliminate the truly deadly teams and then a series of play-off games for the more interesting ones. More play-off games, more wild cards, a little something for everybody, a little nothing for everybody.

All this despite the self-evident law of common sense on the limits of too many play-off games and too long a season, that at a certain point each play-off game detracts from other play-off games and championship games (a good example is baseball, where the World Series had been seriously undercut as a championship because of artificial play-offism).

IF PART OF THE PROBLEM is the game, then, similarly, part of the problem is the fan. We must confess our own guilt. We have, for some fifteen years or so, simply seen too much. If there was a network greed which was matched by an owner's greed, then it was also matched by fan greed. Football was there every Sunday, it was free, or almost free, and so we watched it. One game was not enough and so they gave us two, and so we watched two. A pro football game at its best was something special. But if there are two games back to back they are no longer special. It is like seeing two great movies on the same afternoon; nothing is left defined or clear, they run into each other, become blurred, finally diminish each other. Not satisfied that two games on a given afternoon were enough, we were soon served a third, on Monday night. We gleefully accepted it. Somewhere in some network office there must have been someone looking at those Monday-night statistics and thinking, Friday, Friday night . . . perhaps against the late show on Friday. . . .

IN SOME WAYS I THINK even the networks realized that it was all too much and yet they were imprisoned by the sheer marvel of the economics of it all. People who make $100,000 a year selling what people want to buy do not readily hit the brakes, do not lower the register. One sign of their awareness of the problem is a rising level of gimmickry (CBS has just come up with a woman sportscaster who does interviews so genuinely awful that her work rivals—they said it couldn't be done—the work of Tony Kubek).

ABC, which came into the pro-football market last and at a moment when it was clearly saturated, has most deliberately, I think, put its hype into the broadcasting booth. It sells very consciously the idea that Monday-night football is not so much football, but something different. The ball, which historically takes funny bounces on Saturday and Sunday afternoons, *takes even funnier bounces on Monday night over at ABC.* To this end, ABC "cast" its broadcast booth. Cosell: city slicker, smartass, "controversial"; Meredith: country slicker—a little flaky, like all country slickers—more shrewd and knowing in the long run than city slickers; Gifford: churchgoing father, slightly bemused by his children's antics, ready to settle all squabbles.

This year's cast has been less successful. Fred Williamson has returned to Hollywood. Alex Karras, drafted from the late-night talk shows where he played the role of muscle man–comedian, is no

Meredith. If the present problems remain, perhaps the network can draft Milton Berle to come in next year as the heavy, and recast Cosell as "lovable." (Cosell's controversiality is still somewhat in doubt. In essence he is a comparison gainer. That is, he gains by comparison with Curt Gowdy, who is probably the worst broadcaster of all time, and whose ability to punctuate silence with both banality and inaccuracy is unmatched anywhere else in sports. His employers appear to know this and so he comes to us accompanied by Al DeRogatis, whose job it is to try to correct Curt as gently as possible without really implying that he is in fact wrong.) The significant thing about Cosell is that he is significant at all, that one is so aware of the broadcaster. In the great days of pro football, the game spoke for itself; the rise of the broadcaster is a sure sign of the decline on the field.

When I began this article I was doing it by instinct—my instincts and knowledge of my friends' viewing habits. We are fairly good specimens of the madness—men who were 21 or 22 and just out of college when the boom began, in our late thirties or early forties now. I knew that we do not watch as much, and—this is crucial and far more important—*we do not watch the same way, with the same passion.*

The decline in viewing began about two years ago—almost without our noticing it at first. A tendency to turn off a game in the middle, something unheard of in the old days. Then, gradually, a tendency to think of Sunday in nonfootball terms, that is, the ability to schedule events without first consulting the football schedule. And, finally, a tendency to turn on late, timed for the middle of the third quarter to find out if a given game is genuinely close. Equally significant: we do not gather anymore on Sundays for the game. It is just not that important, and it has lost its awesome pull. We still watch in different ways: an unusually good game, Buffalo against New England, might pull us. Or an unusual situation, Namath against a favored but vulnerable Buffalo. One friend watched the

Minnesota–Los Angeles game because he is fascinated by the last battle of pro football, the coming of the black quarterback.

So when I began to write I thought it was a personal thing: I did not expect to find it in the statistics (indeed, if anything, I thought I was still part of the statistics: the demographics boys at NBC and CBS still saw the light go on at my house, envisioned my rushing out at half time to buy more shaving cream). But I checked around and, happily enough, the statistics are down: right before the dismal Sunday of December 1 (Jets against Chargers, Giants against Bears), ABC was down 5 percent, CBS down 14 percent (CBS is saddled with those old N.F.L. teams which show the erosion of the draft most noticeably), and NBC up 10 percent (NBC luckily has the A.F.C., which means that it has a good share of the few interesting teams around, the Miami Csonkas, the New England Plunketts, and the Buffalo Simpsons).

So there it is, bless it—even the numbers are down and perhaps if they keep coming down they will force the networks to force Rozelle to force the owners to merge rather than to expand. A sixteen-team league. In the meantime, farewell to you, Johnny Unitas, farewell to you, Bart Starr, and semi-farewell to you, Frank Gifford.

THE GAMES HARVARD PLAYS

From *Inc.*, October 1990

IN THE FALL OF 1949, WHEN I WAS 15 YEARS OLD AND CALLOW and unsure of myself, I visited my brother in Cambridge during the Harvard–Princeton weekend. Sometime late that Saturday morning, the Harvard University Band, more than 100 members strong, started playing a miniature concert in the middle of Harvard Yard. Then, neatly dressed in crimson blazers and dark gray slacks—but no pomp, no Ruritanian motorcycle-escort hats—they started marching through Harvard Square on their way to the Lars Anderson Bridge and Harvard stadium.

I fell in behind them, completely enchanted. They were wonderful; they radiated confidence that they were the best in the world at what they did (and they probably were). One manifestation of this high and exalted sense of their excellence was their individualism: they cared not one whit about being in step. That was what first struck me: they were brilliant at what they were doing, and they were all out of step.

They were marvelously hip, though one had not yet come upon the word *hip*. I was utterly drawn to their style, or perhaps even better, their antistyle. Other bands marched with precision, employing rigidly perfect moves, not an eyelash out of sync. The Harvard band by contrast was incoherent: there was at best a kind of communal shuffle. They broadcast by their style, by their body language (a phrase we did not have then), that they were very good and that they were irreverent about being very good. All we had to do, their body language seemed to say, was listen. Princeton crunched Harvard that day, and somewhere in my memory there is a small note that they scored more than 60 points. I remember little of the game; what I remember is the end and the fact that that was the moment I decided I wanted to go to Harvard.

If there is something that sets apart Ivy League football, it is that hip. In the world of hip the strong and powerful do not triumph—they are in fact doomed to fail. It is the cool and knowing who win. Thus almost everyone who opts for an Ivy League education, football player and regular student alike, makes a choice very early on in which football prowess and football success are somewhat peripheral. These are not football powers. The entire nation does not await the game on Saturday afternoon. Keith Jackson, stocked to the brim with cliches ("That big fella can really lay a hit on you"), is not in the broadcast booth. Yet the Ivy League has its own wondrous celebration, and Saturday is important. The football itself is good, better than most outsiders think. (The Ivy League schools, one Big Ten recruiter said, can kill you on a certain kind of bright and talented high school player you badly want. You offer them a chance to play on national television a few Saturdays a year, he added, but those damn Ivy League recruiters, who are the pillars of their communities, can offer them a place in their law firms.)

What makes the celebration special is not just that it is irrevocably linked to tradition (after all, Harvard started playing Yale some 115 years ago), but that those who celebrate are absolutely sure that they are going to run the country in 25 years. At many schools thousands cheer because their players are going to a bowl game. In the Ivy League fans cheer because they believe that they are going to the National Security Council. That defines the proportions. (In my senior year Dick Waldron, my roommate, was the head cheerleader. On the morning of the Yale game he woke my other roommate and me and said with great delight, "Do you know what day it is?" We admitted that we did not. ("This is the last bleeping time I have to cheer, is what day it is," he said.)

The game matters, the sport matters, but above all the celebration matters. It is an event and an occasion of bonding. If we are not that good at this, the unwritten code seemed to say, then it is only because we are so much better at things that truly matter.

No one would dare go to an Ivy League school and, at a rally, talk about the need for school spirit. Spirit is as spirit does, and the spirit is mostly free. ("How we will celebrate our victory / we will invite the whole team up for tea," Tom Lehrer wrote in "Fight Fiercely Harvard.") I have a classmate named Stan Katz, who is today the head of the American Council of Learned Societies, one of the most prestigious jobs in academe. While still an undergraduate, Katz proclaimed Katz's law: Princeton fans, he said, cheer loudly for a touchdown. Yale fans cheer loudly for a first down. But Harvard fans often cheer loudest over vantage points. That is, the people at the south end of the field would cheer wildly if Harvard or the other team (it seemed not to matter) had the ball within the 10-yard line at the north end of the field and the clock ran down at the end of the first or third quarter. They were cheering because the action was coming to their end of the stadium. It was Katz who reminded me of another Harvard cheer during a game when Dartmouth was ahead 28 to 14. The Crimson fans shouted out the score, "Two-Eight-One-Four!" and then in unison added in one great volley: "Now Tell Us Your SAT Scores!"

Mock it we might, but for the first time in our lives we were part of a wonderful pageant. It is almost 40 years since I was a freshman, and over the years those games have blended, scores have faded from memory, yet the colors of the Saturdays have become, if anything, sharper: the huge crowds across the field in blue (coats, jackets, sweaters, scarves) for Yale or orange and black for Princeton or green for Dartmouth. At the *Harvard Crimson* before each game, we had a Puncheon / Luncheon—a pregame lunch at which we ate and drank and to which the visiting editors of the other school's daily were duly invited. We did, though we did not admit it, show our style, our plumage and the plumage of the ladies with us, which was a critical part of our own plumage, though we were loathe to admit it. There is in all of it a wondrous early sense of belonging to something larger.

I think that is what mattered. It was football, but it was never about football. It was about belonging. We had applied to these venerable schools, once the exclusive property of the aristocracy, and they had, much to our surprise, accepted us. But for a long time we were not of them; we went to class, we discreetly (almost covertly) displayed the tiniest symbols that would identify us—the closest thing to an announcement of membership was the color of our scarves. But we did not feel that our place was rightful. Indeed we probably doubted it. This was Harvard (or Yale or Princeton), but did we really belong, were we truly part of it? It was, first and foremost and most readily, on those fall Saturdays when we could have it both ways (participate, be cool, cheer, but cheer almost mockingly) that we belonged for the first time, and as such became part of something larger.

How I Fell in Love with the NFL

From ESPN.com, February 21, 2001

I HAVE SEEN THE NEW XFL AT PLAY, AND IF THIS IS THE future, then for once I think I prefer to live in the past. It is third-level football—mostly taxi-squad players hoping for one last break—married up with young women who seem to have wandered over to NBC from the Playboy Channel.

It is produced and brought to us by people who clearly believe that we as a nation know little about either football or erotica. The league has promised and delivers live coverage from inside the players' dressing room, but I suspect that to be a success it will need to have live coverage from inside the cheerleaders' dressing room instead. Stay tuned, that might be next.

It is, like all too much of American culture these days, deliberately coarse. That seems to be the bet on us as a nation: that there is no way to underestimate the level of national sophistication—or at least of young American males from 14 to 34, about whom today's Madison Ave. marketing geniuses believe coarser is better.

So it is that NBC, a network that should know better, has given us the XFL, and Budweiser, a company that should know better, has given us beer commercials featuring Cro-Magnon young Americans—are they deliberately chosen to be as unattractive as possible?—who grunt, rather than speak, to each other. And so it is that *Saturday Night Live* has slipped in one generation from Steve Martin doing his wild and crazy guy routines to Adam Sandler simply being crude. Can things get worse? Probably.

As I write, the ratings for the XFL are headed toward the South Pole. The truth, I believe (or more accurately, I hope), is that the XFL is failing because the product is not just bad, it is artificial. Its prospects, I think, have nothing to do with whether the NFL is sufficiently violent—it is plenty violent, given the size, speed and power of today's athletes and the nature of the game.

The problem with the NFL is that there are too many teams (like other pro leagues, it drastically over-expanded, and probably the ideal number of teams was somewhere between 18 and 24), too many games, too many playoff games, too many commercials, and too long a season. The product—week in and week out—has been diluted.

The core football season, which once went from October and November through late December, now seems to begin in late August and threatens to last until February. Too few teams have an identifiable character. The game was at its best when, even if your own regional team was not playing well, there was a game on that Sunday between two very good teams—two teams you knew so well, you could look forward to the outcome. More often than not, that's gone.

Clearly, the problem with Monday Night Football is that most of the games are between boring teams no one cares very much about, not whether the nation needs more or less of Dennis Miller as a commentator (I would vote for less).

I was fortunate enough to be a witness to those remarkable years when the NFL came of age as a national sport, roughly from 1957 to 1960, about the same time as the coming of national television, which wired the entire country together visually.

The networks themselves benefited—suddenly, they had a national audience. The leaders of the Civil Rights movement, who were challenging segregation in the South, benefited—they now had dramatic new film clips for the networks' evening news shows, which were very hungry for drama. And pro football benefited, moved instantaneously to parity with Major League Baseball.

At the moment just before this happened, pro football, in terms of the national agenda, was something of a minor league. Unlike baseball, which was well-suited to the medium, it was not a good radio sport. If anything, a few colleges—like Notre Dame—had a greater hold on the nation's consciousness.

But it was a very good game, with great athletes who played at a level well above those of the college game. All in all, it was something of an aficionado's sport; the people lucky enough to have a team in their region—and own season tickets—knew how good it was; to the rest of the country, it was something of a secret. The moment it was married up with network television, it became a huge success.

People instantly knew how good the product was. There was no need for hype, no need for a comedian in the broadcast booth. The camera caught, as radio never could, the speed, power and ferocity with which the game was played. More, unlike the college game, it offered continuity. Instead of roughly a third of a team graduating (or finishing their eligibility) each year, only a small number of players retired. Teams had definable characters.

To understand the sheer magnetic pull of it (hard for anyone to do who was born after the '60s and grew up with professional football as a birthright), think of what we had to contrast it with: Most of us who were avid football fans had seen a great many high school games and a few college games where there were at best two or three pro-quality players on the field at a given time. Even in the Southeastern Conference, whose games I regularly watched in the '50s, there was nothing like it in speed or talent. For most football fans getting a first look at the NFL on television, there was no prologue.

In those years when the NFL burst on the national scene, I was working as a reporter for the Nashville *Tennessean*, 23 in 1957, making $90 a week; I was 26 in the fall of 1960 when I left Nashville, by then making $125. Neither I nor any of my friends owned a television set—I would not own one until 1967, when I returned from Vietnam.

Almost without anyone saying anything, ours was a small football-watching community which simply evolved of itself, a few of us gathering faithfully each Sunday afternoon at a local bar to watch the games. It was all very new. There was no color, no satellite, no instant replay, no FOX channel, no cable. Only CBS carried the games; NBC got into the picture with the coming of the American Football League in 1960. Pat Summerall was still a placekicker with the New York Giants.

We were, I recognize now, a beer commercial before there were beer commercials about people like us. The regulars in our group were my roommate, Fred Graham, then a law student; John Nixon, a college classmate of mine, also a law student; and one of his high school friends, Richard Hawkins, who was an insurance adjustor.

The bar was called Rotier's, which was its technical name, though we still called it Al's Tavern, which was the original name. It was located just a few blocks from Vanderbilt, near 24th and West End in Nashville. The name had been changed from Al's to Rotiers, because Johnny Rotier, who owned it, had done a lot of business with Vanderbilt students, and often cashed their checks from home there.

Apparently, their parents did not like seeing "Al's Tavern" stamped on the back of the checks. Thus the name change to Rotier's to make it seem to the folks back home that the young scions of the South were behaving better. Only a few blocks away was Dudley Field, where Vanderbilt played its SEC games, and where, when I left Nashville in 1960, no black football player had ever played.

I do not think it is fair to say that Al's was seedy, but it wasn't entirely high class either. Certainly there were not a lot of Vanderbilt coeds around. It was an old-fashioned '50s bar, pleasantly dark, and it smelled, as well it should have, of beer both drunk and spilled over the years. There was not much decor; my friend John Nixon recalls a painting of Custer's Last Stand, which was apparently sent free of charge to all taverns by the grateful Anheuser-Busch people.

Johnny Rotier was a quiet man who always wore a sweater. (Some years ago, when he died, his wife laid him out for his funeral in his best suit, but then decided that wasn't Johnny, and he departed us in an open sports shirt and sweater, Nixon reports.) A man named Moose Malteni was the bartender; he had a golden tooth. Mrs. Rotier did the cooking. Nashville was still quite segregated in those days, and so the only black man allowed in was Johnny, a partially crippled man who cleared tables but was not allowed to serve food. The television set was medium size—small by comparison with today's sets—and, of course, black and white.

Al's Tavern served Bud on tap; Jerry's, a competing tavern a few blocks away, had the Pabst franchise and served Pabst on tap. Apparently, if you had one tap beer, it was considered an exclusive franchise. My memory of the beer is that it was 25 cents a bottle; John Nixon agrees, although he thinks somewhere in those years it might have gone to 35 cents. You could also get a large schooner of tap Bud for 45 cents. We tended to be schooner guys.

Cheeseburgers—I was not much of a food critic in those days, but they seemed more than serviceable—were 45 cents. If you were splurging, you went for the T-bone steak and French fries for $1.25. Blessedly, we could spend much of an afternoon there, eat a meal, drink generously and still depart with a tab of only two or three dollars.

We went religiously every Sunday. The games were very good. We were stunned by the way television caught the power and the fury of the game, the sheer ferocity of the hits. It was not by surprise that, as television became an important part of the equation, the defensive players became stars for the first time; they were the ones making the great hits.

So it was that *Time* soon put Sam Huff of the Giants on its cover—unheard of a few years earlier, a pro football player making the cover of *Time,* and a defensive player at that.

Certain players still stand out from that time. In those years, Johnny Unitas was on the rise, cool, confident, above all audacious—the gunslinger as pro football player—coming out there in the late minutes of a game, his team behind, with that slight stoop, working to perfection what would become known as the two-minute drill.

Jim Brown came into the league at almost that exact moment, and he was something completely new, his combination of sheer power, speed and moves, the ability to run outside like a halfback and then inside the tackles like a fullback, on occasion choosing to plow into defenders, and never choosing to run out of bounds. I don't think we had ever seen a running back quite like him before, and I am not sure I have since—which is not to say that there are no running backs who might be as good, or perhaps better, bigger, faster and perhaps even stronger, but I have never again seen a running back who was so much better than everyone else who did what he did at the time he was doing it. He dominated his field in his era like few athletes ever have, perhaps matched only by Babe Ruth and Bill Russell.

No wonder the game took off nationally in those years, and no wonder, with the NFL so limited, there was soon a second league, and it too was successful. We did not need cheerleaders, or hokey camera shots, or too many announcers to tell us what we were seeing and how good it was; the game spoke for itself, and it soon outdistanced the college game, which on occasion when you went in person looked like it was being played in slow motion. We who fell in love with it knew how to find the others among us who also loved it; that is what forms community, of course.

These days I think fondly of those years, and the inexpensive steak and the 25-cent beer, and of the informal community we constituted. I live in New York and still as I did then root for the Giants. Fred Graham is an anchor for Court TV, lives in Washington, roots for the Redskins and occasionally we can still watch the game together. John Nixon is a federal district judge in Nashville, newly advanced to senior judge status, and he roots for the home town, because Nashville, unlikely though it might have seemed 40 years ago, has its own professional team now, and a very good one.

We have not watched a game all together in years, though we still talk about the game over the phone. Our friend Richard Hawkins died tragically some years ago when he was cutting down a tree, and the tree fell on him. Rotier's, which was, I guess, a sports bar before there were sports bars, still exists in a new, milder incarnation today—what is called a family restaurant. Ironically, the most popular sports bar in town is owned by Eddie George, a young black millionaire who, Judge Nixon reminds me, would not have been allowed to play against Vanderbilt in those days. Nor, for that matter, to wait on tables in Rotier's.

INTRODUCTION

From *Super Bowl XL Opus*, 2006

WHEN I WAS MUCH YOUNGER, SOME XXXVII YEARS AGO, I did something that was either un-American or very American—I am still not sure which. Even though I was a moderately obsessed football fan, I turned down a chance to go to Super Bowl III. I was in Miami that weekend in 1969 when the Jets were to play the Colts. I had lectured there on Saturday and one of the members of the lecture committee offered me a free ticket to the game. A very good seat, he assured me. I did not doubt his word, but I turned him down because I wanted to fly back to New York early Sunday morning and watch the game with my pals, Gay Talese, Michael Arlen and the other regulars at our weekly football sessions.

All of us, given the era and our ages, were nominally Giants fans, but in this new age of more flexible loyalties (an outgrowth of the sudden expansion of televised sports) we had committed to the Jets in that season of their remarkable ascent, which coincided with the continued, almost tragic, descent of our Giants. We always convened at Talese's apartment for a number of reasons, not the least of which was that he was the first in our group to get a color television, and he had the largest set, maybe 30 inches across. For every game during that season, we each took what had become in effect our assigned seat in the den, the same seat we'd sat in all season. I sat on the main couch, to the far right. I used to call the den Talese Stadium, befitting a sports gathering place in this modern era when television was still so new and so important, and where the game came to us, rather than our having to go to the game. For the Jets–Colts game that day we were going to have chili and beer. We were, in other words, like millions of other American men— football-centric, beer-centric, pals-centric—depicted in those regular-guy commercials of the era; you know, the one in which you only go around once.

The great new American age of home entertainment, when we no longer had to seek entertainment but entertainment sought us, had just begun. Instant replay was available only in your mind, as you re-ran critical plays from memory alone. ESPN did not exist, and a satellite was still a small East European country controlled by the Soviet Union. Sports hype was also in its infancy—Vince Lombardi was still just a coach, not a demi-god or a trophy, and Chris Berman had not yet made Howard Cosell look shy and modest by comparison. Nor was the Super Bowl yet all that super. Though it was the last game of the year, it was still considered somewhat anti-climactic by many of the fans and by the players themselves. A Green Bay team that had no identifiable weaknesses, or at least none discovered as yet by its opponents, won the first two Super Bowls by methodically grinding down anybody in its way. After their second victory, over the Raiders, several Packers said the game had been something of a disappointment, that beating Dallas for the NFC title—one of the very best title games in the history of the league— had felt more like the real championship game. The idea of the Super Bowl as the ultimate contest had not yet taken hold.

Then came Super Bowl III, the Namath Game. On that Sunday back in 1969 the Colts were an 18-point favorite, primarily because they were the NFL's champions. When Joe Namath guaranteed a Jets victory the press was appalled—it was a violation of the league and the media's unwritten modesty rules under which a quarterback's ego was supposed to exist, but was never to be evident. Namath, as brash as he was talented, not only promised to deliver a victory but had the audacity to say that there were five or six quarterbacks in the

AFL better than the Colts starter, Earl Morrall. This was the kind of thing you were never supposed to say, even though it was obviously true. I agreed, I thought the betting line was way off—dumb, really. As such I have never thought of the game as such a stunning upset. I believed then as I believe now that in a big game one should never bet against the team with the demonstrably better quarterback, and the immensely talented Namath was just reaching the peak of his powers. Morrall—though he'd been the NFL's MVP that season— was, at best, a high-end journeyman, and his back-up was the estimable but now greatly diminished John Unitas, the quarterback against whom I still measure all others. It is hard now, all these years later, to remember how good Namath was before his body betrayed him. He was at his best when the game was on the line—probably the closest thing at that time to a direct lineal descendant of the great Unitas, with the same kind of I've-come-to-clean-up-this-town-even-if-I-have-only-two-minutes-left-on-the-clock iciness. He read defenses well, could throw deep and had so much arm strength that he could throw off his back foot if need be, and he was good at picking up blitzes. He also had very good receivers, and the speed of flanker Don Maynard meant that the Jets would be able to stretch the field against the Colts.

That day the Super Bowl as we know it was born. The Jets were well-coached, they had a sound (if conservative) game plan and they carried it out with a kind of surgical precision. On offense, they played very shrewd ball control with their vastly under-rated back, Matt Snell. Namath took exactly what the Colt defense gave him—a lot of short passes to his receivers and quick drop-offs to his backs. On defense, the Jets secondary cheated, packed in close to the line, dared Morrall to go deep, and intercepted him three times in the first half. The game was something of an execution: the final score was 16–7, but the Jets had been in complete control. What Namath and the Jets proved was that there was now enough parity between the leagues to make this game entertaining. That Sunday the game started the long journey to becoming what is today The Event, not just in American sports, but in American life, where anyone who seeks society's measure of his importance can have it confirmed, can go To See and, even more important, To Be Seen. In terms of marking the success of a career, it is the defining moment for most American men in the Age of Entertainment.

That alone puts it somewhere up on the level of soccer's World Cup (held once every four years) as the ultimate sporting event on Earth, because we Americans have such a powerful hold on the world of entertainment: We do not seek merely to entertain ourselves, we seek to entertain the world. If television has made the world a global village, then we sing and we dance and we act and we even play sports for the rest of the world to watch and hear. We do not do it just for fun, it's our real day job; and that's why young people around the world tend to envy our culture—we appear to be having more fun than anyone else—and why their parents, more dour about the balance between work and play, often despise us. We look like we are at play, even as we work harder and put ourselves under more pressure than ever before. Our greatest export is not cars or machine tools or software, but our popular culture—our music, our movies, our television shows, even our sports. As a nation we live to be entertained, and in the process we have ended up entertaining the world.

The natural, almost inevitable corollary is that, in the process, we have become the world's experts in marketing, and it stands to reason that our ultimate sporting event is also the ultimate marketing event. If anyone is foolish enough to do a remake of *The Graduate*, the man at the cocktail party button-holing the young Dustin Hoffman character should advise him to think "marketing" not "plastics." In this age even the coaches, who at the beginning of the Entertainment Era made perhaps $100,000 a year and were almost anonymous outside their own zip code (and often within it), can now make $5 million a year or more in several different sports and are more often recognizable (and more popular) than their state's senators.

The fact that America's ultimate event for spectators is a game makes sense, and that it's a football game is no surprise. Politics won't do. It's allegedly a non-contact sport and certainly no longer much of a spectator sport—our political conventions are, by and large, devoid of drama and suspense, the outcome decided long in advance, the balloons released at exactly 8:49 P.M., just after the network returns from a commercial break. Besides, while it's all right to go there to peddle influence, you don't want to peddle it too openly.

The Oscars won't do—it's not really a Guy kind of event, and the resident egos out there in Hollywood are too big for their own good, even bigger than those in the corporate world. A good, true-blue CEO, even if he could score the right number of good tickets for Oscar night, does not want to stand around essentially on the outside looking in on people whose work he does not necessarily admire, whose films he probably has not seen, whose lives he does not emulate, and worst of all, who have no interest in him and what he represents. Nor—and this is important—do many of his most significant customers admire Hollywood people that much. Besides, what happens that night is all too predictable—it is not the land of the upset.

Baseball won't do either—it's a great sport, but there are as many as seven games to a World Series, and the league does not control the venue for the event. Ditto basketball, still something of an arriviste sport in terms of big-brand commercial labeling and magnetic pull for CEOs. Boxing long ago lost its magic, in no small part because the men who might have been the great heavyweights of today—the men with speed, power, exquisite reflexes and ferocity of purpose—are instead the NFL's great middle linebackers.

So it's football—one game, one city, ticket of tickets, winner take all. Just as important, the league picks the site far in advance, so it's possible to plan an outing months in advance, take five days to celebrate with the right people, be invited to the right parties, a chance for them to use the new Gulfstream and to bring along their most favored clients and to flex a certain kind of social and commercial muscle. It's the perfect package: You get a vacation, a game of almost unparalleled significance and a tax break.

Pete Rozelle was the prophet of it all, the man who saw the future and understood the possibilities of a marriage between sports, television and the corporate world. He was the visionary NFL commissioner who saw pro football's brightest future and understood that he was selling not just a ticket to a Super Bowl game, but the ticket to a certain kind of Super status. Who else could get away with sticking Roman numerals on a sporting event? Rozelle was the first great entrepreneur-marketer of the modern sports era, a man whose roots were in public relations and marketing. He was a smart, intuitive man, liked by almost all who dealt with him, who caught and rode the great wave of our era—the coming of network television. The Super Bowl game of today is, more than anything else, what Rozelle wrought. It began as a byproduct of the merger between the AFL and the NFL, which was Rozelle's most pressing business at that moment, but he foresaw the game's astonishing possibilities almost immediately. Rozelle's ultimate goal was not merely a merger of leagues, but one between football and American business, between the NFL and America's elite, its most successful men. While the players on the field are celebrating their win in a championship game, there are players of a different sort looking down from the stands and the luxury boxes, the winners in American life.

The rise of the NFL to this extraordinary position began in the mid-Fifties when America became a television nation. Until then professional football was essentially a second-tier sport, almost a minor league game—it had its partisans and they were at once extremely knowledgeable and passionate; they knew how good the game was, but it was still very much a connoisseur's game. There was something just a bit eccentric about the season ticket holders in that era. To the degree that football had a major constituency, it was in the college game, in part because there were so many colleges out there, and people could root for their alma maters.

Baseball had long been first in the nation's hearts, and its almost languid rhythms were ideal for a radio age. The pace was soothing, as were the voices of its best broadcasters. That was an America in which things moved more slowly; professional sports teams traveled on trains instead of planes, and no one talked about a sports market share or disposable income.

Football, by contrast, did not come alive on radio—the medium was ill-suited for its speed and its rare combination of violence and balletic grace. In that era professional football fans saw their favorite game, while fans in other sports more often than not heard theirs. Baseball fit the mood and tastes of pre–World War II America; football was ideal for the post-war boom America, as the nation raced ahead at an ever faster pace in all its endeavors and demanded ever more speed and action in all things, even its entertainment, and when there was ever greater competition for what became known as the entertainment dollar, which was naturally enough in the process of becoming an ever larger part of the GNP. In that era, as the country became connected from one coast to the other by TV's giant new electronic umbilical cord, the nation gathered every night to watch the news on television, in what CBS reporter Daniel Schorr called "a national evening séance." Not surprisingly, we stayed at home and we watched at home. Television was connecting the country to itself and seducing it at the same time.

The rapidly expanding networks needed inexpensive programming, and Americans always needed a sports fix, and the fall schedule was wide open, as the baseball season back then still ended in early October. And pro football was very good on TV. I was there from the beginning, a kind of pioneer pro football fan in the days before it became fashionable. My father had loved the pro game, and he had taken me on occasion to the old Polo Grounds to watch the Giants back in the Forties, and I had seen the beginning of the All-America Conference. I remember a game when the Cleveland Browns, with Otto Graham and Marion Motley, came in, trailed 28–0 at the half (the Giants had the great Buddy Young, whom I later met, an early thrill for me), and then came back in the second half to gain a 28–28 tie. I was only XIV at the time, before the game went on television, but I already loved it. Then pro football was picked up by television, and it was another miracle—no matter where you lived, the game showed up too, and all you had to do was turn on a set.

I started watching NFL games on TV in 1956 with a bunch of pals in Nashville, where I was working as a newspaper reporter. We were all in our mid-twenties, but little did we know that we were the NFL's perfect target audience. We were just doing what came naturally and having a good Sunday afternoon in the process, blissfully unaware that we were a virtually priceless demographic and that an inordinate number of sponsors were zeroing in on us, hoping to sell us beer, cars, razors and a lifestyle. None of us owned a television set, so we would gather on Sunday afternoons at a place called Rotier's, a bar and grille (a rather elegant description of it, to tell the truth) near the Vanderbilt campus to watch the Giants and the Redskins and the Browns while drinking enormous schooners of beer which we chased with steak sandwiches. It was a ritual we fell into naturally; no one ever had to call anyone on Sunday morning and ask if we were going to Rotier's for the games.

It was a black-and-white picture in those days, and the reception was not always perfect—sometimes instead of 22 players on the field it looked like 44, or more accurately, 22 men shadowed by their ghosts. But we, like so many others, got it instantly. Nobody needed to sell the NFL to us. We could see how good it was. When radio broadcasters did football they always had to focus on the men with the ball, runners and quarterbacks. But television showed us the brilliance of the defense—its power, speed and guile. And so, with the coming of television, not only did football gain parity with baseball, but its defensive players gained parity with its offensive stars. A great deal of football's appeal in those days came from the sheer violence of the game, but it was a violence wrought from speed and strength, a fury most often meted out by defensive players. The proof that the game satisfied the most primal appetites of America—all of America—came in 1959, when the Giants all-pro middle linebacker, Sam Huff, was on the cover of *Time*.

The professional game was better than the college game, and it lost far fewer stars each year to graduation. Great college players came and then went all too quickly, but pros might have careers of 10 or 12 years, which gave NFL teams a strong sense of identity, of personality. That sense of identity, of the familiar playing the familiar, is not to be underestimated. It gave fans an abiding connection to their favorite teams, their favorite players, their favorite rivalries, even if they represented cities 2000 miles away. I do not often lament the passing of the good old days; I know that today's players are bigger, stronger, and faster, and that today's better teams would likely beat some of the great teams from earlier eras, but I do regret the combination of free agency (not free agency itself, which is right and just, but its result, which is the overly fluid rosters it helped create) and over-expansion, which has weakened the identity of so many teams, and thus of rivalries in so many games.

As America became a communications society, with TV as its connective link, some things and institutions favored by television grew rapidly, as if in a greenhouse. Think of it this way: Since the early wiring of the country in the mid-Fifties, invention after invention has in some way added to the power of television and its importance in our homes and in our value systems—principally the right (along with life, liberty and the pursuit of happiness) not to be bored at home or burdened with something that you do not want to watch, and an enduring belief that no matter how mundane life appears to be, there is always one more channel to check out. The TV screens have gotten bigger and the fidelity of the picture dramatically better; the cameras at games are more sophisticated, satellites circle the globe at all times beaming down upon us this vast selection of images. It's as if, added together, all these inventions of the last 50 years have ended up turning a little box of flickering black-and-white images into a giant movie screen in our home, which is broadcasting all the time, and we as a society have become ever more addicted to it. Not all of the NFL owners, some of whom were hard, self-made men, embraced television in the early days. They thought that showing games on TV was like giving their product away, rewarding fans for not buying tickets. But the grumbling stopped forever in 1964, when Rozelle negotiated a contract with CBS that put $1 million in each owner's pockets for the next two years. And if there was one thing that grew in that TV greenhouse, it was football.

The NFL benefited greatly from the Communications Era, when the country was wired, and did just as well in the one that followed, the Entertainment Era, which began when cable exploded and the number of channels suddenly jumped to 30 or 40 and soon to 300 or 400. That epoch started with the proliferation of broadcast satellites, the ensuing cable revolution and, in the world of sports, the launching of ESPN and other sports-driven and sports-obsessed channels, guaranteeing a kind of jock nirvana, a world in which the real fan would never again have to watch anything but sports. The all-sports, all-the-time revolution made the games infinitely more important, made the players more important and ultimately and inevitably, turned them into entertainers, as well as athletes. Namath was an early indication that things were changing. He understood long before most of his contemporaries that he was part of a show as well as a game, that he was playing to two separate crowds—the one at the game, and the larger one at home.

Namath (like his contemporary in boxing, Muhammad Ali) understood that his game was as much show biz as it was athletic competition. He was signed by Sonny Werblin, an entertainment guy, a former agent, who watched the young Alabama star walk into the room for their first meeting—cocky, purposeful, with dark, brooding good looks—and saw immediately that his charisma made him the ideal man to lead Werblin's Jets, an upstart team in an upstart league in New York City. Werblin made a point of paying his new quarterback so much money that his signing was itself a media event, and Namath was a star before he threw his first pass. Fortunately for him, he had the talent to match the hype. The same, of course, could be said about the NFL.

Pro football still has a powerful hold on me. I plan my Sundays around it in the fall, and if I'm on the road and don't like the games on the networks, I go searching for a sports bar. I still watch the Super Bowl religiously, a word that is perhaps all too apt in this context.

The Game, of course, has grown exponentially. A few years ago a small group of friends and I were in one of the distant corners of the map, Patagonia, fishing the Rio Grande for ocean-going brown trout, some of which can reach 25 pounds. It was a great privilege to be on this great river at the perfect time of the year, and the fish were very big and very accommodating. But the Super Bowl was on and the Giants were in it, so one of my friends and I stopped fishing early that afternoon and drove for two and a half hours to watch it in a bar. "Are you sure you're fishing with the right kind of people?" the head of the fishing charter company later wired the leader of our little group.

There is a reason the game has thrived. The players are that good, and the NFL action, which builds week after week, is that brilliant, and the Super Bowl is the culmination of it all. I remain enthralled by the ferocity of the competition, and I am intrigued by the knowledge that the players of today—whatever our memories try to tell us about the stars we grew up with, those who first drew us to the game and are forever in our own private Halls of Fame—

are bigger and faster, and thus the game too, with its violent ballet, is greater than ever. I am dazzled that players that big can be that fast, that other players can take such terrible hits and keep playing. In a way it strikes me that these games are about measuring in your imagination what the physical limits of a human being are. How big and fast and disciplined can they be? What is the real limit of human potential? How can a player, a Montana or a Brady or a Faulk, adjust in the tiniest fraction of a second to a changed situation in a given play? I am hardly alone in this; it is why all of us, I think, are drawn to it.

Back in those early days, some 40 to 50 million people watched the Super Bowl broadcast; now, if we are to believe those who claim they can chart it—that is, the people who check on who's watching in Siberia and the Ivory Coast and Kuwait and Patagonia—the game is available to a billion viewers worldwide. In The Game's infancy, a minute of commercial time cost $42,000, and now it is $2.3 million, and many people who are otherwise not much engaged in the ebb and flow of the football season wouldn't think of missing the broadcast, more for the competition for best commercial than for the game itself, which at times is not as entertaining. But in the end, it works; it is The Game, anticipated long in advance and enshrined on our calendars as one more de facto but very real national holiday, this one bequeathed to us by Pete Rozelle, prophet of the future, in a way that even he could not have imagined.

FISHING AND OTHER SPORTS

I am a fisherman and thus a dreamer of a certain quite precise kind, almost always when I am on the water; in my day job I am the most skeptical of men in one of the most skeptical of professions in a world which regrettably holds out fewer and fewer dreams the older I get. But on the water, fly rod in hand, my dreams never desert me; I can look out and even when the river water is murky and deep and running too fast, I can visualize a trout, always of a goodly size, rising to my fly, or if it's a clear day in the Caribbean, I can see a handsome bonefish moving steadily on its anointed course towards our boat, at the last second breaking off the requisite two feet to hit my fly. On the water as I am never without dreams, I am never without hope.

FOREWORD: A MEMOIR

From
The Gigantic Book of Fishing Stories

THE DAY THAT THE STRIPER
—AND MEMORIES OF BOB FRANCIS—
CAME BACK

From the *Boston Globe*, August 12, 1990

FOR TWO YEARS I HAD HEARD REPORTS THAT THEY HAD come back. At first it had been mere sightings and then gradually catches, small ones at first, and then larger ones. I was inclined to discount those early reports, for the departure of the striped bass from these waters had seemed to be fairly complete, and though I was not a dedicated striper fisherman, it was also true that I had not caught a striped bass in 10 years, and it had been more than 15 years since I had had a good day of striper fishing.

There had been times in the late '60s, early '70s of abundant catches. Like many fishermen here, I went with Bob Francis, a man who could catch stripers on days when no one else did.

He was a kind of genius, a brilliant, difficult man. But he knew these waters like no one else and he had stored up 40 years of accumulated knowledge of tides, water temperature, degree of wind, degree of gray in the sky. He taught those who went with him a good deal about how to read water. "Right there," he would say, telling us precisely where to cast, and we would cast out and there would be a large swirl and a strike.

He was not a conservationist. He ran an ad for his charter service in our local paper and it said, "We Catch 'Em. Ask Around," and there was a God-awful photo of him and some client with appalling numbers of large fish sprawled out in front of them. Even in those less sensitized days before we had a striper crisis, there was an uneasy feeling that came with looking at that photo.

His boat was named the *Possessor*, which fairly well explained his feelings about what existed in the sea. He was a tough, feral island man who had never known easy times, but who had ended making his living off the sea, chartering and selling the fish, particularly the stripers which he caught. Fishing and hunting were for him, as they were for many island men of his generation, not a key to a booming tourist industry but simply meat on the table.

He once told our mutual friend, Bill Pew, who runs a tackle shop here, that when he was a boy and hunted for ducks at Eel Point, his father gave him four shells, and that meant he was supposed to bring back four ducks. If he did not, he did not go hunting the next time.

He was by far the best, and he knew it. He wanted no one to know his secret spots.

He hated it when other fishermen tried to spot where his boat was and follow him. If he took too many stripers out of the sea, and he most assuredly did, it was in part for financial reasons, but it was also because he liked to catch fish: It was his way of showing that he was the best. It was almost personal between him and the fish.

I remember one day, probably around 1970, when I went out with him, and we had done well. Not in sheer numbers, but we had taken five fish over 30 pounds. Bob liked to fish with me, for in his opinion, I fished hard—that is, there was nothing of the dilettante in me as a fisherman. When we went out, I started casting and rarely took a break, and that pleased him; what he did not like was that I used light rods, Fenwick salmon rods under nine ounces, which meant that I played fish too long, thereby increasing the odds against boating them and in general wasting time. At the least I caught one fish when I might have caught two. That day, I had hooked the largest fish of the day, and, using my light rod had, after 25 very tough minutes, succeeded in moving it over to the boat. As I played the fish, Francis saw the size, and started cursing me for the lightness of my rod. When stripers finally come in, it is with considerable docility, and there alongside the boat, moving slowly in the water, was an exhausted fish that must have weighed at least 50 pounds. Just as Francis got the gaff ready, the hook pulled out of my lure and the fish, slowly, as if to taunt me, swam away. I was devastated. It was the largest fish I had ever hooked. The sight of that fish swimming on is one I still clearly see; in addition I can still hear Bob cursing me for the lightness of my rods—the fault was clearly mine. No mention was made that it was his lure.

Those years of easy fishing for stripers ended long ago. The striper became an endangered species, and Bob Francis found that hard to accept. He did not come around to conservation. When it was clear that the schools were declining seriously, he would argue that it was not an ecological thing, that it was merely cyclical and that he had seen this happen before. It was almost a generational thing for him; he was an island kid who believed that what was in the water was rightfully his. He did not like to return smaller fish to the ocean, and he did not like the new laws governing the size of catches. The world was changing and he was not. A few years ago Bob took his life; he had been, few of us realized, a manic-depressive.

For a time the striper fishing continued to decline. It was as if we were reduced to one light sport fish, blues. But then gradually about two years ago, the sighting and the catches started again. Something had happened in the ecological system; protected by stronger laws, a fish whose schools had once been plentiful, and then had seemed badly depleted, was coming back.

But I had not gone after them. I fished less often now. Bob Francis was dead, and I missed our unlikely friendship and his shrewd sense of the island and the world, and my own pleasure in arguing with someone who was unalterably opposed to almost everything I believed in. My own life had also changed. For a time my daughter was too young to take on a fishing trip. When I went, I fished for blues.

Stripers seemed to require more time and attention than I had to give.

But recently I called Tom Mleczko about a charter. Tom is Bob's lineal descendant; he is in his early 40s and has been fishing here for 23 years. He is, by consensus, our best fisherman. He represents a different generation of fishermen. He is a gentle man who teaches elementary school in the regular year and is a serious conservationist. I have a memory of him more than 20 years ago, a boy just out of college fishing on the beach and catching a huge striper, unhooking the lure as gently as he could, and then walking the fish back into the water to revive it.

Later I had asked him why he had done it. "Roe fish," he had answered.

When I called him, he asked if I wanted to go after stripers or blues. We were scheduled for a late-morning tide in July, hardly ideal bass time, and the trip was for my daughter Julia, soon to be 10, and her best friend, John Vaughan, already 10.

One of the things which my father had passed on to me was a love of fishing, and I have tried to pass some of that on to my daughter: she casts well and handles the rod well, and I take inordinate pride in seeing her pleasure as her skills increase. I pondered Tom's question and decided stripers would be too hard to get on that tide.

With young children, I decided it was more important to have a guarantee of good fishing and plenty of action. So we would go for blues.

It was overcast and a little windy, and as we came out of the cut near Smith's Point, Tom suggested taking a quick shot at the stripers. He explained to John and Julia the ecological history of the striper, how it had been depleted by pollution and commercial nettings and had come back because of serious conservation measures. Within minutes, both John and Julia were on to fish. "They're both on stripers," he said. In time they boated both fish, about six pounds each, probably just under 30 inches and well under the requisite 36.

We caught a dozen stripers on what was hardly a perfect tide, 10 of them by the children. We put every fish back. One was a borderline keeper. Those decisions, I find, are easy these days. It was the first time in 20 years that a boat I had been on had caught more stripers than blues. There was a special sweetness to it, not just going out with the children and watching them fish and seeing their pleasure, but being able to tell them that with hard work and good laws, nature can replenish what man has done to it.

SEA OF DREAMS

From *GQ*, January 1995

OUR BOAT IS TO LEAVE THE HARBOR AT QUEPOS, ON THE west coast of Costa Rica, at 7:30 A.M. for our first of four days' fishing there. We wait in small, edgy groups, two or three men to a boat, each little group uneasy with the others. Most of us, I suspect, are unsure of our own skills and talents and knowledge of the local waters. I have come to know this feeling well in recent years as I have tried ever more distant and difficult saltwater fishing: the anxiety of the neophyte as he explores alien places, investing in others qualities of expertise that they, too, may lack. This trip marks the second time I have gone after billfish in a year, and on the first attempt I had several chances to hook a fish and failed each time.

It is a few days after my sixtieth birthday, and I am not comfortable with being a beginner. I am seeking the realization of my childhood dream—to catch a sailfish on a fly rod, thereby taking on one of the strongest and most resourceful of game fish with tackle and a technique traditionally associated with much smaller freshwater species. I am (it is almost heresy to say this, for all fishermen tend to inflate not only the size of the fish they catch but also their abilities) a fisherman of quite modest abilities. Though I fished often as a boy, there is something like a thirty-year gap in my biography as an angler, years in which certain skills might have been built into me as second nature. Instead, I perform them now with the awkwardness of one who has come late to the sport. Accomplished in my professional life as a writer, I have journeyed to a place where I am an absolute novice.

But fishing runs deep in my blood; it has been a lifelong passion. I have come back to it, finding in it the pleasure that I remember from my childhood, as well as badly needed solace for a man whose life is beset by constant deadlines and equally constant pressures. My wife tells me that almost all of the things that make me happy are associated with being on the water. This journey, then, to one of the great billfishing regions of the Americas is the culmination of a lifelong dream. The fact that I—a child of the Forties, whose values and expectations were set in a much less affluent time—am actually going ahead with a trip like this still surprises me.

In 1939, when I was 5, my father took me fishing on Highland Lake in Winsted, Connecticut, where my uncle Aaron owned a house. It was one of the first things I was able to do with my father, one of the first ways I could share his love and also, by doing things right, gain his approval. Then, in 1942, he returned to military service. Our family left New York City and moved into my uncle's house. It is always hard to decide in retrospect whether or not you had a happy childhood. I have always credited myself with one, principally because of those four or five years in Winsted, despite the separation from my father. I have come to think of the summers as particularly idyllic. Since my brother and I lived two miles from town, and since there were few other children to play with, the primary reason for that happiness was fishing.

Both my father and his older brother, Moe, were serious fishermen. Uncle Moe, a beloved figure in my life, was far more serious about it than my father; fishing was, as far as I could tell, the essential purpose of his life. He sold used cars, but his work day had never been known to take precedence over his fishing schedule. My father and uncle started taking my brother and me with them when we were very young, and fishing became, in those years, a special vacation within the longer summer vacation. In that summer of 1942, when my father was stationed in Texas, I was 8 and my brother, Michael, was 10. We fished twice a day every day. We fished in the morning, and we fished in the early evening. Sometimes in the afternoon we swam, though half a century later I have no memory of taking any pleasure from swimming.

HIGHLAND LAKE is about three miles long and, if memory serves, about seven miles in circumference. It was in those days, actually, an essentially fished-out lake. It had some bass, pickerel, perch, bullhead, crappie (I never in all those years caught a crappie), sunfish and rock bass, a small panfish about the size of a sunfish. Bass and pickerel were the principal sport fish of the region, and the lake produced remarkably few of either that were of legal size.

My uncle and my father, fishing with live bait—minnows—tended to catch a few good-sized fish each season. My brother and I, using clunky old metal telescopic rods baited with worms or night crawlers, which we dug ourselves, or crayfish, which we got from under rocks or scooped up in the marshes (every bit as much fun as the fishing, to tell the truth), probably caught one or two legal-size bass and one legal-size pickerel each season. We were nothing if not devoted. We had a rowboat and my uncle's canoe. Day after day we went out, and the catch was inevitably rockies and sunfish. Since they were roughly the same size, the two of us argued constantly about which was the better fighting fish. Because Michael was older, he got first choice in the argument and said the sunfish were. I was forced to make the case, weak though it was, for the rockies. We debated this endlessly, summer after summer. He was, of course, right.

We were allowed, as we grew somewhat older, to use my father's short casting rod—this was in the age before spinning reels—and we could cast lures for pickerel and bass. But we were never allowed to use the more delicate bamboo rods. The true sign of coming of age in Winsted, we both believed, would be to own a bamboo rod and use live bait. Both of us presumed this magical event would happen when we were about 15 or 16. As it turned out, it never happened at all.

But the limits of the tackle had nothing to do with the limits of our passion for the sport. We not only fished every day, we thought about it all the time and talked about it incessantly and read about it constantly. We haunted Rank's, Winsted's one tackle store. Mr. Rank (I do not remember his first name; he was always Mr. Rank) ran the only truly enchanted store in town. It was filled with the most beautiful bamboo rods imaginable and the lightest of reels. Even the fly line he sold—a rich, luminescent green—seemed far fancier than the rather conventional black line we used. Mr. Rank was also the local tobacconist, so there was an aroma of pipe tobacco in the shop, which only added to the manliness of the atmosphere.

We were the ultimate careful shoppers, two boys showing up at least once a week, geared to make the most minute purchases as slowly as possible. Each of us would be armed with perhaps a dollar; more often than not, we ended up buying nothing grander than a packet of hooks with catgut leaders. But we always took our time, carefully studying all the items that were far beyond our means. The only thing that we didn't like about Mr. Rank was that he always called each of us "Sonny." He did not do this condescendingly, but to us it seemed so, as if it prevented us from being what we thought we were—fully formed fishermen—and turned us into what we were, little boys.

Mr. Rank also sold the countless wonder plugs, or lures, that we saw pictured in the great fishing magazines of the time, *Field & Stream* and *Outdoor Life*. In both those monthlies were advertisements for these very same lures, complete with photos showing fishermen displaying strings of awesome bass, each one, it seemed, weighing more than ten pounds. I still remember plugs like the Heddon River Runt, which lurched as it moved through the water;

the Hawaiian Wiggler, a pickerel plug with interchangeable skirts; and the Jitterbug, on which I actually caught some bass.

The magazines formed a gateway, in that pretelevision era, to the fantasy world of Better Fishing. We were allowed to buy one a month. (You could read the other one in the barbershop.) It is possible that the first byline I ever came to recognize belonged to the best-known fishing writer of the time, Ted Trueblood. He and his fellow angling writers portrayed a world that existed somewhere beyond Winsted, a world of larger fish (and a great many more of them) and cool, patient, skilled fishermen, men of uncommon expertise who knew where to go, which lure to use and where to cast; men who went readily to distant places to nail down the lunkers—very large game fish—that always awaited them.

Back then, freshwater fishing was a great deal more popular than saltwater fishing, and the articles more often than not were set on lakes. The lunkers tended to be bass, muskie or pike. Muskies made for particularly good copy because they were big but not beyond reach as they lurked behind partially submerged tree stumps in northern Minnesota and Canada. These fish, it seemed to me, were the same ones that had eluded magazine writers the previous year, getting away with a desperate jump that would throw the plug or snag the line on a stump. These articles were always accompanied by an artist's rendering of an intense, anxious angler standing in the boat, his rod bent double as the huge, prized fish breaks water and tries to throw the hook.

It was a wonderful dreamworld, because it did not belong to people like us. We knew no one who fished like those super-anglers, with the skill of guides and the resources to go wherever they wanted. Not even Uncle Moe, the most serious fisherman in the family (by consensus, it was the only thing he was serious about), made any of these trips. The limits on our fishing were set by finances and geography. Even someone as gifted as my uncle fished only the nearby lakes of the region. On occasion he'd show up at our house in the early morning with a string of very big fish, about which he was unusually secretive. That led my brother and me to believe he had spent the night illegally fishing the nearby Winchester Reservoir. This only gave him added cachet in our eyes.

Time passed. My father came back from the war, and we moved to suburban New York. He died of a heart attack in 1950, and our lives changed radically. There was no more talk of bamboo rods. Both my brother and I worked in the summer and went off to college in the fall. After graduation, we began demanding careers, and fishing became an even smaller part of our lives, although we never lost our love of it. Looking back now, I realize our father had given us an exceptional gift: He had shared his love of a sport with us when we were very young, so that his love of it became our love of it. And we were well taught. We learned not just the mechanical things—how to cast a minnow with a certain strong but soft toss so the bait did not fly off—but also a larger philosophy of fishing. There were certain verities: We were to use the lightest tackle possible in each situation in order to give the fish the best possible odds; we were to keep nothing we did not intend to eat; and, finally, the most elemental rule of our entire childhood (other than the mandatory ones about doing homework), we were never, *never*, to horse a bass. That is, never to try to force a bass in but to let it run and only then apply pressure.

TWENTY-FIVE YEARS AGO I bought a house on Nantucket. I also bought half of a boat and began to fish for blues and stripers in the waters off our island. Blue fishing with light tackle is particularly exciting, and I started using spinning gear for the first time. My friends Dick Steadman (the other owner of the boat) and David Fine and I became part of a generation of Nantucket fishermen who used much lighter equipment in pursuit of blues than our predecessors had. Our friend Bill Pew, who owns a tackle shop there (and who is a leader in the light-tackle movement), estimates that in the past twenty years the test weight of the line has dropped from twenty-five-pound test to ten, eight and even six, and the weight of the rods has dropped accordingly.

My brother often came to visit me on Nantucket in the ensuing years. Our relationship, which had been exceptionally close when we were young (we were just twenty months apart, and my mother, for reasons that remain greatly puzzling to me, often dressed us as twins), had become quite difficult once we were grown.

Given the transient nature of our childhood—in the course of which we followed our father (before he was shipped overseas) to New York, Winsted, El Paso and Austin, Texas, among other places—we had become much more dependent on each other than most siblings. That closeness and friendship began to unravel later in our lives. There was too much knowledge, too much heat and too little space between us. We felt a rising sense of competition as we grew into middle age—especially after my brother, a doctor, announced in mid-career that he intended to be a writer as well—and in our later years we became edgier and edgier with each other.

But it was during that period that he came to Nantucket each summer, and by far our best times together were spent on the water. Fishing removed the tension of modern life and adulthood from our relationship and restored to us the far simpler moments of our boyhood. We once again became easy with each other, and we unconsciously measured the great good fortune of each day's bounty against all those years of barren fishing in Winsted. What we could not resolve as grown men we could at least put aside, by dint of going out on the water and becoming, momentarily, little boys again. Some fourteen years ago, a terrible tragedy took place: My brother was surprised in his home one night by a burglar and was shot and killed. When I was told, my mind immediately floated back to the endless image of the more than forty years we had spent together, often in strange and seemingly inhospitable settings. By far the best and happiest—and most enduring—of all my memories were those of us fishing together as boys and men.

A YEAR AGO, on the eve of my fifty-ninth birthday, I walked into Urban Angler, a marvelous store in New York City that sells only fly-fishing gear. I wandered around for an hour or so, just as I had in Rank's some fifty years earlier, knowing all the while exactly what I had come for. When I left I had spent some $1,500 for an outfit I could use in pursuit of sailfish. I had bought a twelve-weight rod, the standard for going after sails and tarpon, a modern graphite of great strength and flexibility and remarkable lightness. And it was the most money I had ever paid for a toy in my life. But I wasn't anxious about the money; I was anxious about taking a chance on something new, something I could easily fail at. No one likes to do that late in life, least of all someone who has been successful in his career. It is this fear of failure more than anything else, I think, that deters us from taking on our secret adventures as we get older.

For the kind of fishing I had dreamed about as a boy was now readily available to me. Travel had become infinitely less expensive; it was no longer a barrier between an angler and the great fishing waters of the hemisphere. With changing tax regulations, places that were once the exclusive haunts of the very rich—the distant lodges of the wealthy created to be shared only by pals or favored corporate customers—had become commercial retreats open to the public. Fly-fishing for saltwater big game had become an increasingly popular sport.

This did not mean I was ready to take a sailfish on a fly rod. I had nothing going for me save desire and my expensive new rig. Fly-fishing for sailfish, it should be noted, is very different from all other forms of the sport. In some ways it is more like trolling, since the actual cast is to a spot only about fifteen feet behind the boat. First, the captain trolls teasers—hookless lures to attract the fish; when a fish surfaces, the teasers are reeled in just fast enough to excite it and bring it ever closer to the boat. At the critical moment, these rigs are yanked from the water; the sailfish switches its attention to the fly and strikes.

That may sound easy, but it isn't. It does not account for the sheer disruptive madness when a fish so large comes so close to the boat and is about to hit so delicate a lure. It is very easy to blow it, and I had blown it several times on my last trip; to be honest, I had panicked. Each time, I jerked the fly too early or too late. I was not cool and loose the way those great fishermen in *Field & Stream* had always been.

So it was last April that I was on the dock at Quepos waiting to go out for my second shot. The fishing had been good, said our captain, Javier Chavarria, who seemed pleased that we wanted to fly-fish. To him it was clearly more exciting and more sporting than using the usual heavy trolling rigs.

On the first day, I fished like a donkey, managing to blow my first two strikes. On the second, I tried to set the hook by using the rod as instructed, yanking the line with my left hand. The sail threw the hook on the second jump. But I was getting there; for the first time, I sensed that my learning curve was improving. Meanwhile, my friend Gerry Krovatin, a young lawyer from New Jersey (who had been wary of coming with us because he was the least experienced fisherman in the group), took his turn, struck his first fish and boated it a half hour later.

The next morning, we had been enjoying two hours of leisurely talk on the boat when a big fish came up on the rigs very quickly. Once again there was an explosion of action and everyone ran to a station to handle the teasers while I prepared to cast. I tried to be cool and not to panic, to remember the requisite technique. The captain yanked the teaser out and the fish switched to my fly, took it, turned sideways and started to run. I hammered the line to set the hook so hard with my left hand—I had forgotten to wear a glove—that it cut my skin very deeply in two places. But I nailed the fish and the hook went in; then, as the fish made its first ferocious run, I slammed back on the rod to drive the hook in deeper. For the first time I felt sure I had done everything right. The fish ran about 150 yards and then it jumped.

The sail is a majestic fish. There is something both thrilling and terrifying about the power of that first run; skilled technicians have spent years trying to develop a reel that will not burn with the heat caused by a speeding fish. For the novice, it is a brand-new world. The first run is an introduction, both thrilling and terrifying, to a great fish. The angler feels the shrinkage of his own power and mastery even as he feels the quantum increase in the power of the fish.

It ran and then it soared, a jump that was about as definitive a statement on the desire for freedom as I have ever seen. It flashed silver in the sun, shaking wildly, and then it jumped again. I held my breath, but this time the hook held. There was yet another run and a series of jumps, all of them equally regal. I was torn by the combination of my awe at what the fish was doing and my certainty that somehow the hook would be thrown. For all fishermen there are special moments, and for me there are these: the first legal-size bass I caught in Highland Lake, with my father smiling approvingly; the nineteen-pound bluefish I once took off Nantucket with six-pound tackle; the first bluefish my daughter caught on her own; and finally this moment, a good-sized sailfish solidly hooked on a fly rod, breaking the surface again and again.

The fish jumped, I was told later, eight times. The fight lasted about thirty minutes and would have been an hour if the captain hadn't used the boat to close in. The fish, Captain Chavarria said as we released it, weighed about ninety pounds. My shirt was soaked through with sweat. My arms were tired as they never had been from any other kind of fishing. My left hand bled badly. It was a glorious moment.

In a way, it was not that much about skill (I lost the next two fish I hooked, both after long runs and several jumps). It was more about will and determination, the willingness to try something late in my late life even though I might fail at first. It was also about the preference of catching one sailfish on a fly rod instead of six or seven or eight of them on a heavier trolling rig. I had been right in trusting my instincts and sensing that this sport, which put so slight a rod against so powerful a fish, would touch something deep in me that had been waiting there all those years.

WHY I FISH

From *Town & Country*, April 2000

WE HAD GONE OUT EARLY TO CATCH THE LIVE BAIT, OUR boats hitting the water by 6:30 A.M. We spent the first twenty-five minutes catching the bait, casting for small fish on the surface, stockpiling them, so to speak, and keeping them alive in small tanks on the boat in order to use them as bait for the larger fish. Catching the bait is great fun in itself, with a feeding frenzy on the surface, as the skipjack and bonito corral tiny minnows and drive them to the surface of the water, and the birds swirl around them overhead. We use the birds as a marker to find the skipjack and bonito we will need for bait. In this case the fish that are the hunters will be caught and immediately used for bait for the giant fish we now seek. On this particular morning it took only about twenty minutes to load up with bait. This was the second day of our fishing trip on the Pacific coast of Panama, and the first day had not gone all that well for me: the good news was that I had caught one sailfish; the bad news was that a relatively small yellowfin tuna, a brute of a fish, had smashed the spinning rod I had just bought for this trip—a rod that, compared to the ones I used fishing off Nantucket, had seemed much too heavy when I bought it but had lasted for only one fish. That did not bother me too much—what I really wanted on this trip was my first marlin, and if a small tuna could smash the new rod, I had cause to fear what a giant marlin might do. Thus, I gladly switched over to the rods supplied by the lodge.

It was a clear, beautiful day: by early morning the sun was out, the sunscreen was being slathered on, and we had a brilliant back-drop as we worked about a mile or so off the Panama shoreline. There is a sense, on a day like this, of simplifying everything in your life. I have fished all my life. My father shared his love of it with me when I was a little boy; he died when I was young, and it remains one of the rare things we were able to do together. There were special days in the period when we lived in Winsted, Connecticut, when we would fish Twin Lakes, fifteen miles away, instead of Highland Lake, the local lake, which were particularly treasured. Twin Lakes not only meant far better fishing, it meant that my brother and I could catch fish like grown-ups; that is, it meant that we could use live bait (minnows) instead of worms. That love of being on the water has always remained with me: the one way I know that I can leave behind the rest of the baggage of my life. I think of it as being a form of therapy. It is on the water where I am most serene, and I am a fervent believer in the ancient fisherman's motto, "Allah does not subtract from the allotted time of man the hours spent fishing." Because of that, I have over the last six or seven years tended to make one trip each winter to a fishing resort like this, usually in the Caribbean, sometimes in South America, usually accompanied by four or five friends. We tend to be fishing connected; that is, we have all fished together back in the States—usually in Nantucket, where I have a home—and more often than not of an age (now in our 60s), although we have in the last year or two tried to bring in some younger friends. Though fishing is at the core of the trip, and we all fish hard, it is also true that these trips are the only all-male things that any of us do. None of us belongs to an all-male social club, and none goes to an all-male poker night. So there is something old-fashioned about it, and the conversation, particularly for men who are in general loath to reveal their inner feelings, is often surprisingly intimate, particularly as the week progresses, and we become increasingly candid with each other. My wife tells me that this is the male version of what she and her friends do every year when they go off to a spa. Certainly these trips are more about friendship than they are about catching giant fish. We have done this in a number of places: fished for peacock bass in Venezuela, for sail-fish on a fly rod on one coast of Costa Rica and tarpon on light spin-ning tackle on its other coast, and, of course, for bonefish in the Bahamas. This is our second time in Panama.

On this, the second day, we had been fishing for only about forty minutes when the strike came. We fish two to a boat, and we rotate turns, trying to be as fair as possible as to what constitutes an at-bat, so that no one gets shortchanged. On this day I am fishing with Pete Van Horn, a Texas businessman, and I am up when the fish moves on the bait. "Marlin," said the captain as the fish approached, and he whispered the word, as if not daring to speak too loudly for fear of driving the fish away. When a marlin strikes, you are supposed to let it take the bait and run until the fish turns the bait in its mouth. Only then do you try to nail the fish. So I watched nervously as the fish ran with the line, endlessly, it seemed to me at first, and then fi-nally on the appointed signal from the captain I drove the rod hard and set the hook.

Because it was my first marlin strike, I became a little boy once again as the fish made its first casual run with my bait, my heart beating too fast, the doubts about setting the hook properly all too real. I grew up fishing every day of the summer as a boy on a fished-out lake in northwestern Connecticut, always optimistic, but catch-ing, if I was lucky, a couple of legal-size bass a season; then, in my mid-30s, I bought a house in Nantucket and became reasonably adept at light-tackle saltwater fishing just offshore. In addition I've done some trout fishing in the Rocky Mountain area, but I grade myself as a competent, if somewhat marginal, fly-fisherman. For most of my life big-time deep-sea fishing was, if not beyond my reach, certainly beyond my imagination. But in recent years that has begun to change, because of the democratization of travel, the drop in the cost of long-distance travel, and the transformation of once private homes into hospitable commercial fishing lodges.

I had caught sailfish in the past, and properly encouraged by the size, strength and beauty of the fish, I even went out and bought a fly rod strong enough to cast for a sail (though in truth it is more like trolling than fly-casting), and a few years ago I caught my first sail on the fly rod. But I had never caught a marlin, nor had anyone else in a boat in which I had fished, and the excitement of it, why it seemed to move other fishermen so much, had so far eluded me. Yes, I had thought, they are bigger than sails, but I still wondered what all the fuss was about.

On this day I found out. Our first visit to Pinas Bay had been several years ago, and it had not gone all that well. We had liked the lodge very much, but the fishing that year was quite poor. The people who ran the lodge had been very apologetic; our fishing had been way below normal because of that year's El Niño, a major change in the normal weather that had thrown the temperature of the water off significantly and driven most of the big fish away. Pinas Bay, otherwise famous as a game-fish base camp, we were assured, was undergoing the worst fishing it had offered in several years. It did strike me that I had heard variations on this theme before: if only you had been here last week, or, for that matter, next week, the fishing was/would be far better.

But, as I say, we had liked the lodge very much and were delighted to be back. It is simple and clean, carved out of a mountainside in a gorgeous spot on the west coast of Panama. It was built in 1961 by a Texas oilman named Ray Smith, who used it for a time as his personal preserve; for the last thirty-four years it has been open for sportfishermen. A flight of about an hour in a chartered Twin Otter from Panama City gets you there. It is located in a beautiful setting, and the view is always spectacular as you work your way up and down the Panamanian coast. Of the different resorts I have stayed at as a fisherman, Pinas Bay strikes me as being by far the best, extremely well run, and the courtesies, befitting the simplicity of the location, are greater than the amenities. The people who work there are all very nice, and the food is quite good to very good, particularly, it seems to me, if you order the fish every night (grilled fresh yellowfin tuna, grilled fresh mahimahi, grilled fresh snapper). As my fishing partner Dick Steadman says, everything they have control over, they do very well. The one thing they do not have control over, of course, is the quality of the fishing.

That certainly wasn't a problem on the morning I learned what the fuss about marlin was all about. The fish was fierce, unspeakably strong, and with a mind of its own. It began as a match of strength, his against mine. To my strength, of course, we added the skill of the captain, who readily maneuvered the boat to take up the line every time the fish had made one of its long and powerful runs. When I was a boy of about eight, the first lesson of fishing taught me by my Uncle Moe (who was the most serious fisherman in our family; indeed it was said to be the only thing he was serious about) was never to horse a bass; that is, never try to overpower a fish. With a marlin that rule remains true, but also absolutely unnecessary—there is no possible way to overpower a fish of that size and strength.

And so the battle began, my job, it seemed to me early on, to survive, and to keep reminding myself that all of this was a good deal harder on the fish than it was on me. It was already hot by that hour, and within a few minutes I was soaked with sweat. Although I am in very good shape and my arms and hands and wrists are all strong from working out and rowing a single scull, some twenty-five minutes into the fight I felt a weariness in my arms, and for a brief moment I wondered whether it was worth it all; then I thought of all those fishermen whom I had heard about who had battled giant marlins for five and six hours and more, and I wondered whether in fact after a certain point it was fun.

What was fun, of course, was watching the marlin, which began to jump and to make dazzling leaps in the air, sometimes jumping straight up, and sometimes hurtling through the air like some kind of low-flying luminescent projectile. The marlin is a simply beautiful fish, the beauty, silver and dark blue, shown to maximum advantage by these spectacular leaps. If I had been moved at first by the sheer strength and power of the fish, now I was moved by its innate beauty, and by the pleasure of watching the struggle of a fish that large, that strong and that handsome. It was the first time in my life that I had been in absolute awe of a fish that I was hooked into.

And that, I think, finally made it fun, the beauty and the explosiveness of the fish, and the respect that I immediately came to have for its lionhearted courage: Van Horn told me later that the fish jumped some eight times, and on every jump, he added, I let out a huge roar, cheering, it seemed, as much for the fish as for myself. So it was that the battle went on for some forty-five minutes. The fish, our captain said, probably weighed about 350 pounds, not that big on the Richter Scale of marlin, but quite big enough for me. In the end we brought it in, close enough for the mate to touch the leader, which made it an official catch, and then we cut the leader, and the fish seemed to give a lazy half-roll, and then swam away (the hook, we were assured, would eventually come out of the marlin's mouth on its own), leaving me in the boat, a man who had always heard about how marlin were somehow different, and was now a believer.

Homage to Patagonia

From ESPN.com, February 7, 2001

IT HAD TAKEN ANY NUMBER OF PHONE CALLS TO FIND OUT that the one place in Rio Grande, Argentina, which was showing the Super Bowl was the Posada De Las Sauzes, or as the gringos might say, the House of the Willowbrushes. There we could see the Gigantes of New York play the Cuervos of Baltimore.

Patagonia is home to both awe-inspiring scenery and outstanding trout fishing. For on the sports world's most sacred day, the Sunday of all Sundays, my friends and I were fishing for brown trout in what is virtually the end of the earth, the southern part of Patagonia, by dint of a trip scheduled nearly a year in advance. That is a trip agreed on well before the most unlikely of all scenarios had become reality: My beloved Gigantes, 7-9 last season, and a somewhat sloppy 7-4 in mid-November, had gone on a surprising roll, getting better by the week, ending up in the Super Bowl, their chances greatly enhanced by an amazing dissection of the Vikingos of Minnesota.

My friend Dick Steadman, who was also a serious Gigante fan (and a former football star himself, having played center for Punahou High School in Honolulu in the late 1940s at roughly 150 pounds), and I thus found ourselves caught between two formidable athletic pulls, the desire to catch some of the largest and most formidable fresh water fish imaginable, and the love of and commitment to a favored football team making a most unlikely championship appearance. For that tiny minority of my fellow

Americans who take football more seriously than fly fishing, I should point out that fishing for brown trout in Patagonia is a kind of championship in itself, a rare opportunity, or perhaps more accurately a rare privilege.

The Argentinean Rio Grande is exceptionally difficult to get to, requiring almost two days of travel; the conditions under which you fish are extremely demanding, winds up to 40 miles an hour; and the trout themselves, which are sea-going, but which come back to fresh water to spawn, are well worth the immense effort, and can easily run up to 35 pounds.

Thus the choice between fishing and watching the Super Bowl was between one kind of madness in irreconcilable conflict with another kind of madness. When the shocking contradiction of our schedule finally manifested itself, Steadman and I had flagged our group leader, an ebullient friend of mine named Richard Berlin, to explain the gravity of our problem. Berlin, who lives in the Boston area, was not personally affected by the crisis—his Patriotas had disappeared from serious contention on about the fourth week.

Still, Berlin is a good pal, and he knows obsessive behavior when he sees it (after all, he owns some 20 fly rods), and he phoned Pat Pendergast of the Fly Shop, which was midwifing our trip, and explained the dilemma carefully. He had these two good friends, he said, both of them almost normal under most conditions, who were now caught between their conflicting obsessions. They wanted, in his jaundiced view, to do the unthinkable, to interrupt, however briefly, some of the greatest fishing on the continent in order to see a football game.

The trout in the Argentinian Rio Grande can run up to 35 pounds. Pendergast, a man who clearly had his priorities much better ordered—there was trout fishing and then there was everything else in life—listened patiently, as if to the counsellor for two madmen who was loyally carrying out the most undesirable of instructions, and then said he would do what he could to find some place where the game was on. Then he had paused and added his own view of things.

"Richard," he said, "I think you're fishing with the wrong kind of people."

That might or might not be true. But there we were at last, a mere 6,000 miles south of Tampa, hoping that somehow a television set which carried the game could be found. Even then there was, of course, a serious conflict in our schedules: the visitors to the Maria Behety Lodge fish twice a day, from roughly 8:30 to 12:30 in the morning, and then again from about 6:30 to 10 P.M. at night. The game itself was to start at 8:30 Rio Grande time. The trip from the fishing pool to town was about an hour, which meant that we would barely have time to start fishing before we left the river for the game.

Nonetheless, the evening started auspiciously. Richard quickly caught two fish, and I caught one (a 10-pounder, which while not big for the Rio Grande, was big for me, since few of the trout I had caught in the past had ever gone above 2 pounds). Both of us were quite sure that our good fishing luck was also a harbinger of how the game might go.

So it was that we picked up and left one of the greatest trout streams in the world, the action clearly still hot, and driven by our guide Jorge Castro (gracious enough neither to say anything nor to show any obvious disbelief), raced for downtown Rio Grande. Never in my life had I left such good fishing so early with a promise of much more to come. But life is clearly full of sacrifices; besides there was still almost a full week of fishing ahead.

We got to the hotel with six minutes gone, the game scoreless, the Gigantes stumbling around on their own goal line, almost turning the ball over. As I pulled up a chair I was struck, not for the first time, by the contrast between the richness and privilege of my life and the particular era we live in, and that of my father, who was, like me, both a passionate fisherman and a committed football fan.

(There was, I discovered years after his death, a note in his 1925 Tufts Medical School yearbook to the effect that getting Charley Halberstam to describe a football game was as good as going to the game itself.) He had loved to fish, but had largely been forced by finances, a lack of time, by service in two wars, and by lack of access to prime fishing water to spend his time casting to ghost fish in fished-out lakes in northwest Connecticut. His reward, one or two keeper bass a summer.

His ability to travel, after all, was prescribed in a different, much poorer age, when jet travel did not exist and those remarkable bonus miles which had enabled me to get to Buenos Aires had not been invented. His foreign travel had been confined to two trips, France and Germany in 1917, and France and Germany in 1944–45, both of them, at least, financed by his government. He died some 17 years before the first Super Bowl was played. The idea of athletes like these, so big and fast, playing before us on an immense television set, virtually an indoor movie theater, located so many thousands of miles from where the game was being held, would have been beyond his imagination.

The difficult journey to Argentine fishing spots is usually worth it. So even as I watched, I pondered the cumulative technological miracles of which I am the beneficiary, grateful for my good fortune, and wondering at the same time what it will be that my daughter will do and be part of in her lifetime which is beyond my own comprehension.

The game was on, live and in color and in Spanish. Clearly the Super Bowl was not that big a draw in Rio Grande. Steadman and I were the only people in the hotel den, other than a somewhat puzzled waiter, who seemed to have no special loyalty of his own, but who, in an engaging and warm manner, seemed to want our team to do well, and was quite willing to grimace whenever fortune smiled on the Cuervos. Nonetheless there was something absolutely charming about watching the ultimate football game from so great a distance in an environment in which no one else seemed to care.

There was, after all, a certain modesty to the setting that the game badly lacks almost everywhere else—it was almost as if we could think of it as being in normal numbers, rather than Roman ones. It was marvelous being spared the hype; I am, after all, one of those people who believes that the Super Bowl is more often than not a disappointment, in no small part because of the two-week layoff, so much of it devoted to the hype. (One of my cardinal rules as a journalist is that any event that attracts media people in regimental or division strength is almost sure to disappoint and is not worth attending.)

What I liked best, I must admit, was the absence of noisy commentators. The announcers were speaking in Spanish, and with all due respect to John Madden and Pat Summerall, it was a pleasant change. Actually, I can easily imagine that when Madden watches at home, he, too, turns down the sound at a game like this. He is one of my favorite commentators, and I savor the idea of Madden the fan turning down the sound of Madden the announcer. The lack of words helped to bring the game down to scale. In addition, the self-important hand of Madison Avenue was blessedly absent in the Spanish version, and I loved that.

For the normal show within a show—the Super Commercials at the Super Bowl—was gone: the great American beer and auto companies paying so much to unveil glimpses of their products, clips which are more often that not about the talent and inventiveness of their ad agencies than they are about the advantages of the product being showcased. Instead, there were ads in Spanish for the Spanish audience.

As for the game itself, it turned out to be hard going for the Gigantes, who seemed to get smaller throughout the evening. I had taken the Cuervos quite seriously—they clearly had advanced to the game through a more rigorous schedule, but in truth I had feared the Titanes of Tennessee more than the Cuervos, because they seemed to have more offensive weapons at hand. It was my hope, forlorn as it turned out, that while the Cuervos were stronger on defense, the Gigantes would have more weapons on offense.

Kerry Collins and the Gigantes were dominated by the Cuervos. I believed the Gigante secondary could cheat on the Cuervos and Trent Dilfer, as the Cuervos could not cheat on Kerry Collins. My game plan was for the Giants to imitate the Jets in their victory over the Colts some 30 years ago, and take what was given, short passes to the tight end and the backs coming out of the backfield, effectively using the pass as a run until the defense finally opened up deep.

I thought it could be done, and I was very wrong. Either the Gigantes had no comparable game plan, or the Cuervos linebackers were so quick that they took even the shortest pass away. Whatever happened, it was not our day. Be that as it may, Steadman and I accepted our fate and decided that the Cuervos had dramatically outplayed our señors.

We also decided that it was a lot easier to accept the dismal outcome so many thousands of miles from home, not being part of a large group of New York fans clustered together, expecting victory but watching their hopes systematically evaporate in the second half. So, one season ended. One form of madness was over for the day, and in fact, for about eight months. So be it. Football is football, not life itself, unless of course you're a professional football player.

For the rest of us life must go on: We survive as mortals, and as sports fans, and as fishermen based as much as anything else, not on truths which can often be barren, but on hope and faith, that life holds possibilities for tomorrow that are more expansive than the realities of today, that Kerry Collins will grow in confidence next season and throw less into double coverage, that our next cast will entice a fish larger than his predecessors.

And so the next day, I went back to the Rio Grande and in the middle of the evening a huge fish took my fly, made one grand jump, displaying itself in full glory—at least 30 pounds, said Castro—then stripped much of the line with a fierce run, jumped again and bent the hook completely out of the line, thus departing forever from my life. But on the day after that, I went out and hooked an immense trout. It put up a magnificent fight, lasting some 25 minutes, and this time neither I nor my equipment failed, and I finally landed the brown, 22 pounds, the largest freshwater fish I had ever caught.

Anatomy of a Champion

From *Vanity Fair*, May 1996

THE AMERICAN FENCERS SPENT THREE DAYS LIVING THE comparative high life in Madrid after competing in La Coruña, on the western coast of Spain. They practiced during the day at a Madrid fencing club, and they lodged in two rooms at the Hotel Lisboa, which cost them $20 each a night. On tour they sometimes stayed in one room—breaking down hotel beds to put their mattresses on the floor was a necessary skill for American fencers. But at the Hotel Lisboa they had their own bathrooms, as well as telephones and television sets, so it was a considerable bargain. With a World Cup event coming up in Venice, they had to decide whether to stay on in Madrid or go to Rome.

It was not an easy call. On the side of Madrid was the relative luxury of the Hotel Lisboa and the fact that Madrid was significantly cheaper than Rome. In Rome's favor was the fact that Nick Bravin, at 24 the senior member of the team as well as its de facto travel agent, translator, and general mentor, spoke better Italian than Spanish. Also, Bravin believed that the younger members of the team, who did not know Rome well, would benefit by wandering through the streets of one of the great cities of the world.

Rome it would be. The next morning Bravin went to a local travel agency, where he found that it would cost them some $700 each to fly to Rome, but less than $200 each to get there by train (second class)—a grim, cramped, exhausting 23-hour trip. The airfare represented a good deal of money for the team; their dilemma was of the kind shared by many amateur athletes from America who, while representing one of the richest countries in the world, play sports that do not televise well or about which the American public cares little. Bravin was certainly used to these kinds of problems and was skillful at getting around them; he soon found just what he was looking for—a leg of a Thai Airways flight that would take them from Madrid to Rome for about $100 a person.

At the Rome airport Bravin consulted his tattered notebook containing a list of the cheapest hotels in the world's capitals and started calling around. At the first seven places, he struck out, but at the eighth, the Hotel Contilia, he found one room still available, at $120, or $30 a head. On this trip there were only four of them, rather than the usual five, since teammate Peter Devine was sick with the flu and had gone ahead to Venice to rest for the World Cup event there. They played hearts to see who got the worst bed—the one they jokingly called "the crippler."

FENCERS ARE MARVELOUS ATHLETES, smart and surprisingly strong, with great footwork and great hand-to-eye coordination. The three events (and their weapons) in fencing are the foil, the épée, and the saber. Foil fencing, which uses a thin, rectangular-shaped blade, is athletically and intellectually demanding because it has the smallest target area—the torso, back, and groin. Bravin, in addition to being a world-class poor person's travel agent, was also a star of the individual foil in America, a three-time N.C.A.A. champion as a Stanford student, and a three-time national champion. He had been the first American in years to show that he might be able to compete at fencing's highest level—against the mighty Europeans, who dominate the sport and who subsidize it handsomely. According to Carl Borack, a former Olympic fencer who now serves as the captain of the American team, the annual American budget is roughly $400,000, while the Italian government gives its team more than $6 million.

Nevertheless, Nick Bravin had come to believe that adversity had its own rewards, that by dint of being forced to economize he knew not only Europe's castles and museums but also its working-class bars. He had made friends as he might not have had he been protected by wealth and celebrity status. Best of all, he and the other American fencers had learned to make sacrifices and to take care of one another; they had learned to be teammates and good friends, even as they had to be fierce competitors.

This current group of Americans in the foil—Bravin, 24; Cliff Bayer, 18; Peter Devine, 19; Sean McClain, 20; and Zaddick Longenbach, 24—were surprisingly closely matched in skills and the most talented team this country had produced in years, thought Bravin's old college coach, Zoran Tulum. Tulum, originally from Yugoslavia, had come to America 10 years before and developed a grudging admiration for the toughness of American fencers, whose rewards had to be completely internalized.

Among the teammates that Nick Bravin was steering to the Hotel Contilia was a young man named Cliff Bayer. As a high-school senior, he had burst onto the national scene to become the wunderkind of American fencing, stunning Bravin in particular by coming from behind in the 1995 national championship finals and beating him. When Bravin looked at Bayer he saw nothing less than the image of his younger self. "Cliff is extremely hungry—just like I used to be," he said. "He has a lot of physical gifts, but above all he has the gift of attitude. He wants to beat you on every point, and he is afraid of no one, afraid of no reputation."

Bravin himself had won the first of his three national championships in 1991 at age 20. In the words of Zoran Tulum, he was as hungry as a wolf then, as audacious as he was fearless, and he had taken particular pleasure in knocking off better-known fencers. By 1994 he had begun to beat some of the best fencers in the world, Elvis

Gregory of Cuba and Dimitri Chevtchenko of Russia among them. There was talk that he might become one of the giants of the sport.

THEN, TO TULUM'S DISMAY, Bravin entered Columbia Law School and lavished the singular intensity he had previously given to fencing on his studies. By March of this Olympic year his ranking had fallen to No. 4, just behind Bayer, Devine, and McClain. Since only the top three will make the Olympic team, decided in June after the national championships, Bravin found himself in a tight spot. He was certain that technically he was a better fencer than ever, but he had begun to wonder whether he still had the hunger that Tulum talked about so often. The wolf, according to Tulum, was always the hunter. It sized up its prey and thought of nothing else. Hunting was a matter of life and death to the wolf; so should fencing be to the true champion. Bravin was still fast—Rápido, his Cuban competitors had nicknamed him—but fast was not enough. The antelope is fast, but you cannot fence if you are an antelope, Tulum would say. The wolf triumphs because it thinks of nothing else, it is always the hunter.

As a fencer, Bravin knew that Tulum was right, but at this point there were other things in his life. He found, as had other athletes before him, that the ascent was the easy part. On the way up you had no title to lose.

He had been drawn to the sport almost by chance while growing up in Los Angeles. His older brother, Jess, had tried fencing, and Nick, who was then about 12, tagged along. He immediately decided that he too wanted to take fencing lessons. Shawn Bravin, his mother, was skeptical. She knew her youngest child was bright and gifted at many things, but he was also easily bored. She had seen many of his fads, including Bravin piano and Bravin violin lessons, evaporate overnight. Yet eventually she gave in and bought him all the requisite gear.

At first he had not particularly liked fencing, but he stayed with it, in no small part, he decided later, to prove his mother wrong. He had always been quick, no matter what sport he played, and almost from the start his coaches saw great potential. Soon, with their encouragement, he began going more than once a week.

It was not the dashing, swashbuckling swordplay he imagined from the movies, the glorious pleasure of sticking his opponent with a sword. Rather, it was technical drudgery, footwork drills, using muscles in his arms and legs in ways he had rarely used them before. But after six months or so, his coaches finally let him compete, and he loved it.

He won his first four tournaments. At the start, perhaps, he loved competitions too much. He was brash and impatient, hotheaded and unwilling to listen to his coaches. He loved the individual nature of the competition, and he found out something about himself: he hated to lose. His coaches homed in on that instinct. "How many fencers in the final eight actually want to win a tournament?" Ed Richards, one of his first coaches, asked him. "All eight," Bravin answered. "No," said Richards, "four of them are happy just to be there, two want to do well, and *two* want to win. Remember that and be one of the two."

Jess Bravin, who was six years older than Nick, went off to Harvard and fenced on the Harvard team. Coming home from college for a holiday break, he was stunned to find the change in his little brother. Not only had he become a superior fencer, but all his exceptional qualities, intellectual and physical, had been fused together through this demanding sport. It was also who Nick Bravin had become as a person—skillful, strong, confident, audacious.

He fenced at increasingly higher levels, while still playing football at Alexander Hamilton High School in Los Angeles—he was one of the smallest men on the team. His schedule was brutal: up at six A.M., school starting at seven, football practice from two to five in the afternoon, fencing practice at six. His biggest decision in those days was whether to go home briefly for a bite to eat after football practice or go directly to fencing.

He was 16 years old, still growing, and perpetually exhausted. But his friend Al Carter would not let him sleep through his fencing lessons. They were about the same age and the two best fencers in the area. Carter would call up, listen to his friend's complaints that he was tired and in pain, and then tell Bravin he would pick him up in 15 minutes. The two thought of little else but college and future Olympic glory; the vanity license plate on Carter's car in those days read: 92 GOALD. They would attend the same college and lead it to a national championship. Many schools courted them and the University of Pennsylvania, a traditional fencing power, seemed likely to get them.

BUT BRAVIN VISITED STANFORD and was overwhelmed by the beauty of the campus if not the quality of the fencing. Stanford was hardly known as a powerhouse in the sport. That meant the level of competition in daily practice was not nearly as good as it was at Penn or Columbia. Also, Tulum, the new coach, was unknown to Bravin, and in fencing the personal relationship of the coach to his fencers is considered critical. Tulum was wary of the ways of American college recruiting. When Bravin asked Tulum for a trial lesson, Tulum said no, he did not do auditions. What do you mean, no? thought Bravin. I'm twice as good as any fencer you have, and I may be the best fencer you ever get, and you're saying no to me? "No," Tulum repeated as Bravin stood there dumbstruck. "I'm not going to give you a practice lesson. You're not going to try me out." Zoran Tulum had his rules, and he had his suspicion that altogether too many middle-class American kids were spoiled. "We'd like to have you, but if you want to take your talent elsewhere, that's fine with me."

Bravin was stunned. Every other college in the country with a fencing team wanted him; his choice meant committing four years of his life to a school and a coach, risking his chances of becoming a national champion. Yet this man would not even give him a trial lesson. "All I can offer you," Tulum added, "is hard work and good weather. Period."

IN A WAY their meeting was like a fencing bout, Bravin later figured out. Tulum was pitting his ego against Bravin's. There was something about that and something about Tulum's sheer bluntness that Bravin liked. In the end it was a hard decision, so he called his older brother and asked his opinion. Jess told him that fencing was important but that competitive fencing was not forever—he might break a leg on any given day and end his career. Jess told him to make his decision based on the school, not the fencing team or coach. So, while his friend Al Carter went to Penn, Nick Bravin decided to go to Stanford.

Bravin and Tulum were both driven and willful, and at first the two constantly battled. Bravin did not consider the competition among his teammates good enough, so he would go off to practice at a club in San Francisco. This meant missing practice, which irritated Tulum and his teammates. Tulum threatened to kick him off the team. "We're better off without you," Tulum would say.

Yet Tulum was a very good coach. He was shrewd at knowing how to challenge his young star. One of the first things he did was print up a sign for Bravin: SECOND SUCKS, it said. Not only did Bravin become a better fencer, he became more passionate about fencing. His objective was not merely athletic but in time spiritual as well. He wanted the peace of mind that came with reaching the highest level of his abilities. He wanted to try to be the best at one thing even if he did his best and failed. He was aware of the danger implicit in so singular an ambition, that it demanded an overwhelming amount of sacrifice—exams taken on airplanes to tournaments, fitting in homework while his classmates were having fun. He knew he was giving up part of his youth. But the alternative was worse: to stop just short of true excellence. There were, he thought, altogether too many people who did that, who were haunted for the rest of their lives by the question of how good they might have been had they tried just a little harder. Whatever else, he vowed, that question would not go unanswered in his life.

Tulum preached that fencing was 50 percent athletic and 50 percent psychological and intellectual, that in addition to the physical talent of a Michael Jordan you needed the strategic ability and the psychological acumen of a Garry Kasparov because you had to stay several moves ahead of your opponent. Attitude was crucial. In fencing, if you think someone is better, he'll end up being better. For years a kind of national inferiority complex had plagued American fencers. At international meets they saw foreign teams that were so well subsidized they even came with their own cooks. Such wealth and power engendered a certain amount of swagger. The Americans felt like the poor stepchildren of the sport and were beaten all too readily. To draw an American in an international tournament, Bravin noted, was virtually regarded as drawing a bye. He himself had done poorly in the 1992 Olympics. But then he had been only 21, and since fencers reach their peaks in their late 20s and early 30s, he still had a bright future.

Two years later he was coming into his own and just beginning to beat some of the best fencers in the world. It was at this point that he entered law school, and he found it was hard to be a wolf both at fencing and at his studies. Tulum, of course, had not been happy with the idea of law school—it was a terrible distraction, he thought. "Every day you don't practice all out," he said, "is like losing three days: the day you lose by slipping just a little, the day you lose by not getting just a little better, and the day you lose because your opponent gets better." Bravin had tried to stay in shape, but it was difficult. In 1995 when he arrived in Louisville for the nationals he thought he was fencing well and was confident he would win his fourth national championship. But Tulum thought he had been coasting on his name for a while.

NOW, AS BRAVIN NEGOTIATED ROME for his younger colleagues, Cliff Bayer was No. 1. When Bravin was winning his first national championship, Bayer had been only 13, still collecting baseball cards. True, he collected them feverishly, determined to have a better set than any of his friends. The son of a New York City doctor, he walked a neighbor's dog for $20 a week so he could buy more cards. He also became so skillful at trading cards, his brother, Greg, later remembered, he picked up the nickname Rip-off Cliff. There were complaints from neighboring parents to the senior Bayers that Cliff had snookered their kids.

Bayer, like Bravin, took up fencing because his older brother had done it. He had become impatient with baseball—he thought his teammates did not play as hard as he did. In fencing he found a sport where there was no one to blame but himself when things went wrong. His first coach, Miklos Bartha, a Hungarian émigré now in his 70s, was a distinguished figure in New York fencing circles. Bayer's father, Dr. Michael Bayer, remembers when Bartha told him his son would make a champion: "I looked out and saw nothing, but Miklos had a practiced eye and he knew what made a great athlete—the willpower and the instinct. He could look at a little boy of nine and see it all: the character, the inner toughness, and the drive." Like Bravin, Bayer did not enjoy the drudgery of the early training—the repetitive drills of advance and retreat, the dancing classes with swords. But he rose to competition, often beating older and seemingly more talented boys with the intensity of his will.

The first time he saw Bayer at a tournament, when Bayer was only 15, Tulum was struck by the boy's courage and instinct for combat. "That child has a heart the size of his chest," thought Tulum, "the heart of a champion." Bayer himself did not think he was a natural for the sport, but he knew his desire was so strong that he could turn his weaknesses into strengths. "Some people know instinctively why it is important for them to be the best," says Dave Micahnik, the University of Pennsylvania coach who successfully recruited Bayer for next fall. "Cliff is that way—it is vital that he be the best."

On occasion the pressure of school and fencing was almost too much for someone so young. Once, he fenced at the Junior World Cup in Giengen, Germany, with melancholy results. To get there he had to take an international flight to Stuttgart, a train to Heidenheim, and then a bus to Giengen. He was tired upon arrival, which affected his concentration, and he fenced poorly, not even making the top 32. Then he had to retrace his steps, lugging all his gear, trying to do his homework on the train, in order to rush back to school in New York. Unable to get a decent night's sleep on the plane, he wondered whether it was all worth it and thought about quitting.

But he knew he was getting better. In 1994, while still a high-school junior at Riverdale Country Day School in New York City, he came in third at the U.S. national championships. It was a stunning achievement. He was amused by the response of the older fencers to his success: "Who's this upstart kid who's doing so well, they were thinking, and I was thinking, Third, *that's not good enough, I can do better. I can win this whole thing.*"

By the time of his high-school graduation, at age 17, he was already ranked No. 3 in the country. He defeated Zaddick Longenbach, an Olympian in 1992, at a senior-circuit tournament in New Jersey. Both Longenbach and Bayer had worked out at Salle Santelli and the Metropolis Fencing Club in New York City, and Longenbach had been beating Bayer since Bayer was nine. Bayer's older brother, Greg, a former captain of the Princeton fencing team, had watched the match and was startled by what he saw. For the first time, he realized, his brother's physical abilities had caught up with his competitive in-stincts. Bayer himself felt he was ready to take on Bravin in Louisville.

IN THE FIRST ROUND of the 1995 nationals, Bayer was nervous. Yefim Litvan, his coach, sensed it immediately. "Relax," he said. "Just have fun here." That helped and as he relaxed he began to see his opponents' moves more clearly. He made the semifinals and thus qualified for the Senior World Championships and the World University Games.

The semifinal match with Longenbach was intense. For a while it was touch for touch. Bayer had never seen Longenbach so focused in a bout. But Bayer won, 15–13. That meant he would face Bravin in the final.

In 1994, Bravin had beaten Bayer, 15–11, at the nationals, but Bayer was not intimidated. His hero was the great Italian fencer Stefano Cerioni, the 1988 Olympic gold medalist, who was known as the most aggressive of fencers, a man who approached every match as if it were a street fight. Bayer wanted no part of a silver medal. He and his friend Sean McClain had their own saying: "Silver sucks." Now Bayer was sure that he could beat Bravin—after all, Bravin had not been much older when he had won his first national.

AS THE TWO PREPARED TO FENCE, the air was electric. Bravin knew that he was now the hunted and that it was much harder than being the hunter. He knew also that the physical gap with Bayer had narrowed. He sized up the younger man and found he was alto-gether too much like he himself used to be, with little respect for existing hierarchies. Bravin remembered his second N.C.A.A. cham-pionship, in 1992. He had been ranked 24th, which annoyed him greatly, because in his own mind he deserved to be the favorite that year. He had responded by winning.

They both were fencing well. Bravin took an 11–8 lead. He was pleased and felt certain he would get a fourth national title. He began to think that Bayer too believed that the old order would hold, that Bravin was the champion and would continue to be so. Here he made his mistake. He relaxed and became overconfident. Certain he had established his superiority, he became less focused, less aggressive. Watching the match, Dave Micahnik saw Bayer go to the end of the strip after Bravin won a point, slap himself on the leg in anger, and let out a roar, as if he were waking up from some long hibernation. Then he came back and stormed past Bravin to win the bout, 15–12.

Yefim Litvan now believed that Bayer would become an Olympic medalist, but perhaps in 2000—this year, 1996, would be one in which to gain international experience. But Bayer, with the fearlessness of the young, thought otherwise, that there was no reason to enter a match thinking of it only as experience for the future.

In defeat Bravin realized he had probably lost something of his edge and certainly something of his mystique. He decided to take a year off from law school to work on his fencing and get ready for the Olympics. He needed to find out whether he still had the hunger, whether he could still be the hunter.

ICE BREAKERS

From *Condé Nast Sports for Women*, February 1998

ALL LAST FALL AND WINTER, AND THEN INTO THE SUMMER, she gave up almost everything. She took leave from her senior year at Harvard, putting aside the mundane but sweet pleasures of life that any bright, attractive college student is entitled to. Instead, on days when the Boston winter was unspeakably gray and depressing, when her body still ached from the last workout and she most demonstrably did not want to do full-body pull-ups and squats and hoist free weights, Allison Jaime Mleczko, 22 (A.J. to her family and friends), gathered herself and went to the varsity weight room at Boston University. There, four times a week, along with about a dozen other talented and dedicated young women who hoped to become members of the first U.S. Olympic women's hockey team, she put in a grueling three hours under the watchful eye of Michael Boyle, a BU strength and conditioning coach. Her body was so depleted by the intensity of these workouts that she quickly realized she had to give up any attempt to hold down a part-time job.

For Mleczko (pronounced muh-LESS-ko) and some of the other women, these workouts were exhilarating. The access to the weight rooms most of them had received at their own colleges had always been marginal, and they had been treated, more often than not, as amiable but not entirely serious stepchildren. But at BU they were the charges of one of the most gifted trainers in collegiate sports; more, the weight room pulsed with a sense of seriousness and excellence. Working alongside them were not just some of the college's best athletes but also, in the spring and summer, a group of highly accomplished NHL and NFL players, already budding millionaires, who were training with Boyle to get in shape for the seasons ahead.

In Mleczko's case, the tour of the weight room began with considerable humiliation. At five feet eleven inches, she was one of the biggest women trying out for the team, a formidable prep school and college hockey star who had usually dominated the women's leagues, using her height for extra leverage. Over the years she had come to think of herself as strong. Yet now that she and her colleagues were on the verge of competing on the international level—where every player is strong and in superior condition—for the right to go to the Olympics in Nagano, Mleczko discovered that she was surprisingly weak. The new women's Olympic hockey coach, Ben Smith, already had Mleczko pegged: a good deal of size, a good deal of talent, a dominating player on a relatively weak college team. Not nearly as much strength as she would need to play to her true potential. Moreover, he thought, she was still very young, a player who wasn't yet aware of the great gift she had for the game, and who needed to assert herself more on the ice. The question was whether she was willing to go through the torturous procedure that would raise her strength and therefore her ability to the next stage.

Back in the summer of 1996, as he began laying the groundwork for this year's Olympic team, Smith told Mleczko and the other candidates that he would not and could not make their career decisions for them. He knew all too well the kind of financial sacrifices he was about to suggest to them, since if they did what he advised they would not be able to hold jobs. But if they wanted to make the Olympic team, he said, they would be well advised to spend the entire year working out under Michael Boyle's strict supervision.

THUS IN MLECZKO'S CASE the ultimate challenge had been offered to a passionate and committed athlete. But the first day of weight training under Boyle was devastating. She couldn't do a single pull-up or a squat worthy of his demands. She bench-pressed only 65 pounds, far too little for a player of her size. Size clearly did not equal strength; if anything, her size now worked against her. Because she was taller and heavier than almost all of her teammates, it was harder to do pull-ups. She reached a point that Boyle knew all too well, where many a gifted male athlete decides that the price for doing what has always come so naturally has gone up too much. But she did not tell Boyle that she was going home; nor, he noted, did she do what many athletes often do at this point: ignore the weaknesses and reinforce the strengths. Instead she asked, "What do I do next?"

She stayed with the program. For the first two months there was little in the way of reward and a great deal of pain. When she picked up the bar to do the bench press, she often had to take off the weights that the other women were using. But by the third month the workouts became, if not exactly fun, more acceptable, because she could see results, not just in the weight room but, more importantly, on the ice when she skated. What kept her going in the hard times, she later decided, were two things: First there was her dream of becoming an Olympic hockey player, of getting a chance to play at such an exalted level, a chance so many women who had gone before her had never had; secondly there was the support of her teammates, all of whom hoped to be a part of history on this first Olympic team.

By the summer, she could do three sets of eight reps on the bench press at 105 pounds, no mean feat, and three sets of five pull-ups. By then Boyle would needle her, saying, "A.J., I really wish I had a video of you when you first started—I'd use it as a before-and-after commercial for the program." To Smith, her improvement was equally impressive, a test not just of strength but of something perhaps more important—character—because he knew how easy it was for someone who had led a charmed athletic life to unravel after running into an obstacle like this.

What also helped keep her going was the attention of Boyle, a coach who could easily have been using his time in other ways but who seemed gender-blind. Boyle took the female athletes as seriously as he did some of his more celebrated male athletes. He had come aboard at the request of coach Smith, who was a pal. In the beginning, he had regarded the assignment as a lark, but working with these women had turned into one of the most enjoyable things he had ever done. In the world of sports, both he and Smith decided, they had found something of a sanctuary, a place where there was a sense of excellence and dedication but none of the countervailing egotism, born of the intense new materialism of sport that is so destructive to the concept of team. No one was spoiled. No one had an attitude problem. "Coaches who haven't coached women before," Boyle said recently, "don't know what they're missing. It's very different from coaching men—with some of the men these days it's like pulling teeth to get them to do certain things, and on some days they make you feel more like a dentist than a coach."

What Smith and Boyle were watching in these athletes was the unleashing of an immensely powerful force that came with the removal of a ceiling that had for so long suppressed the dreams and possibilities of young women. Here were all these talented and dedicated athletes, who had worked so hard for so long and had excelled at every level, but had always known there was a limit to their dreams and expectations that would not have existed if they were men. They had all been the best in junior high, in high school and in college; had they been men, they would have been superstars, brazenly recruited by colleges and courted by agents and pro teams. (In Mleczko's case both her talent and the likely elusiveness of her dream had been underlined by a sentence in her ninth-grade yearbook that predicted she would be the first woman to play in the NHL.) All these young women were acutely aware that the Olympic spotlight had a unique capacity to illuminate the importance of women's sports. Ordinary American sports fans, a preponderance of them male, who would never bother to watch women's rowing or volleyball or softball, would do so if the United States was competing against some feared rival—the Russians, or the Chinese, or, as in this case, the Canadians. That had happened in the summer of 1996 in Atlanta with the women's softball, soccer and basketball teams; this year it might well happen with women's ice hockey.

As Mleczko's strength began to increase significantly, so did her athletic ability. If anything, she now became slightly embarrassed about the hockey player she had only so recently been, someone who because of a lack of leg strength had too often skated straight up, instead of bent over, simply because she was not in good enough shape. "I used to think that I skated that way because that was the way I skated, but then when we started doing weights I realized that it had been because I had so little leg strength—that you skate straight up when you're tired, but that you can skate bent over for a long time if you have the leg strength."

If it is true that adversity breeds strength, then this group of young women was unusually strong, not just from Boyle's weight training but from the inner resolve required to follow a dream against such odds for so many years. From the beginning, people had tried to keep them from playing because of their gender. They had been challenged in numerous ways, by officials who did not want them on teams and by boys who tested them with cheap shots in order to show that hockey was a masculine sport.

Many of these women were in their mid-twenties and were delaying career decisions in order to try out for the Olympic team. Lisa Brown-Miller turned 31 in the fall. She had been the head coach at Princeton and had tried to recruit Mleczko several years before. But now they were teammates, for Brown-Miller resigned the Princeton job to try out. Or, as Sandra Whyte, 27, a former Harvard captain who left her job as a lab research assistant to train with the team and who lived with her family to save money, says, "Part of my competitive instinct is the need to survive against considerable odds and to prove to myself that I can do this [play hockey] despite all the various people who for so much of my life kept telling me that I couldn't."

Even at this level of accomplishment the economics are hard: The subsidies the women receive from the American Olympic organization are infinitesimal, somewhere between $10,000 and $15,000 a year from USA Hockey to be used against living expenses (those who were members of the last national team, which came in second to the Canadians at the world championships, get an additional sum). Not everyone accepted the subsidies; Mleczko turned down both of them in order to retain eligibility for her final year at Harvard. A teammate told her she was crazy—she obviously needed the money, and going back to Harvard and playing after the Olympics would be a step down. "Well, that may be true," she answered, "but I love playing for Harvard, and I can't imagine being there and not playing for them. It's been a great school for me, and I've loved going, and I think I owe them something—like playing one more year. Besides, we've never done things for money in my family anyway." She comes from a family of modest means: Until his retirement in 1996, A.J.'s father, Tom, was a teacher at a private day school in New Canaan, Connecticut; he is also a skilled charter fisherman in Nantucket, Massachusetts. Her mother, Priscilla (known as Bambi), runs a small clothes shop. Mleczko attends Harvard on scholarships and loans, which means that she will need to carry her debt that much longer.

THE WOMEN'S GAME, it should be said, is very different from the men's. There is no checking, or at least no legal checking. That means speed is of the essence. It places a premium on skating well and fast, and on passing. It is, says Ben Smith, "a purist's game—it is all about skill." When he and the other coaches he has assembled to work with this team, many of them men, talk about the quality of the women's game at this level, they talk about it as a reflection of the way hockey used to be before the hard checking and fighting became (with the encouragement of television) so much more important. Smith believes the good women's teams bring back memories of the famous 1972 Russian national team, one that absolutely delighted hockey aficionados with its passing and speed.

This is the pioneer generation of women's hockey. These women all began as rebels, astonishing their friends and families when they were young by preferring to play hockey with boys rather than follow the gentler track of figure skating, as they were supposed to do. "I just don't know what to do with her," defenseman Vicki Movsessian's father, Larry, once said when his daughter was about 6. "She's supposed to be a little girl, but she likes hockey better than figure skating, and even when she's doing her figure skating, she refuses to wear her figure skates and she wears hockey skates." Hockey, Vicki thought from the start, was much more fun. It was a real, live, honest-to-God game. There were more kids playing. Besides, figure skating was not only lonelier, it was not really fun. Instead, it was filled with the terrible tension that came from constantly being judged and critiqued, and at the ages of 6 and 7 Movsessian did not like being critiqued. When she was about 8, her father tried to sharpen her figure skates himself and somehow managed to grind down the distinguishing toe picks at the front. He was distraught, sure that he had ruined an expensive pair of skates. She immediately comforted him: "Don't worry. Figure skating's over for me anyway. I'm a hockey player."

Some of them had brothers who were hockey players. Cammi Granato, perhaps the best known of the women players, has several brothers who have played hockey at the elite levels, including one, Tony, who's now an All-Star with the San Jose Sharks in the NHL. (Ironically, of the two, only Cammi is going to Nagano.) Meaghan Sittler's father, Darryl, played in the NHL for the Toronto Maple Leafs, and her brother, Ryan, was a high draft choice a few years ago. A.J.'s father was the hockey coach at the day school where he taught. It turned out that he had always loved the idea of her becoming a hockey player.

A.J.'s entrance into the world of skating was somewhat draconian. She was 2 years old when Tom Mleczko took her out to the center of the frozen pond by their house, put skates on her and walked off the ice. It was, she later learned, exactly what he had done with her older sister, who had quickly fallen in love with skating. (The skates, it should be noted, were not double runners.) It was fall, crawl or skate, and the first time she tried, A.J. fell and broke into tears. Then she crawled across the pond, absolutely convinced that her father didn't love her. At least her mother had prepared hot chocolate for her in case she made it to shore, a sign of some parental love.

But soon afterward, perhaps the third time she tried, she began to skate, awkwardly but doggedly. She quickly decided that she had accomplished something important and, moreover, that she liked skating. She was not as innately talented as her older sister, Wink: Wink skated gracefully; A.J. skated forcefully. When A.J. was 6 and Wink was already passionately involved with her figure skating, A.J. came home one day and announced that she wanted to be a hockey player. It was a moment of complete innocence: She had no idea that there was such a thing as a gender barrier in hockey or in life. "Hockey looked like fun. There were all these kids, and they were *playing together*. I didn't notice that they were all boys."

The gene pool in the Mleczko family is formidable. Tom was a good schoolboy athlete and played several sports at Bowdoin College. He is to this day a skilled outdoorsman; during the crunch of summer, he can take three separate charter fishing parties out during a day and never seem to tire. His sister, Sarah, was a star athlete at Harvard and won 12 varsity letters there. A.J.'s mother, the former Bambi Gifford, was a club champion tennis player and part of a large Nantucket clan whose members tended to be tall, powerful and athletic.

Tom Mleczko would later say that the day his daughter announced her intention to be a hockey player was the greatest day of his life. He immediately went to a meeting of the organization that ran the local boys' hockey leagues and said that his daughter wanted to play. No one could see anything wrong with his suggestion, and so the league heads decided that she could play. Tom then went to the lost-and-found at the New Canaan Country School and gathered up various stray pieces of equipment for her, including, A.J. remembers with some amusement, a cup.

Tom is a talented coach, a man who could easily have succeeded at a much higher level if he had been so inclined. He is also a man of relentless enthusiasm, who believes that talent should not be wasted. He was not a Little League dad, and he did not demand too much of either daughter, but he treated their athletic aspirations as he would a son's—that is, he took them very seriously. If he did not pressure them to excel, he quite skillfully convinced them that the pursuit of excellence was fun, as well as something they were doing of their own volition.

When A.J. first started playing, there was an undertow of protest from some of the boys and their parents, who presumably believed the intrusion of a girl on this particularly physical sport would make hockey just a little less macho. From the beginning A.J. played with boys, largely because women's (and girls') hockey as an organized sport did not really exist. For many of those years she was the only girl on her team, and often the only girl in the league.

In suburban Connecticut at that time, there were all kinds of leagues—the Mite (ages 7 to 8), the Squirt (9 to 10), the Pee Wee (11 to 12) and the Bantam (13 to 14). Things began to get reasonably serious when she wanted to play at the Squirt level (the Mite team did not travel, whereas the Squirts did). There were tryouts for the Squirt team. No girl had ever tried out for it before. A.J. was very nervous, not at all sure that she was playing or skating well. After her workout, Bill Emmons, the local coach, told her she would hear about the results in a few days. Never had she wanted anything so badly, and those few days seemed to last forever. When Emmons finally called, a little unsure of the path ahead and a little nervous, he spoke to her mother. "Are you sure you want her to do this?" he asked Bambi Mleczko.

"Is she good enough?" Bambi asked, wanting no special treatment either way.

"Ability-wise she's right up there at the top," Emmons said, "but it *is* a boys' game."

"Well if she's good enough and she wants to play on the team, we want her to play on the team," Bambi answered.

A.J. THOUGHT HOCKEY was the right sport for her. She loved to skate, and she was by nature aggressive and competitive on the ice. That competitive spirit probably stemmed in part from a natural rivalry with an older, talented sister who seemed to do all things gracefully and easily. And in part it was probably orchestrated by her father, who sensed from the start that his second daughter was an uncommon athlete with an uncommon commitment. In those days the Mleczko home had two avid young athletes: Wink, preoccupied with figure skating, who rose early in the morning for long jaunts to distant rinks for lessons, and A.J., by no means a natural skater but most assuredly a natural competitor, who had hockey all to herself. The sport fit her personality. She might have looked like the girl next door, someone just off a Norman Rockwell *Saturday Evening Post* cover, except perhaps a little bigger and stronger, but she was a natural-born tomboy, and there was a certain toughness and resilience to her personality.

In those years hockey became something more than her sport, something equally important, a critical part of her identity. It was not just the local boys who were on occasion irritated by her commitment: The mother of her best friend, a girl her own age, was quite irate when A.J. missed going to the friend's birthday party in order to play in a scheduled hockey game. "How can you let her do this?" the mother asked Bambi Mleczko, both puzzled and angry. A.J. herself had made the decision, Bambi answered. "We don't make decisions like that for her."

On occasion there was the smell of gender bias or gender prejudice. Sometimes she would skate onto the ice and hear someone from the other side asking who the guy with the long hair was (even though she had cut her hair quite short in those days), and then someone else would shout out, the secret revealed, *Oh-my-God-it's-a-giiirrrll!* Most people handled this sports breakthrough, small though it was, relatively well. Her teammates were usually good about it: This may not have been what they wanted, but she was a pretty good player and she never asked for special treatment. If there was an occasional problem with one or two of her teammates, it was probably because they were being teased by other boys for playing with a girl.

There was no checking in the lower leagues, but when A.J. graduated to the higher ones, where checking was permitted, some adults were concerned about how she would fare. In her last prechecking game against the Darien team, an opponent (a boy who had played with her on her day-school team and who had been bad-mouthing her for months—a rare, fully developed child male chauvinist) skated over and gave her a hard check. It was completely gratuitous. Without breaking stride, she wheeled around and whacked him as hard as she could, knocking him absolutely flat on the ice. Hers was an illegal hit, but she had answered the question of whether she would be able to play at the next level.

But it was also an early warning that because A.J. was moving to a league where checking was permitted, she might become a target. From time to time that happened. In a club game against Central Connecticut when she was 13, she brought the puck across the center line, passed it off and was holding her position along the boards when a player from the other team skated halfway across the ice from behind her and blindsided her, nailing her against the boards, full force, a shattering hit with his elbow to her face. She was very lucky; if her face had hit the boards, she might have sustained serious injury. "That's not a hit—that's a mugging," Tom Mleczko shouted. The boy was thrown out of the game. A.J. missed just one shift and never once complained.

She later viewed those years as a series of tests. At first it was some of her teammates who were wary. Then as she passed muster with them, it was the parents of opposing players who complained that she was not good enough. Things got a little more complicated as she and her teammates began to enter adolescence. She knew she had finally been accepted when she was sitting on a bench in the dressing room before a game, already in uniform herself. One of her teammates looked up, saw that the door was open and asked her to close it because there were some girls outside. "Hey," she said, "I'm a girl, too." "Yeah," he said, "I know you're a girl, but you're . . . you're A.J."

When she was 14, she played on an all-girls' team for the first time. Of course, the team—the Connecticut Polar Bears—had to play boys' teams. Suddenly there was a change in her game. In the past she had always played defense, but now she was a much better skater than most of her peers, and she played center and forward, handling the puck much of the time. That was helpful: It improved her puck-carrying skills, passing and sense of the play. Recognizing that the boys were becoming stronger, she took lessons on the weekends to improve her speed and strength.

In the tenth grade she went off to the Taft School, a prominent Connecticut boarding school with a good hockey program. There, she played with and against only women, and her ability propelled her to a higher plane. Instead of fighting her physical limitations against bigger male opponents, she found that she was stronger and more gifted than most of the other players. Taft had a very strong women's team, yet she was clearly better than her teammates. In the finals for the New England championship against Holderness in her sophomore year, she scored all four of Taft's goals in a victorious game that was decided in overtime. During her three varsity years, Taft was the New England prep school champion.

By now there were clear signs of the player she was to become. She had marvelously soft hands, which meant that when she controlled the puck, her teammates were likely to get it not only at the right place at the right time but also in a way that they could handle. Most important, she had great rink vision and an uncommon ability to sense where different players would be as the play developed. "Her athletic vision is almost unique—it's a gift. Some of it may be physiological, coming from great peripheral vision," says her prep school coach Patsy Odden, "but some of it I think is a thing that great athletes are born with, a wonderful anticipatory instinct for the game. Because she was not the flashiest player on the ice or the best skater, she was not always the player that a lot of ordinary fans noticed. But she was always the one that the other coaches and the real hockey fans noticed—the player who made other players better."

If there was a flaw here, it was a tendency to be too self-sacrificing and a willingness to pass up shots that she probably should have taken. It was an odd personal signature for a player who obviously loved the game and was fiercely competitive. In this one way she tended to hold back, as if not wanting to call attention to herself and become too big a star. It was, some friends thought, the most natural by-product of her own unusual road to stardom. Enough attention had been paid to her early on, and for all the wrong reasons. Now even as she played among girls, she wanted to do nothing more that might set her apart from her teammates. Her modesty turned into a desire to set up other players. In her senior year Taft made two trips abroad, where it played against the Russian women's national team and the German national team and won every game but one. "It was fascinating—everywhere she went the

other coaches picked up on her and her sense of the game. Who is
that girl? they would ask, singling her out," notes Patsy Odden. In
St. Petersburg the coach of the Russian national team asked Tom
Mleczko, who had gone along as an assistant coach, if his daughter
would entertain the idea of staying on in that historic city and playing with the Russian team. The coach reasoned that it would be a
great cultural exchange for her.

A.J. was heavily recruited for college, and finally decided on Harvard over Princeton although the latter seemed to have the stronger
hockey program. Among those who worked to get her to Harvard
was her sister, Wink. Two years ahead of A.J. and, at six feet, too tall
for figure skating, Wink was beginning to surface as a quality hockey
player in her own right. "If it's a choice between playing with A.J. or
against her, I'd much rather play with her," she once noted. In time
she chose Harvard, which was not yet a powerhouse in women's
hockey, and where the recruiting was somewhat low-key, based on
a certain Cambridge-based presumptuousness that anyone with
the chance would want to go to Harvard. On the school's largely
mediocre team, A.J. quickly emerged as a great star. As a freshman
she was Ivy League and Eastern College Athletic Conference Rookie
of the Year. From then on she made the All–Ivy League team every
year, and by the end of her third year she was already the leading
scorer in Harvard history. But trying out for the Olympic team was
going to demand a stronger commitment than ever before.

She was facing an important choice, because, while hockey was
important to her, it was not the only thing in her life. She was also a
good student and she led a normal social life. Her cousin Caroline
Apple Gifford, 24, says, "I've been with a number of other athletes—
both men and women—who have reached that level of excellence,
and if you're around them for even a few minutes, you know immediately that they are *athletes* and it's the dominating part of their
lives. There's a kind of natural arrogance to who they are and what
they've accomplished. They really let you know in the first instant

you meet them that they are jocks. But A.J. is different—you could be around her for a long time, and unless she had to go off to practice, you might never know that she was a jock playing at that high a level. Maybe it's the nature of women's hockey at this moment—it's so new, and these women have had to fight so hard for their place in the sports world, and they've gotten so little recognition that they're all able to remain very modest."

For coach Ben Smith, who is exceptionally popular within the world of hockey, working with the women has been an epiphany. When USA Hockey suggested he give this a try back in 1995, he was wary. He was a men's coach at a big-time hockey school, Northeastern, and he had been an assistant coach for the 1988 men's U.S. Olympic team. He had accepted the offer of working with the women, he later noted, because it was proposed on a winter day and he had forgotten that by taking it up he would lose a summer of sailing and golf. But soon he was hooked. "These are wonderful, focused athletes," Smith says. "They want to go to the rink each day for the same reason I do. They love hockey, pure and simple. There are no agents around, no big bonuses awaiting them, no commercials to be filmed. I love it."

The first thing he learned was that he had to be very careful of what he said, because women are unusually coachable, and they take seriously everything he says. On his first day he noticed that as they loosened up before practice by skating around the rink, they had their sticks with them, but no pucks—a contrast to the way most men warm up. At the time they were soon to leave on a trip to Scandinavia. Smith immediately blew his whistle. "Look," he told them, "unless they've changed the rules and I haven't been told, even in Finland and Sweden when you play hockey you do it with a puck." So they skated over and explained to him that the previous coach had told them they were never to warm up with a puck, and so unless told otherwise that was the way they practiced. "I learned from that," he said. "I try not to say too much."

Right after the first selections had been made in late August, the team flew to Scandinavia for a series of games—three with the Swedes and then three with the Finns. International travel was often hard for these young players. They had to deal with jet lag, time zone changes, eating different foods and being away from home. Besides, it was a new team just beginning to come together. But what took place abroad pleased Smith. Sweden was not a powerhouse, and the Americans won all three games rather easily. But the Finns were another matter. They had come in third earlier in the year at the world championships and had almost achieved parity with the U.S., and now they were playing on their home ice. Again the Americans swept all three games. Mleczko emerged as one of the most important players on the team, a player who, in Smith's words, made things happen. She played well on the trip, with four goals and six assists—the high scorer on the U.S. team. She played particularly well in one game, a blowout of the Swedes, and the next morning Smith stopped by to see her at breakfast. She looked a little tired.

"Hey, A.J.," he asked, "how'd you sleep last night?"

"Not very well, Coach," she answered. "I don't know. For some reason I was wired and couldn't fall asleep."

"Well, A.J., when was the last time you scored four goals in an international competition?" he asked. "Do you think that could have something to do with being so wired?"

THE U.S. PLAYERS, Smith believes, have a good chance for a medal. They lost in overtime to the Canadians last April in the finals of the world championships, and though hockey is considered a Canadian sport, the Americans think they are closing in fast on their rivals. There is an added edge to the competition now, because after the game some of the Canadian players began to talk about how high-powered the American financing is, something that was particularly offensive to these young women who had sacrificed so much to get where they were and were receiving so little support. At the 1997 championships, it was clear that the American women, in terms of their skills and their overall talent bank, were as good as the Canadians. But what they lacked was the inner toughness and confidence that comes only with experience. As A.J. says, "We know that we're as good as they are. What we have to do now is prove it on the ice, as much to ourselves as to them."

Ben Smith, for one, thinks that those fans sitting at home watching will be pleased by the aesthetics of the sport, by how fast and artistic a game it is. The women's college game is not yet there in terms of talent, he says; the talent, though considerable enough to form a national team, is not deep. In a few years, with the help of a showcase at the Nagano Olympics, more and more women will want to play, and soon the college game will benefit from that. Smith hopes that women's hockey will not be corrupted if it becomes more successful. He is wary of the game becoming big-time too quickly. It is important in life, he believes, to be careful what you ask for, because you might actually get it.

ALI WINS ANOTHER FIGHT

From ESPN.com, March 21, 2001

MUHAMMAD ALI WON ONE OF HIS MOST IMPORTANT VICTO-
ries the other day. It was a long time coming, almost 30 years, and it
was over one of his most difficult opponents, himself—or perhaps
more accurately, his lesser self. He finally admitted he had trans-
gressed by going far beyond any acceptable line when he had belit-
tled and taunted Joe Frazier during the hype for their three historic
fights.

Back then, he had called Frazier an Uncle Tom, said he was
much too ugly to be a champion and called him, on the occasion of
their third fight, a gorilla. Frazier, unable to fight back verbally, for
words were never among his weapons, remained hurt and bitter
long after the fights were over.

When Ali finally apologized, he accepted the fact that he had
wounded another, very worthy man. "Joe's right [to be bitter]. I said
a lot of things in the heat of the moment that I shouldn't have said.
Called him names I shouldn't have called him. I apologize for that.
I'm sorry. It was all meant to promote the fight."

Ali's apology was both magnanimous, and long overdue. What
he had said at the time was cruel and unacceptable. He had taken
Frazier, the least political of men, and cast him in the most unlikely
of roles, that of the great white hope, a role that Frazier in no way
deserved.

Included in the apology was a covert admission on Ali's part that
he owes no small amount of his own remarkable claim to greatness

to Joe Frazier, innately far less physically talented an athlete, but every bit as indomitable of spirit. The simplest of all the many truths of Ali's magnificent career is that without the three Frazier fights, Ali is not Ali. For their fights represent one of those great moments in sports when two superb, lion-hearted athletes—with vastly differing skills—arrive at the same place at almost the exact same time.

Because of Frazier, we know how great Ali was, how strong, how resilient and how resolute, and how courageously he could take a punch—for early in his career it was said of him that that was a particular weakness and vulnerability. When he was on the way up, and when he first won his crown, we always knew how great Ali said he was; when it was all over, the fights with Frazier done, we knew that the reality was greater than the hype, the walk better than the talk.

The Liston fights, after all, are not defining—the Liston that Ali beat, however threatening, was old, out of shape and the shadow of the mob still hangs heavily over the second fight. The fight with George Foreman in Zaire is the equivalent of one Frazier fight, but it is a relatively small part of what would eventually become a much larger body of work.

Let me be absolutely clear in what I am saying, because Ali is such a complicated and controversial figure, particularly for writers who came of age in my generation, when a great many people quite deliberately got him wrong and resented his changing his name, becoming a Muslim and, more than anything else, refusing to serve in Vietnam. I am a huge Ali fan. I thought him a great fighter, a remarkable, luminescent personality, a genuine original (unlike so many thin imitators who have come along since), in the end someone so large on the landscape that he transcended the smaller world of sports for the larger one of American history.

I was still a young reporter covering Civil Rights in the South when he burst on the scene in the late '50s and early '60s, and like many of my friends I was taken by his talent, his youth and joyousness. On that night in February 1964 when he fought what still seemed like the invincible Liston, I remember going to the theater with my friend, Gay Talese, and being frightened for him, scared that something young and fresh and original was going to be destroyed by something heavy and menacing.

His becoming a Muslim did not bother me. It seemed like a legitimate choice, a serious one for a complicated, bright, but alienated young man. Most important, it seemed to be a choice made out of conscience, which is the only thing that counts.

But a generation of older sportswriters, many of whom already disliked him because he seemed too boastful, were now even more offended—he had changed his name, and joined up with a group that seemed to them to be outside the mainstream of American life, more openly hostile to their way of life than anything they had yet encountered. For a generation of men made uneasy by anything save the conventions they already accepted, what he represented was immensely threatening.

When he refused induction, they became even angrier, though among the most vociferous there were few who had ever heard a shot fired in anger. That hardly bothered me: I had already spent two years in Vietnam as a correspondent, and my negative reporting about the war had angered two Presidents of the United States.

But the world of sportswriting which defined him in those days was immensely conservative; it is part of Ali's unique power and uncommon intelligence, the fact that he was well ahead of the curve, that he survived, true to himself, without changing, and it was the world of sportswriters which had to change in the coming years.

Sportswriting then reflected not merely older American values, but older unrecognized American prejudices, and Ali in so many ways seemed an affront to them, and to the extremely thin fabric of that era's tolerance.

There were a lot of sportswriters at that time who thought they were liberal because they had accepted the arrival of Jackie Robinson: in their view it was all right for black athletes to play against whites—thus they were more enlightened than those who had gone before them—but it was not all right for them to have opinions on anything except sports. If they spoke out on racism in general, then they had gone too far. (It was all right for Jackie Robinson to play baseball, but it was not all right for him to complain about how hard it was to find housing in a white neighborhood.) That was the generation of sportswriters who, deep into their careers, tried to call him Cassius Clay.

A generational faultline ran through American society in those days, and Ali (who spoke against the war publicly a year before Martin Luther King did), as much as anyone on the national scene, seemed to reveal it and define its prejudices and conflicting values: How you felt about Ali put you on one side or another in something much larger.

Ali, by the prevailing dominating opinion of the day, was supposed to be grateful for his right to fight; after all, the traditionalists would argue, look how much money he was making. He should accept his good fortune, and refrain from being a critic of America's domestic racial policies, let alone its foreign policy.

To me, his stand on Vietnam was the rarest of things, a genuine act of conscience by a prominent American on a compelling moral issue about which he felt passionately, and for which he was willing to pay a very high price. It meant that someone at the very top of his profession was willing to give up the thing he cared about the most because of his beliefs—extraordinary in any circumstance, but more so with someone like a fighter who has so brief a career. I remember the moment when all the top black athletes of the era gathered to meet with him, some of them trying to talk him out of it, suggesting that he play the game, go along with the draft, fight some exhibitions for Uncle Sam and not risk so much for, what seemed to many of them, so little.

But he refused to compromise his beliefs. That made him unique. Not just among fighters, not just among athletes, not just among blacks, but among all his fellow citizens. There were all kinds of people in the upper level of the U.S. government in those days, all of them better educated and seemingly more sophisticated than Ali, who dissented from Vietnam but who did not act on their beliefs. Because of that, Ali remains special to me—the only high-level American who in effect resigned his job because of his beliefs on Vietnam.

I thought he was a brilliant figure, something of a comet who had burst upon us and for whom we had remarkably little preparation: joyous, funny, talented. He sometimes seemed like a great one-man, multi-act Broadway musical that was both tragedy and comedy, and for which he was author, director, and principal actor. With Ali everyone else got second billing.

But there was a dark side as well, the occasional cruelty to opponents both in and out of the ring, and that detracted from the rest of the performance; for whatever political baggage that they brought to the fight, it was unbecoming, hardly worthy of him.

He was unnecessarily cruel to Floyd Patterson. More, he behaved badly with Frazier as well, talking about how ugly he was, and calling him an Uncle Tom. It was ugly stuff, mean and gratuitous. The hype of the fight hardly needed it, and it was unacceptably demeaning to Frazier.

Frazier after all was a great fighter, but not in any other way as gifted as Ali, unable to play the game with the media (and thus the public), a man who could only be a target in the game Ali was orchestrating. He could never, because of his limitations, quite get out of the box that Ali had consigned him to. Ali was born to do as well with the media as with his opponents; he could always speak for himself, Frazier never could. But in doing this, in letting the game become too cruel, Ali diminished in the eyes of those of us who admired him and wanted him in every way to be worthy of his own greatness.

The truth was that Joe Frazier was never a Tom, and he was not a white man's fighter, nor in any way was he political. When Ali was barred from fighting by the U.S. District, Frazier had spoken up for him and his right to fight. Frazier's only politics were his fists. Fighting was his only ticket out of the cruelest kind of poverty.

Frazier was the son of sharecroppers in South Carolina, closer in his roots to slavery than Ali, darker of skin when that still mattered a great deal more in this country, less advantaged than Ali in all ways, most especially physically. All he had was his will, and courage, the willingness to pay an awful price to maximize the one ticket he had been given to get out of poverty.

Only in courage were he and Ali equals. Lest we forget, they fought three times and in each fight there was little definable difference between the winner and loser. In the first fight, in March 1971, Frazier won in 15 rounds in an awesome bout; when it was over both fighters had to go to the hospital, and Frazier was unable to fight for another ten months.

The second fight, some three years later, was won by Ali in 12 rounds. The third, in September 1975, when Ali was 33, and Frazier 31, was the famous Thrilla in Manilla, perhaps the greatest fight of all time. At the end of it, when Frazier had tried to answer the bell for the 15th round, Eddie Futch, the referee, had stopped him, ended the fight, and had cut off Frazier's gloves.

"Sit down, son, it's all over," Futch said. Then he added: "No one will ever forget what you did here today."

Nor in 26 years have we forgotten yet.

THANKS, SOCCER, SEE YOU IN FOUR YEARS

From ESPN.com, August 2, 2002

THIS IS SOMETHING OF A CONFESSION. IT HAS TAKEN ME some 36 years to realize it, but I am a fan of World Cup soccer, but not of soccer itself. For a long time I was loath to admit this. I realized that I was hooked on the World Cup one morning this year when I got up a little early first to walk the dogs and then to watch the early games, even though the U.S. team had already been eliminated—thus it was not pure Yankee chauvinism. But truth be told, I do it for the pleasure of the nationalism involved, not for the love of soccer. Nor do I think, as things currently stand, I can be cured. I like, within reason—no assassinations and really rough stuff—the nationalism at play at moments like this in World Cup years and Olympiad years, this time all those wacky Koreans cheering like mad, and trying to get even for what happened to one of their skaters during the Winter Olympics.

Bobby Charlton, since knighted, will be remembered for sobbing tears of joy when England eventually lifted the Jules Rimet Trophy as 1966 World Cup champs. My erratic relationship with the game—it is not love-hate, it is not love-love, and it is most surely not hate-hate, started some 36 years ago when I was working for the *New York Times* in Europe, I had just been expelled from Poland for writing articles that displeased the Warsaw regime (whose representatives had often complained to me about my referring to the government as a regime, which I, despite the frequent warnings, continued to do, and in fact still enjoy doing today). Since I had also been asked by the Prague regime—there it is again, that word, but they really were regimes—not to come back, that left of the three principal countries assigned to me, only Hungary where I was now welcome. And it was obviously time for me to go. Departing Warsaw (or deported from), I was stationed temporarily in Paris.

That was 1966, a World Cup year. I was, after more than a decade of covering civil rights in the U.S. South, Vietnam and the Congo, quite underemployed in Paris, and more than a little bored. So I had a lot of time to watch soccer and I watched at a small bar near the *Times* bureau on Rue Caumartin. There was a small black-and-white set there, and if on occasion when the reception was poor it looked like there were about 40 or 50 players on the field, it was nonetheless good fun. There were a number of us regulars who went there for the games, and there was an easy camaraderie for an American not easily attainable in Paris—especially because there was no U.S. team for me to root for. I could not be chauvinistic, and I don't think the French team was very good that year, so the locals could not be very chauvinistic either.

Nationalism, I assure you, mattered that year. Two games stand out in my memory from that championship run. In one, during the quarterfinals, the Hungarians played the Russians. This was still the height of the Cold War, only 10 years after the Russians had crushed the Hungarian insurgents with their tanks, in one of the cruelest instances in the era's big power suppression of a small nation. As such, the Russians were considered most properly at that moment, as much in Europe as in America, the thugs of the developed world. French intellectuals, apparently never having heard of the Gulag, might be more than a little soft on them, but in the bars and coffee houses, working-class people knew who they really were and how they held power.

The Russian team, as I recall, was favored, but the Hungarians played fearlessly and joyously, indeed exuberantly. They never thought defensively: they were aggressive, and they attacked again and again. It remains one of the best soccer games I have ever seen. Interestingly, in my memory, the Hungarians won—they remain eternally young and full of fire. And yet when I started writing this, Mary Buckheit of ESPN kindly checked the score for me, only to find that the Russians had in fact won 2–1. Sometimes you can win but lose, and lose but win, I guess.

The other game was the championship one, Britain against West Germany. Again nationalism mattered. It was 21 years after the end of World War II, and that might seem like a long time for today's sports generations, but for those of us then, given the historic quality of two wars, and given the particular darkness of German atrocities in the second one, the shadows of the past still hung heavily. It was, after all, a time when a great many upper middle class Americans loved the idea of buying a Volkswagen bug as a second car, but still agonized over spending money on it and thus sending money to Germany—and we are talking about a VW, not a Mercedes.

That made it very easy to root for Britain, especially because, as I recall, the Germans were favored and played a tough but methodical game. The Brits were very good that day, and they won, as I recall, on a disputed goal by Geoff Hurst. But I had liked the idea of the best teams from all over the world gathering to play for a soccer championship, and playing on national teams.

And it has stayed that way. I like checking out national characteristics as reflected by playing styles—the great truth about national clichés, that is, the easy broad judgments we make about the national characteristics of other countries (if not our own), is that they are all unfair, and they are all generalizations, but they are also more often than not true. The Brazilian team is likely to be more expansive and athletic; the German team more stolid. The Germans are less likely to make mistakes, but they are also less likely to play with flair. The Italians will play like, well, Italians. Then there is the rise of the African teams—an intriguing subject for someone like me who has watched the coming of black athletes in this country, and who was himself a correspondent in the Congo in 1961 and 1962. At what point will the coaching—and the diet—be good enough for some of the African teams to rise to their rightful place in the world's athletic order? I wonder. A few years ago—I think it was in 1990, the Cameroon team played with great exuberance and virtuosity, and terrified a number of the more phlegmatic, European teams.

So the World Cup is always good fun, perhaps even more so because now the U.S. team is better, and on an ascent, and the question for someone like me, with a bit of a sociological–cultural bent, is how much our new immigration patterns, some legal, some illegal, have changed our athletic pool, and enriched our soccer feeder system. We know in addition to that source that any number of private day schools now favor soccer; in the middle class and upper middle class, it's the soccer moms (now seen by political consultants as a definable political entity, once Republican because of basic economics and the prejudices of their husbands and their parents, but now swing Democratic because of their feelings on abortion and other women's issues) who do not want their sons to play football, and want them to play soccer instead. (The price of damage on a soccer field is more likely to be a twisted knee, but not $10,000 in dental work.) So there are two intriguing sources of talent—the newest immigrants who brought the game with them, and some of the children of our more established families, who being schizophrenic, play soccer during the week, but watch football on television on Saturday and Sunday.

So here's my problem—and this is my confessional. I like the World Cup, but when it's over, I'm gone. The game itself doesn't hold me. It should, but it doesn't. It's wonderful when two great teams are battling late in a big game and the score is tied. But that happens all too rarely. I remember some years ago when the World Cup was to be played in the United States and there was a great deal of talk about the fact this was going to do it, was going to put soccer over the top as a popular sport here. And, of course, it didn't happen. People were enthralled by the World Cup, and then very much like me, they went back to their old ways when it was over: baseball, football, basketball, tennis, golf, and, of course, stock car racing.

Now, I know what I'm going to say is heresy to traditional soccer lovers, those who know the game well, the true aficionados, and that they will put the blame on me and others like me. They will think it's our fault for not being better fans, and perhaps they're right. But I think the problem is the game itself—or more specifically, the rules of the game. Very simply, the rules favor the defense against the offense much too much, and they take the game's best players and limit their offensive ability. It allows mediocre players from mediocre teams to bunch up and reduce the possibilities of artistry from the game's best players. A mediocre team can lay back, keep a game close against a more exciting, more talented team, and hope for a lucky score to win. Or at least a score that implied a boring game was close. It's as if Michael Jordan arrived in basketball, and there was no 24-second clock, and opposing teams could keep the score close by simply holding the ball. I am hardly alone in this—my colleague Tony Kornheiser wrote of, I think, Brazil early in the championship game, holding in his words, "an insurmountable 1–0 lead."

Despite restrictive rules, Ronaldo flashed his artistry by scoring twice in Brazil's 2–0 victory over Germany in the 2002 World Cup title game. It's important to understand that if in a sport like this, I'm something of a beginner as a fan, it doesn't mean I don't get it. Tennis is in many ways equally alien to me, but I understood very quickly the quality of the Connors-Borg-McEnroe matches, what their respective strengths, both physical and psychological were. The camera is a very quick teacher, and most big-time network sports have announcers who are exceptionally good at explaining the intricacies of the sport. Many of us watch with friends who fill us in on points a newcomer might otherwise miss. I don't have to be an aficionado of golf to understand what Tiger Woods represents, especially on the last round of a big tournament, when he's only a stroke or two behind the leader. After all, I've seen what Jordan does to his would-be competition in the fourth quarter of big games.

The world changes. Television changes what the potential audience is (it already has)—it opens up Europe and much of the rest of the world for basketball, and it potentially opened up this country for soccer. But it never really happened as a spectator sport here. Expectations for those sitting at home change too, people have less time, and want more excitement when they watch. More and more competing forms of entertainment are out there. I realize those who love the game love it the way it has always been, and I am sure they disagree with me and they probably think changing the rules to juice the offense is the first true sign of the apocalypse still to come, but the truth is, I think, without some kind of dramatic change, the game is less artistic than it should be, and less fun, and we see less of the pure talent of the best players. So until they change, I bid farewell to soccer until the next Olympiad, or World Cup.

Olympiad XXVIII

From *Vanity Fair*, September 2004

I STILL CHERISH AND ADMIRE THE OLYMPIC IDEAL.

I know it's tarnished these days, in a world of big-money rewards, too much hype, and too much doping, but it's an ideal nonetheless. It still rings true to thousands of athletes from all over the world, especially those who have not been corrupted by the modern sports-entertainment world. In the more arcane sports, an athlete devotes 8 or 10 years of his or her life with single-minded obsession, waiting for that one luminous moment when he or she can compete against the best in the entire world. For these men and women the Olympics is the one chance to make their otherwise obscure sports become, thanks to the magic of global television, momentarily less obscure, perhaps even the focus of the entire world.

I did not much like the Dream Team of the 1992 Barcelona Olympics. To me it was the opposite of the Olympic ideal. It was (allegedly) good for America (we were still No. 1 in basketball, our sport—thank God), good for basketball, most particularly international basketball, and certainly good for the N.B.A., but it seemed to me to violate the Olympic spirit. It was not just that we were sending professionals to play on an amateur field—the Eastern-bloc countries had been doing that for years. Rather, it was the idea of celebrating already celebrated athletes, whose real sponsors were the new nation-states of sports-equipment empires. The players themselves were already rich and famous beyond any acceptable level, and their attitudes all too often seemed to shout out that they did not need the Olympics, the Olympics needed them. That rare moment in the spotlight that Olympic exposure gives most athletes had for them already taken place again and again; they had lived their careers in the spotlight, and had come to believe that, though it had made them rich, the spotlight was essentially an intrusion in their lives. They were too grand to stay in the Olympic Village, unable to mix easily with the other athletes, with whom their only real contact was signing autographs for them. The Dream Team at the Olympics seems to reflect an America made immodest, an America of which I have had a growing sense in recent years. In truth, I got no pleasure from their victory, and I wished that they had all stayed at home.

I have written about the Olympics a few times in the past, and when doing so I have always chosen to spend time with athletes from the periphery—men and women from those sports not favored by the television cameras and by the new entertainment culture. Twenty years ago I spent a wonderful season with America's male single-scull rowers, about whom I wrote in my 1985 book, *The Amateurs*. I figured that, as men who had devoted their lives to something that the rest of the society largely ignored, they would be superb athletes, and that they would be both interesting and accessible. I was right on all counts. They welcomed me into their world; their phone numbers, if they had phones, were listed in the local directories; they had no public-relations people; and they were as curious about my project as I was about their personal and professional journeys, which had taken them to the Olympic sculling trials in Princeton, New Jersey, and then to the 1984 Los Angeles Olympics, where they remained hypeless in the land of hype.

When, eight years ago, the editor of this magazine asked me to write an article to accompany a photographic portfolio of athletes bound for Atlanta, I decided to travel with America's fencers, and once again had a marvelous time. At the moment when I joined them they were in Rome en route to a World Cup event, living on, as far as I could tell, about $8 a day apiece, which included both room and board. Yet they were loving every moment of it. They were smart, curious, and talented, and it was fun to meet them and travel with them, and fun to write about them.

So, when I think about the Olympics at their best, I think about athletes from the more arcane sports, people who see the Olympics as a rare, glorious, shimmering moment in the spotlight. I think of Alberto Juantorena, the Cuban 400- and 800-meter runner who won two gold medals at the 1976 Olympics. One of the greatest athletes in the world, he was seen far too infrequently on the international stage.

And I think of the legendary runner Wilma Rudolph. Probably my first great Olympic experience came in 1960 when I watched her win three gold medals. Women's track is not as big in this country as it is in some parts of the world, where fans are infinitely more knowledgeable about the sport and its records, and where ordinary track-and-field meets regularly sell out. Here it is secondary to men's track, which itself is never quite big-time unless a rare superstar like Carl Lewis is competing. During the Cold War, Olympic track became temporarily more important than usual, I suppose, because the head-to-head competition with the Soviets and their Eastern-bloc satellites seemed to matter, as if it directly reflected the arms race. If we won fewer medals than the Soviet Union, did that mean that we were over the hill as a superpower, that we had gotten soft as a people? Had the Soviets, despite their failures in so many areas, managed to raise a tougher breed of athlete (read: would-be soldiers)? And were the East Germans, with all their medals and their ferocious sense of purpose, the society of the future? (No, it turned out. Just an overly mechanistic, rather authoritarian society, much given to doping and other practices that did no one any good in the long run.)

Wilma Rudolph burst onto the scene in 1960, and she was magnificent, not only a great runner but also a great story. Her father was a railroad porter, her mother a maid for rich, white families. A strikingly beautiful young woman, Wilma, one of 22 children, had had to overcome a series of illnesses, including polio. By chance I had met her before she became famous. I was a young reporter for the Nashville *Tennessean* then, all of 22 years old myself, and one day, just before the 1956 Melbourne Olympics, I was sent by my editors to the track-and-field complex at Tennessee State University. It was a black college, and Ed Temple, the coach there, already on his way to becoming a legend in the sport, apparently had a great relay team made up of four young, black women who were going to compete in the upcoming Olympics.

Ms. Rudolph was 15 or 16 and still in high school then. She was not yet physically imposing. Though she later became tall and powerful, at the time I think she weighed less than 90 pounds. I suspect that this was the first time she had ever encountered a reporter from a metropolitan newspaper. It was all very primitive in media terms; there were no public-relations people present that day. Ed Temple seemed to think that she was on her way to becoming a great athlete, and that she might have a shot at a medal in the 200 meters. She was also going to run a leg in the 4-by-100 relay. I knew little about women's sports then, and Temple did much of the talking. What I remember most clearly is that when I filed my story back at the office I led with something to the effect that out at Tennessee State four remarkable young coeds were zeroing in on the 400-meter relay and were going to run in Melbourne. When I handed in the piece, there was a great internal debate at the paper over the phrasing in the lead, and eventually the "coed" reference was taken out—for though we were one of the most liberal papers in the South and very aggressive in covering civil rights, a decision had been made at the top that young black women could not be called coeds. At least not yet.

I watched the Melbourne Olympics, and Ms. Rudolph did all right. She had clearly not yet grown into her body. She did not medal in the 200, but got a bronze on the relay team. I did not cover her again, did not keep track of her progress, as a wiser, more experienced reporter, aware of a great story about to happen, might have. In 1960, when she reached stardom, I was busy covering the civil rights movement in Nashville and had not followed her ascent as a dominant runner. But in Rome that year she simply exploded into the national and international consciousness. She won gold in the 100 meters, the 200 meters, and the 4-by-100 relay, for which she ran the anchor leg, took the baton in fourth place, and brought it home to win.

It was a dazzling exhibition, and I can still remember my pleasure in it. More than the three medals, there was something special about her, I thought, an elegance and grace. The Europeans seemed to sense her extraordinary qualities even before her fellow countrymen did. I have a memory of the French journalists starting sometime that week to call her "the black gazelle." Black power and the "black is beautiful" part of the civil rights movement were then still to come, but that summer Ms. Rudolph provided a startling preview of the idea that black was beautiful, as did her fellow Olympian the young Cassius Clay. For one shining moment, in my mind, in a world which was not yet overloaded with hype, the Olympics had a truth and authenticity—the Olympic ideal lived—and I have watched ever since, hoping to see the next Wilma Rudolph.

PALS

It soon became obvious that we had hit a great river with giant fish at an almost perfect moment. Even fishermen of no distinction, like Steadman and me, caught five or six fish a day. The average size was fifteen pounds. More important, it was not just the catching; it was the ongoing pleasure of it all.

MEN WITHOUT WOMEN

GQ,
September 2002

He Got a Shot in the NBA, and It Went In

From the *New York Times*, February 7, 1999

IT BEGAN ABOUT A YEAR AGO AS THE MOST CASUAL KIND OF palship, one formed in a New York gym. We were working out next to each other on stationary bicycles. He came over and said that he understood that I was working on a book on Michael. Michael, of course, is Michael Jordan. He knew Michael a bit, he volunteered, because he was a Carolina guy, and had played ball there a very long time ago. Perhaps he could help with the access. That did not strike me as likely. Somehow he did not look connected to the high-powered modern-day world of basketball. Instead, he looked quite ordinary, just another man in his 60's, a little shorter than me, perhaps 5 feet 9 inches or 5-10. His name, he said, was Tommy Kearns, and for a long time the name meant nothing to me; during most of the ensuing three or four months of our regular conversations I did not think of him by his name, but rather as the pleasant, helpful Carolina alumnus from the gym, a man who was, judging by the sweat on his workout clothes and the slightly chunky outline of his body, working even harder than I to keep his weight down. In the modern age when a player is usually at least 6-5, and with a body fat content of under 7 percent, he did not look like a player; that was emphasized by the fact that the New York Liberty players practice at our gym and from time to time as we talked we would look at the sleek, powerful bodies of young female professionals, all of them, it seemed, stronger and taller than we were.

But our palship progressed. We both liked to talk basketball. He was smart and likable, and he clearly knew the inside of the Carolina program extremely well, who was in and who was out. Dean Smith was Dean to him, yet he clearly was not a name dropper. After a few weeks during the early months of the legwork on my book, he began to guide me through the intricacies of the Carolina hierarchy, and at a time when I was still struggling to gain access to Smith himself, he tried to be helpful.

The Carolina basketball world, it should be noted, is tightly bonded and largely sealed off from the outside world: a cult, Chuck Daly, the former Penn and Detroit coach once told me, a good cult instead of a bad one, but a cult nonetheless. Outsiders, particularly writers, are likely to remain outsiders forever. Kearns was clearly in the club; he played golf with Smith at Pinehurst each summer with many of the best-known Carolina alumni, a kind of Dean Smith Invitational. That is very much an insider's game; Carolina coaches, Carolina alumni and a few trusted outsiders who had treated Carolina players well, like Jerry West, Rod Thorn, Kevin Loughery and Daly, were the ones asked to play.

Our friendship progressed over the year. We talked about the game, and about Michael, and Kearns tried, unsuccessfully, to get me to try spinning, a hyped-up form of stationary bike riding. Then, late in the season when I was checking out the Carolina basketball brochure, looking up some of James Worthy's statistics, I happened to stumble into some of Kearns's records. Tommy Kearns, it turned out, had been a third-team all-American in the mid-50's, but even more, he had been the playmaker—that was before they were known as point guards—on the Carolina team that in 1957 had gone undefeated and beaten Kansas and Wilt Chamberlain for the national championship.

I mentioned this to him with some measure of apology the next time we spoke at the gym: "You really *were* a player, weren't you?" And with that he started telling me a very good basketball story from a very different era. He had been in the vanguard of New York City kids whom Frank McGuire had recruited back in the mid-50's and put on his reverse underground railroad to North Carolina, as part of a plan to bring winning basketball to a school (and region) which, in basketball terms at least, was largely an underdeveloped area. Basketball was not yet a truly national sport and the game was still more often than not a city game—played best, it was believed, in New York. But it was a bad time for the college sport in New York. The point-fixing scandals of the early 50's had destroyed the sport locally. Once-powerful programs had been closed down. McGuire himself had coached at St. John's before seeking a kind of sanctuary at Chapel Hill.

After landing at Chapel Hill, McGuire had almost immediately started to import his own boys. He was the son of a New York cop and he was good at recruiting city boys; if in Carolina he had something of a strange accent, and if he seemed a little flashy, very much the outlander, then neither of these things was true when he went after kids in the boroughs. He was very good at visiting kids in their homes, usually accompanied by someone very successful from the same neighborhood who vouched for him. He liked to do most of his recruiting in the homes—where he could make a better read on the lifestyle and the ambitions of the parents and therefore tailor his pitch accordingly—rather than in fancy restaurants where the parents might be uncomfortable. He visited the home of Tommy Kearns, who was a big-time schoolboy star in New York, some four or five times. In those days the Catholic high schools held tryouts for scholarships—the players the coaches wanted got them, and Kearns had played for Lou Carnesecca at St. Ann's, a traditional powerhouse; he had been an all-city playmaking guard, quick, scrappy, and smart with the ball, with a good outside shot. Under his direction, St. Ann's in 1954, his senior year, had been national Catholic school champion.

McGuire badly wanted Kearns, and the fact that the senior Kearns was also a cop living in the Bronx did not hurt—it was an easy house in which to make a read. The recruiting sessions were, Kearns remembered, largely devoted to McGuire's attempts to overcome the doubts of Kearns's parents about sending their son to so alien a part of the country. After all, Chapel Hill was in the heart of the Bible Belt South, and Tom Kearns Sr. was wary of what would happen to a good Irish Catholic boy down there. But, Kearns remembered, McGuire was a masterly recruiter, and if you listened to him, the conversion was going to be quite different—he and his boys were going to convert the Protestants to Catholicism, and do it through the Trojan horse of basketball. And so in time Kearns became one of four New York City kids McGuire recruited for his class of 1958, fittingly enough, all of them Catholic. Already waiting for them down there, a year ahead of them in school, was a young man of consummate talent who was a great pure shooter, Lennie Rosenbluth, also a New York boy, who was Jewish. That would make their team essentially all New York, four Catholics and a Jew: Kearns; Pete Brennan from St. Augustine's in Brooklyn; Bobby (no kin to Billy, who came after him) Cunningham, from All Hallows in the Bronx; Joe Quigg from St. Francis Prep in Brooklyn; and Rosenbluth from James Monroe in the Bronx.

Their arrival marked the beginning of big-time basketball at Chapel Hill. They knew the game, they were well ahead of the national curve in basketball savvy, they knew how to shoot and set picks and make cuts and, above all, how to pass. They compensated for a lack of height by deft defensive positioning. Freshmen could not play for the varsity in those days, but the Carolina freshmen were undefeated and often beat the varsity in practice. As sophomores, they played regularly and went 19-7, and then in their junior year everything tumbled right and they went 32-0. The heart of the team, as the *Raleigh News and Observer* later noted, was Kearns. In the National Collegiate Athletic Association semifinal, they beat Michigan State in three overtimes. Then, playing in Kansas City, Mo., they had to play against a Kansas team led by the seemingly unstoppable Wilt Chamberlain. They were ranked No. 1 in the country because they were unbeaten, and Kansas, which had lost once, was ranked No. 2, but there was no doubt which team was favored; it was Kansas by about 8 points, playing virtually at home and led by the mighty Wilt.

Before the game, McGuire, wanting to fire his players up and wanting to end any possibility of intimidation, had turned to Kearns, the smallest player on his starting team, and said, "Tommy, you're not afraid to jump center against Wilt, are you?" and Kearns had shouted out, "Hell no!" So he had jumped center, and Wilt had got the tip, but having Kearns jump center had set a tone of Tar Heel cockiness. ("My wife still says that jumping center against Wilt in the national championship game is the defining moment in my life, the one sure thing which will be in my obituary," Kearns said the other day.) The message had been given, Carolina was not afraid of Kansas, and it eventually won, again in triple overtime. The game, little underdog Carolina against awesome Kansas, had caught the imagination of the country and the region; from that time on, noted the writer Jonathan Yardley, who was about to enter Carolina, basketball became not merely a sport, but a religion in the area—in that sense, what McGuire had promised the senior Kearns proved to be true.

Their next year was not so successful. Rosenbluth was gone, and Quigg was injured and they did not do so well. The irony of a great athlete's story—deeds once so important to so many people, thousands cheering, but deeds now largely distant memories for all but those few who actually played, men who had regained anonymity in their lives—struck me forcefully as he finished the story. He had told this story outside the locker room of our gym and as we were about to part, he said, almost casually, "I played in the N.B.A., you know." He paused and added: "Briefly. I still hold the record for the best field-goal percentage. One for one." And then he was gone. Not sure whether to believe him or not, I went home and took out my trusty

National Basketball Association record book, and there it was, a great line: one game, one field goal attempted, one field goal made.

It was a statistical line for the Walter Mitty in all of us—and I thought based on that we ought to have lunch so I could hear the rest of the story, and so we met again. In 1958, when he had graduated from Chapel Hill, there were only eight teams in the fledgling N.B.A.—with 10 players each. The year that Tommy Kearns came out, the league was just beginning to change and there was the early surfacing of black players—Elgin Baylor went first in the draft that year. Even more important, Syracuse, which took Kearns in the fourth round, took a seemingly unknown guard from Marshall named Hal Greer in the third. Kearns, who had played in a number of all-star games, had never even heard of Greer. Basketball drafting and scouting was hardly big time, and Tommy Kearns had never, as far as he knew, been scouted. It was several weeks after the draft when a letter arrived from the Syracuse owner, Danny Biasone, setting Kearns's salary at $7,500 if he made the team. Nothing in those days was guaranteed.

The numbers, he soon realized at preseason camp, were going to be tough given the limited 10-man rosters and the need to keep the payroll down. The veteran guards on the team were Larry Costello, Al Bianchi and Paul Seymour, then 30 years old and a 12-year veteran. The question was whether Seymour would be a coach or a playing coach. If he only coached there was one more spot on the roster. But Biasone was not a wealthy man—his money came from the ownership of bowling alleys, and so all economies were critical. The competition was tough: the coach himself if he chose to play; Costello, who was very, very quick; Greer, clearly an ascending star ("a little bigger, a little quicker and a little bit better shooter than me"); and Bianchi. Some teammates thought it was going to come down to a choice between Greer and Kearns, and that was ominous to Kearns.

Kearns had a good camp, but in one of the last preseason games he came down off balance from a rebound and hurt his ankle and it cost him several weeks. When he was finally ready to play, it was in a game against Cincinnati. Syracuse, as Kearns remembers, was well ahead in the second half when Seymour sent him in: in time, the ball had come to him on the outside ("four or five feet outside the foul circle") and he had taken his shot and it went in. "It would be a 3 in today's game," he noted proudly. All told, he had played seven minutes. The next day Seymour made his decision. He called Kearns in and said: "Tommy—it's been great. We really like you and your game. But I've decided to stay on and play, and so we have to let you go." That was it. There were no agents to call European teams in those days; he was gone that day. Hal Greer, who came in with him, went on to play for 15 seasons (39,788 regular-season minutes to Kearns's 7), becoming a Hall of Fame player who averaged 19.2 points a game. Kearns played for a time in the Eastern League and then went back and married a girl who had gone to Duke, and worked in Greensboro for 10 years as an investment banker before returning to New York. He was, he told me, a man with no regrets: he had got a great education from a great school, he had helped win a national championship, and in the record book it still shows that he was the best shooter ever in the N.B.A. You could look it up.

MEN WITHOUT WOMEN

From *GQ*, September 2002

ON THIS FEBRUARY MORNING, MY FRIEND DICK STEADMAN and I looked more like little Michelin Men than fly fishermen. We were fishing for giant brown trout in Tierra del Fuego, on the Río Grande near the southern tip of Patagonia, and had layered ourselves in lightweight long johns, chinchilla long johns, sweaters, Gore-Tex waders, windbreakers, river boots and mudguards. Fly-fishing should be graceful, but there was nothing elegant about our movements on this day. No decent bureau of tourism would have wanted to photograph us—the fish perhaps, but not us.

We were at the bottom of the American hemisphere, 7,500 miles from home. If you go any farther south, you get penguins. What makes the Río Grande worth the time and cost of the journey and the stay at the lodge is that it offers the rarest of fishing possibilities—to catch the giant brown trout, which, being anadromous, live in the ocean and return to freshwater at this time of year to spawn. They eat a far richer diet than their freshwater kin and can easily reach up to thirty pounds.

It was the second time that Steadman and I, along with our friend Richard Berlin, had come here: A year ago, we had fished the same river at roughly the same time of year, but it had been much harder for us. The water had been high, the wind had been very stiff, and it had been extremely difficult for even some of the more skilled fishermen to reach many of the pools; for Steadman and me, locked as we are in a kind of perpetual apprenticeship as fly fishermen, it had been exceptionally hard. A year ago, when we would return from our twice-a-day outings the first thing I would do was hit the Advil bottle. Nonetheless, I had caught about ten fish during the week, and the largest had been twenty-two pounds. A bad week here is like a superlative week anywhere else.

This year, by contrast, we had been told that all the stars were perfectly aligned. The runoff from the mountains had been marginal. The water was way down, from high on our chests in 2001 to knee level most of the time. We would be able to reach any pool we wanted. There were lots of fish in the river, we had been told, and they were big. Our week may well be the best in years, we thought. And yet, and yet . . . I would believe it when it happened.

But even if we fished under optimum conditions, it would not be easy. On this first morning, Steadman and I, despite all the predictions of easy success, were being skunked. The wind was well over thirty miles an hour, and I was not able to cast easily. I tried casting right-handed, but I kept hooking myself on the back. Fortunately, I am partially ambidextrous and can cast left-handed, and that helped, but only so much. It was a hard morning, and I was wondering by late morning whether I was doomed, whether there was some kind of mark on me—and on Dick Steadman as well—whether we simply had tried to go above our proper station in the universe of fishing by coming here and the fishing gods were telling us, accumulated American Airlines miles or not, that we did not deserve to fish here.

For there was a certain hard truth here, one that no fisherman likes to admit, especially in print: I am not a particularly good fly fisherman. My grade, if I am being generous, is a C+. I handle light spinning gear with considerable skill, but I remain embryonic at fly-fishing—I came to it late in life, and my schedule is not built around it. I handle a fly rod every two or three years for a few days at a time, and just about when I get into a rhythm my fishing time is over and I regress. Moreover, I am reluctant to bring the obsessive quality that drives so much of the rest of my life to my time fishing. Far more than most of my colleagues, when I am on a river I am guide driven, reluctant to be pulled into the aficionados' discussion about hatches and choices of flies. I fear trading innocence for excellence, that in the process some of the sheer pleasure of the doing will be lost, although I am aware that my attitude remains something of an affront to the purist.

Dick Steadman is a more serious student. He has been my friend for thirty-two years. We have fished together with questionable results in all sorts of lodges—Panama, Costa Rica, Venezuela—over the years. We met in 1970, when I was working on *The Best and the Brightest* and he had just finished a tour in the Pentagon as a deputy assistant secretary of defense. We became immediate friends, and for about twenty years we both had houses in Nantucket and owned a boat together and would fish two or three times a week for bluefish and striped bass. He is an uncommon man; I don't think I know anyone else who has so high a level of intelligence and yet is so grounded and so in control of his ego. He is one of those rare people who can always see the equities in any question, even when they go against their own interests.

Steadman's ability to command respect—instantly—from other men is like nothing I have ever seen. Normally, to do this a man has to have excelled at something other men admire—athletics, war— and has to be over six two. These things matter greatly to men, as do looks. I am convinced Robert Redford's appeal has always been greater to men than to women because he has the looks and the manner most of us would have liked to have had—and of course did not—when we were in high school, when these attitudes about how we should look and behave were indelibly set. Steadman, though very attractive, has no war record, did not command a battalion and was not a great athlete. He is about five eight. Little of this helps him on the normal Richter Scale of male charisma. Yet he possesses a palpable sense of command, purpose and grace, and there was no doubt in my mind that if our group was in some kind of crisis during this trip, it would be only a matter of minutes before he became, without anyone saying anything, our leader.

Steadman and I would have been good friends without fishing, but we are much closer because of it. What we were hoping to do this week was to put an end to the bane of our fishing lives, what we call the Week-Before Syndrome. This refers to our tendency to arrive at some fabled lodge the week or month after it had had the greatest week for fishing ever and the fish had all gone elsewhere. The manager of the lodge is always apologetic when he breaks the sad news of this to us—it is not his fault, and certainly not our fault, but nonetheless, he implies, if we'd had the good sense to come at almost any other time, the quality of the fishing would have been guaranteed. The truth is, it is hard for him to bring himself to say this, but they have never had a week this poor in the lodge's history. Would we, by the way, he adds, like to see the lodge's register to see how many fish were caught last week, month or year?

When I was a younger man, I thought of fishing as an end in itself; you went fishing because you wanted—needed—to catch fish. The more and bigger fish you caught, the better fisherman you presumably were and the better man you were. Now, much later in life, in a world greatly changed from that of my young manhood, with gender lines much more blurred in most professional and social situations than in my youth, with fishing still a primarily male pursuit (or at least the way my friends and I pursue it), I am intrigued by the relationship of fishing and friendship and the social dynamics of these all-male trips. I have found that the men I know talk more openly and candidly with one another about personal things on these trips than they do back home.

On most of my fishing expeditions, the people I have gone with have all been close friends. This trip would be somewhat different: There were ten of us in our larger group, and we were only loosely connected. We had been put together by my friend Richard Berlin, and most of us tended to have a link with him rather than with one another. Thus there was among us as men, as it had always been, even when we were boys, the hidden, unannounced matter of male shyness and uncertainty: Would we be good enough at this, or would we somehow fall short of our expectations and the expectations of others? As such, the social dynamics were intriguing: Would the social order be dominated by the man who catches the most or the largest fish, or would other factors emerge? Would we be more macho than normal because we were in a new and uncertain social setting, doing something that some of us were not that confident of? Would we be unusually successful on the water, and if we were, would that create an unspoken competition in terms of the number and size of fish being caught? I had seen that happen on occasion, if not in our group then in other groups at lodges we have stayed at—men becoming truly unacceptable in their behavior toward others because they have had several very good (or very bad) days on the water. Or would it, if we are unusually successful, make us more comfortable with ourselves and thus with one another? I looked forward to seeing how all of this would play out on this trip.

The new social order surfaced at the end of the first day of fishing. Jock Miller, a newcomer to the group, had caught two huge fish, each more than twenty-seven pounds, and he was, not surprisingly, in a somewhat expansive mood at dinner. He is an old friend of Berlin's; they had known each other as boys, when their fathers worked for the same New York company. Miller is a truly sweet man, and he would emerge by the end of the week as the gentlest—or kindest—man in our group. We, of course, did not know this yet. What we knew was that he had caught not just one but the two biggest fish of the day.

Then, in a celebratory mood, he talked about a competition he'd had with his father when he was a boy. At issue had been the question of who had caught more fish in terms of poundage over an entire summer. On the last day of the summer, trailing his father slightly, Miller had slipped a three-pound stone into one of his fish as it was weighed. That had put him ahead in the competition. We were shocked—shocked!—to hear this confession. We were, after all, on a fishing trip, men behaving like boys, and so we acted accordingly. What Miller did with this self-mocking story would be momentarily hard on him but exceptionally good for our group dynamics.

Just by chance, a few minutes before, a friend of mine named Ken Aretsky, who owns three restaurants in New York, had volunteered his story of being arrested for selling Cuban cigars at Patroon, his midtown-Manhattan steak house. The charge was trading with the enemy. For a time, Ken faced the likelihood of a year in jail. In the end, he dealt with this threat with considerable grace and came to regard it as an experience not without its upside (part of his probation was training young people from underclass neighborhoods for work in the restaurant business). It was also a quite terrifying experience. A good many of his friends, myself included, thought the passion with which the U.S. government went after him was truly scabrous, given modern-day geopolitics and the open way many powerful politicians from both sides of the aisle, as well as leading corporate executives, somehow manage to have access to Cuban cigars while also helping to sustain the embargo against Cuba. If anything, these thoughts were certainly reinforced after September 11: Did this country have so few real threats against it that its prosecutorial energies could be used so carelessly against something that presented so little threat to the public good?

By chance both these stories—the Cuban-cigar story and the stone-in-the-fish story—were told near the end of the dinner, when several members of the group were about to light up cigars, Cubans, of course, bought a day earlier in Buenos Aires. The juxtaposition of the two stories became irresistible for us as a group. Almost immediately, someone asked which was the greater crime: weighing a fish with a rock hidden inside to win a family fishing competition or selling Cuban cigars in your steak house? A vote was called for. Suddenly, Jock Miller was facing a hanging jury: twelve men, all of them, of course, fishermen who had traveled a great distance to be here, at least six of whom were serious cigar smokers. It was, given the democratic nature of the group, to be a secret ballot. Fat chance of an acquittal here. Miller was judged to be the greater offender by a 12–0 count. This was a bit hard on Jock at first—later he had to be convinced it had in fact been in good fun, that we were not angry that his first two fish were so much bigger than ours (well, it is quite possible that this information did factor in a bit in our vote) and that, most important of all, he helped us to bond.

Suddenly, instead of being a group of several smaller factions, we started to come together as one, a raucous, rather joyous group. There was no homage to the man who had caught the biggest fish— if anything, his catch made him something of a target. Everyone seemed infinitely more comfortable with the others; it was as if we had been together in the past.

This was what Richard Berlin, our group leader, wanted. He and I have been friends for eight years. His daughter and mine were in the same class at boarding school and were among suitemates who, on the first parents weekend, decided that since they were all friends their parents should be friends as well. As such they took us all to a dreadful Chinese restaurant in exurban Boston, where we were all on our most proper behavior—all political and religious and other potentially controversial subjects went unmentioned.

At that dinner, Richard—exuberant, joyous, a true man-child— emerged as the glue that held a number of couples together in a loosely formed group for the next four years; he is a man able to get across the normal borders of reserve in embryonic social situations—no small skill, I think. He is, I soon learned, a man of wonderful enthusiasms, chief among them fishing. I like to fish, too. But there is a difference: I fish; he, by contrast, is a fisherman. Richard technically is the founding partner of a New England–based insurance brokerage, but in truth fishing is at the core of his being. Much of his life seems to be governed by the habits, moods and peculiarities of various prime game fish; as they migrate, so does he.

Our gear reflected our relative fishing status. Both last year and this year, I arrived at the lodge with one rod, one reel (albeit two spools) and about thirty flies; he arrived with four rods ("only four," he noted later, "all eight weight"), five reels ("but eleven spools") and 1,200 flies ("but I gave away at least 200"). He owns every fishing toy and gizmo ever sold in any tackle shop, he knows every good trip to every distant trout or salmon river and every worthy lodge, and he knows the guides—he would invite Alberto Molina Gomez, his guide from Argentina, to fish for salmon in Nova Scotia with him later this year. He spoke a language of wooly buggers, bitch creek nymphs and gold bead prince nymphs and 200-grain and 300-grain lines, a very different language than the one I use. When he started out in the morning to fish the Río Grande, he looked very much like one of our Special Forces men ready to take down an Al Qaeda base camp.

In the world of Richard Berlin, the pleasures of fishing must be shared to be enjoyed, and his enthusiasms have a certain communal quality. As such, there are absolutes: You *have* to go to Argentina, all the way down to the tip of Patagonia, to a lodge called the María Behety, because it is the best lodge there, with the *greatest trout fishing* in the world, and the fish are the *biggest* trout in history, and late January and early February are the best two weeks, because the fish are just coming in from the ocean and there are *lots and lots* of them. Some run as big as *thirty pounds!* Two years ago, when we were making plans to come here, he was nervous that I might pull out. Just to make sure I did not, and to be sure I had the right equipment, he called the Fly Shop, which runs the trip, and ordered all the clothing and fishing gear for me, using, of course, my credit cards. It became quite clear to me that if our friendship was to last, I was obligated to go to Patagonia. The remarkable thing about Richard as a group leader, Ken Aretsky noticed, was that his only concern was how well the rest of us did, not how well he did. His particular anxiety this week was that the less experienced members of our team, like Steadman and me, would do better than last year and that the newcomers would do well.

He and I did not seem, early on, destined to be close friends. Richard Berlin, I thought at the time of our first meeting, Richard Berlin. The name struck something of a bell. I remembered the early Vietnam days, when I was a skeptical reporter in Saigon and among the people making my life a small hell were the Hearst writers of that time, who seemed to want to use me for target practice and to distort everything I was writing for the *New York Times*. These attacks were quite systematic. Some years later, when I was working on one of my books at the Lyndon Johnson presidential library, I came upon a number of memos to and from the Johnson people about Vietnam and their press problems. One of them said that Dick Berlin, the top Hearst official and a close ally of the Johnson administration's, would take care of the dissident reporters in Saigon. A few months into our friendship, I asked Richard what his father had done. "Oh," he answered, "he was a top executive for Hearst." Still, the political struggles of the father should not be passed on to the son, and we have become very good friends over the years.

If the first day started slowly for me, there was redemption during the evening session. The evening shift also started slowly. I had a few strikes and landed one very good fish of about eighteen pounds around 9 P.M. Although Steadman and I were both working hard, the results seemed marginal. Last cast was scheduled for 10:30. The moon started to come up about 10:05, and then came the fish, obviously summoned by the moon. The water exploded. All of a sudden, I was on fish after fish. Every cast resulted in a strike. I hooked a big one, busted off it, hooked another and brought it in, a seventeen-pounder, and then on my next cast caught a fifteen-pounder. I lost one of comparable size and then caught one more of sixteen pounds. They were all ferocious—and they challenged all my skills, especially fishing in the high wind in the dark. Steadman had comparable luck. Our jinx was broken. For once we had arrived on exactly the right week.

Back at the lodge, the group seemed unusually compatible. Last year had been very different: Of the twelve people at the lodge, three of us—Berlin, Steadman and I—had come together and formed a small group, but the larger group had had no central social focus or order. There had been a couple of Brits, as well as the Howertons, John and Jason, an attractive father-son team from California, and some people who were not connected to any of the others. We had all gotten on reasonably well, and near the end the Howertons had seemed to blend in with our threesome, but we hadn't had any sense of community. The conversation at night had been pleasant enough but hardly rich, and we had remained somewhat shy and tentative with one another for the week.

Of the twelve in this year's group, ten of us were in some way or another Berlin connected. In the off-season, Richard had been in constant contact with the Howertons, and they'd been annexed to our group by E-mail and the sheer force of Richard's personality. They made an easy fit—John, it turns out, was droll and funny, and Jason, thirty years younger than most of us, was a wonderful athlete. I think the rest of us took an additional delight in seeing a father-son team so comfortable with each other. It was a reminder for some of us of the all too rare shared moments with our own fathers.

Richard was also determined to fill as many slots as he could with people who he felt would be amenable to the larger family he wanted to form. When two of his original choices had to drop out, it was not enough for just any fisherman merely to apply through the Fly Shop. He had to clear it with Berlin as well. A man named George Lee, who is a brilliant fisherman and a genuine eccentric, wanted to take one of the slots, but first he had to be screened by

Richard. If it was the equivalent of a job interview by phone, Lee was well prepared in advance by mutual friends as to what to say, since Berlin had just been through (1) a divorce and (2) a mild heart attack. "George, tell me a little about yourself," Richard had asked him. "I'm recently divorced, and I just had a heart attack," George said. "Well, George, I think we just might have a place for you," Richard said.

Among the others in our group of ten was Bob Kruse, a formidable figure and a friend of Berlin's from Dartmouth, a powerfully built man (he apparently captained every team at Andover before going on to college) who turned out to be a very good fisherman and who had worked as a charter captain in the Key West area for many years. Even better, he was smart and funny, with a uniquely rich laugh that seemed to ring through the lodge early in the morning when we went to bed and early in the morning when we got up. Before we met Bob, we had heard Berlin talk about him with his usual excitement; it sounded as if they had been fishing together twice a year since the day they'd left college. Instead it turned out— to my considerable surprise—that they had not seen each other in more than twenty-five years. This turned out not to be a problem: Bob, open and joyous, was perfect for our group.

Berlin, as group leader, added a number of colleagues, including his childhood friend Jock Miller. When there had been a last-minute vacancy, I had suggested Ken Aretsky, a longtime pal. Like Berlin, Aretsky is something of a fishaholic, and he has almost as many toys—he arrived with, among other things, a sixty-year-old classic bamboo rod and an antique fishing tote bag that looked like it was left over from the time of Zane Grey.

Ken was an immediate success with the others: He is a subtle man, an instinctive sociologist who reads people well—he had better be, running three restaurants in New York, where people's egos and wallets are often vastly greater than their internal comfort zones. He all too often hears the magic words from some million-aire and now billionaire disappointed with his table assignment, "Do you know who I am?," a phrase uttered not as a question but as a statement of fact. Over the years, I have come to understand that Ken knows all too well exactly who these people are; he often knows more about them than I suspect they know about them-selves, and this week his dissection of some of the more prominent but grotesque financial types and social lions of New York was quite wonderful.

When another rod slot had opened up, Ken had arranged with Berlin to invite a friend of his named Ted Buchanan, a man so suc-cessful on Wall Street that in his early forties he had pulled back from the rat race, moved to New Mexico and committed himself more to a life in conservation than in finance. The two of them fre-quently fished together on the Beaverkill in upstate New York.

Added to George Lee and Jock Miller, that made eight, and add the Howertons, that made ten. The two outsiders were patent lawyers from the Bay Area, Gary Aka and Charlie Krueger. They are both relatively quiet by temperament, and given the rather noisy na-ture of our group, one where everyone else seemed connected, they were for the first few days quieter still.

It soon became obvious that we had hit a great river with giant fish at an almost perfect moment. Even fishermen of no demonstra-ble distinction, like Steadman and me, caught five or six fish a day. The average size was fifteen pounds. We considered a nine-pound fish to be small. Over twenty-two pounds was large. More impor-tant, it was not just the catching, it was the ongoing pleasure of it all. The fish were so big and strong, and we were obviously going to land enough that we took as much pleasure from the big ones that broke us off as we did from the ones we brought in. On my third day, I hooked up an enormous fish and kept it on for a long time, perhaps fifteen or twenty minutes, and it made four beautiful jumps, all of a piece, all very high at exactly the same angle, all against the current, each done perfectly as if by instruction from the Argentine Bureau of Tourism. The fish must have weighed between twenty-five and twenty-eight pounds, and when it finally broke off, I felt no sense of disappointment, just awe.

One of the things that made the group work was that we had no hierarchy, other than the fact that Berlin had put us together. But he was enjoying too much pleasure in our success to want to dominate the group. He was fishing very well—the largest fish of the week would be his thirty-one-pounder—but what he seemed concerned about was that everyone do as well as he was doing. Some members of our group who might nominally have been the most dominant figures at the table based simply on accomplishment in other fields, like Steadman, were among the lesser fishermen. Everyone kept his ego in check. George Lee, the late arrival to the group, was obviously the best fisherman. Yet he was low-key and self-contained about the fishing, a man obviously antihierarchical by nature. To him, fishing is an end in itself, and he was, if anything, less a score-keeper as the week progressed than the rest of us were. That helped: The best fisherman among us was the least interested in receiving the unofficial gold.

The rest of us maintained a light veneer of scorekeeping—because if we were not in some kind of zone ourselves, then most assuredly the river was, and therefore some sort of score demanded to be kept, if only by the rules of the lodge. So the rest of us returned after every shift, and partially seduced by the brilliance of our good fortune, we inevitably talked about how many we'd caught and how big they were, the ritual benchmarks of fisherman talk. But George was content to say, very simply, that he'd had a very good day. He was, Kruse, who was his roommate, told me later, deliriously happy to be fishing here; it was for someone so talented the rarest kind of fishing, as Kruse noted, the fishing of a lifetime.

But he had no need to talk about it. "To appreciate how wonderful the fishing is for him this week," Kruse added, "you have to do a lot of shitty fishing on a lot of shitty occasions. That way, maybe you earn the right to fish like this once in a lifetime." Gradually, George became the secret star of our group, not just because he was the best fisherman but because he might also have been the most interesting man among us, funny, smart, unconventional, mordant. He was the most unprepossessing looking of us. If we were not exactly fashion plates ourselves, we all nonetheless wore the casual clothes of the upper middle class, successful American men at serious play: sweaters, corduroy pants, cool understated albeit expensive vests. George, by contrast, more than a little overweight and balding, looked a little like a rogue figure with a bit part in a Shakespeare play. His clothes seemed chosen precisely to offend the style preferred at a cold-weather lodge (he looked as if he was dressed for a not really good Caribbean bonefishing lodge just about to close: loud orange T-shirts in combination with green pants); Ralph Lauren most assuredly would not have approved.

Yet we all were becoming aware, day by day, that looks and clothes and medical reports aside, George Lee was our prince, the one seigneur of fishing here, the man who not merely carried himself with the greatest skill but advertised himself the least and went about it for nothing but the inner pleasure; it was for him the most private expression of self. Moreover, he had become by the third night something of the star at the table as well, wickedly funny, sardonic and self-deprecatory. He reads widely—it had been a long time since I had talked with anyone about the novels of William Humphrey. I was intrigued by him, and his darker sense reminded me of two of my brilliant outlaw writer friends, Hunter Thompson and the late Freddy Exley; he seemed like someone from their pages. He struck me as exceptional, authentic and, finally, real.

He did not seem a man for a conventional life, not a readily domesticated species. Fishing is his life. A brother, Art Lee, writes about fishing, and apparently George is a great aficionado and collector of arcane fishing gear, which he occasionally sells on the Internet—right now there is a truly ugly mounted carp that he may well sell for $45. I don't understand why anyone would want to mount a carp; that anyone else would want to buy and hang a mounted carp seems stranger still. When, with a rare bad cast, he buried his fly deep in the back of his head this week, he joked about wanting to keep the fly there permanently as his first true fisherman's pierce, which seemed oddly appropriate. When his marriage had ended recently, he had immediately gone to see the talented outdoor artist Galen Mercer and had him draw a steelhead trout, which George took to a tattoo artist and had emblazoned on his left forearm, as if to symbolically demonstrate the change in his life—first things were now first.

He seemed to have a number of fishing places of his own: a trailer in upstate New York; a small place in Newfoundland, which he was not quite sure he actually owned even though he had bought it and there may or may not have been a deed to it; and a place on the Umpqua River in Oregon. At first George was apparently a little nervous about meeting the rest of us, fearing we might be a group of Darth Vaders of the fishing world, a bunch of men who, all having made our first $100 million on Wall Street, now intended—as a parallel birthright—to do as well with the trout of the Río Grande. What George really feared, Kruse told me later, was that if we did well on a river like this with fish this big, we would think it was because we were that good at fishing, not because we had the good luck to be at the right place at the right time. Would we really know, George wondered at the beginning, the difference between larger good fortune in life and true fishing skill?

I knew better, and I think most of the others did as well. Though modesty is not necessarily one of my—or, I suspect, the others'—virtues, the sheer good fortune of being here on a great week imposed its own involuntary humility. I knew my limitations and that the good luck I had enjoyed, catching five or six big fish a day, had little to do with talent. If talent had been the basis for the trip, I would not have made the cut. There was one blessed period on my last day, when within one forty-minute period I took a twenty-six-and-a-half-pounder and then on the next cast a twenty-four-pounder. I was smart enough to know it was about the river and the stars and the fish and the guides. I knew I was still a marginal fly fisherman—perhaps after twelve sessions in high winds down here, my grade had moved up to a B−. That upgrade was the extent of my illusion about my abilities.

That did not lessen my pleasure in fishing—perhaps it made the pleasure even greater. I retained the sweet pleasure of the truly innocent at play in wonderful water among the obsessed. I remember not just the big fish I caught but also the beauty of the ones that got away, especially the one that made those four great jumps. What I liked as much as the fishing was the group. Day by day, the pleasure of the water seemed to blend into the pleasure of the group dining. We seemed to be intrigued by one another and surprisingly open to one another. Oddly enough, we did not talk much about fishing during the meals—that was mostly taken care of during the predinner cocktail hour. Sometimes we were light, and sometimes we were deadly serious. One night one of the Californians asked the New Yorkers where they were on September 11, and we all spoke informally. By far the most moving was Jock Miller, two of whose sons were employed in the World Trade Center area, and as he described what it was like trying to get in touch with them for a crucial three or four hours (all the phones were down)—it was, he said, the worst day of his life—he broke into tears.

Gradually, we melded into one group. Gary Aka and Charlie Krueger, the two California attorneys, shy at the beginning in the face of all our noise, were annexed and talked about fishing with us next year. At the final dinner, we gave out awards. George Lee was named Patagonian Rookie of the Year, and he received a uniquely ugly ashtray. Jock Miller won the Truth in Competition award: Aretsky handed him four stones to help weigh his fish in the future. Someone talked about the rare quality of friendship in this group so casually put together. Steadman later shrewdly suggested that it was not quite friendship; he had carefully tracked who we were and how we had gotten there and what the lines of connection were. We are not really friends. What we have is something more unusual: We have an almost perfect example of fellowship.

Schaap Was a Pioneer . . . and a Good Guy

From ESPN.com, December 24, 2001

DICK SCHAAP WAS ONE OF THE VERY BEST JOURNALISTS OF his generation, a man whose career reflected the enormous generational changes in his profession forced upon it by technology. He was a man of newspapers, magazines, books (lots of books) and, finally, as print began to decline in the middle of his career, of television, a world into which, unlike so many of his print colleagues, Dick made the most natural of transitions.

He was also a very good man. He treated a vast range of people with respect and dignity, and he conferred on them uncommon good will. As such, he was unusual—almost unique—in the richness and breadth of his friendships in a world where relationships are increasingly adversarial. He was simply one of the best-loved people in this profession. That is rare. Not many journalists can manage to do high-quality work and yet retain the friendship of many of the people they cover—and compete against.

He wrote his own memoir this past year, and he subtitled it, in self-deprecating satire of all the ghostwritten books he had produced, "Dick Schaap as Told to Dick Schaap." When he finished the manuscript, he sent it by for a blurb. I read it and enjoyed it, though when I put it down, I was touched by no small amount of melancholia, and even a bit of envy. Dick, it was clear, though we were almost exactly the same age and had covered many of the same things, had had a great deal more fun than I had had over the years.

We met for the first time as college journalists, representing our respective school newspapers at Harvard Stadium in the fall of 1953 at a Harvard-Cornell football game, he on his way to being the editor of the *Cornell Daily Sun*, me on my way to becoming managing editor of the *Harvard Crimson*. We were, in the way of ambitious young college journalists, properly wary of each other. (If both of us knocked on the door of the *New York Times* or the *Herald Tribune* after we graduated, what would happen if there were only one opening?)

There was, it would turn out, plenty of room for both of us, and we ended up longtime colleagues over what is now more than six decades of reporting. Eventually, I went to the *Times*, and he went to the *Trib*; I went overseas, he stayed in New York and became one of the last *Trib* city editors and, in time, a columnist for the paper. Though his column was citywide, his best work was always in sports, in no small part because he never saw sports as a narrow, enclosed place—as the Toy Department, as it was scathingly known in most newspaper circles. Rather, he enjoyed it not merely for the athletic competition inherent there, but he saw it as serving as an important window on the larger American society.

Because of that, he became at a rather early age—in his 20s—a very important figure in the world of modern sports journalism. Long before it was fashionable, indeed beginning when it was quite unfashionable, back in the late '50s, he was far ahead of the curve in writing about the rise of black and Hispanic athletes. More, he wrote not merely about their athletic abilities, but about their feelings as well.

This was at a time when few black athletes had made their way into the top level of professional and college sports, and were still greatly outnumbered by white athletes. But where blacks were even more outnumbered was in the ownership-management hierarchy of sports—and, to be blunt, in the world of sports journalism.

That world was very white, too, and surprisingly inflexible. Most of the more influential figures in it had come up in a very different era, some 20 or 25 years earlier, accepted far more rigid racial premises, and had little tolerance for athletes who were in any way different from the norm, or in any way outspoken. Many of the sportswriters and editors of that era thought they were greatly advanced in their thinking if they wrote that it was all right for Jackie Robinson to play for Brooklyn. They did not, however, want to hear about his off-the-field grievances, his troubles in finding a house or getting a meal in a restaurant.

It could be said that the empathy factor in this world was rather marginal. Most of the leading people in sports and sports journalism reserved what little empathy they had for themselves, or for people as much as possible like themselves.

Dick was dramatically different. He was not just talented but sensitive, and he had something which would serve him well for the rest of his career—the gift of instant friendship. He reached out to a generation of young black athletes, some talented, some not-so-talented, at a time when few other reporters were doing it, and he brought to his reporting a sense of what it was like to be different.

Dick intuitively understood that something very important, indeed profound, was taking place in our society in terms of race. He was right, of course—nothing less than a revolution was taking place. And if one of the great windows on it was in the South, where the Civil Rights movement was just getting under way, then perhaps the other exceptional window on it was sports, where for the first time the descendants of slavery were being given a chance to display their talents.

In 1956, Dick voted for the great Syracuse running back Jim Brown for the Heisman Trophy. Brown was self-evidently the greatest college player in the country, but a jury of white journalists from another generation obviously thought that it was a bit precipitous to honor him. He came in fifth. Yes, fifth. To Dick's credit, when he found out that Brown had been jobbed, he boycotted the Heisman voting for more than two decades.

Nor was the Heisman incident unique. Some two years ago, along with Glenn Stout, I put together a collection of sports reporting to be called *The Best Sports Writing of the Century*. One of the things we wanted was not merely the very best writing over those 100 years ... we wanted to reflect the broad social changes in American society that had taken place over the years. Obviously, that meant we had to pay a good deal of attention to racial shifts as they had evolved over that span.

Here Dick's work was invaluable, because he had focused on such issues so early on. Originally, I wanted to use three of his magazine pieces (the only magazine writer from whom we ultimately took three was the estimable W. C. Heinz). One of Dick's pieces, written in 1958, detailed the anger of Pancho Gonzales, the great tennis player, brought on by his years of mistreatment by the white tennis establishment. Another was a piece in which Dick told of taking Muhammad Ali around New York in 1960 when he was very young, very innocent and still known as Cassius Clay. And the third was a lovely early piece on Wilt Chamberlain.

In the end, because the book was already a bit too long, we had to cut the Chamberlain piece. But Dick was pleased—two out of three, he said, was not bad.

It is hard to think he's gone. He seemed in recent years as youthful and exuberant as ever. Nearly 50 years of covering sports had not worn him down or made him cynical. He was, at the end, as optimistic and enthusiastic as when he started out.

His puns were as bad as ever, his heart as generous as ever. He had become silver-haired, and was a good deal more handsome than he was as a young man.

No one was nicer to younger reporters. One of the few people I ever heard him bad-mouth was a colleague who he thought had mistreated women and younger reporters when we were all much younger.

He remained remarkably tolerant of those he covered. If he

could see their flaws as some of us did, he could also find in some athlete who seemed (at least to me) absolutely without redeeming qualities something likable. Redemption came easily to him. He could see in someone else's lesser qualities otherwise submerged signs of their humanity.

He always thought what he did was fun, and as such he made it fun. It is hard to think of his not being at the center of some group and having fun, oblivious to the clock.

When I was young and just starting out, I thought there would be a lot of people like Dick in this business. But now that I am older, I am grateful for the few like him, and that I was lucky enough to meet them.

A Full Life of Football, Till the Very End

From the *Washington Post*, November 22, 2005

THERE WAS, AS THE CLOCK WAS RUNNING DOWN IN THE FINAL seconds of the Super Bowl this year and the New England Patriots were about to win their third NFL title in four years, a wonderful scene that might easily have been scripted in Hollywood. An older man, 86 years old to be exact, who always stayed in the background whenever there were television cameras around, moved from his spot on the sideline to be with his son, Bill Belichick, the coach of the Patriots, in that final sweet moment of triumph, arriving there just in time for the traditional Gatorade bath.

And thus did Steve Belichick, a classic lifer as a coach, 33 years as an assistant coach at the U.S. Naval Academy, who coached and scouted because he loved the life and needed no additional fame (and in fact, much like his son, thought fame more of a burden than an asset), get his one great moment of true national celebrity, the two men—son and father—awash in the ritual bath of the victorious.

Steve Belichick died of a heart attack Saturday night. He had spent the afternoon watching Navy play and win, in the company of some of his former players, and the evening watching another college game, USC against Fresno State, and almost surely rooting for Fresno State because Pat Hill, the Fresno coach, is a former Bill Belichick assistant, and thus an honor's graduate of what might be called Belichick University.

Steve Belichick viewed his son's extraordinary success, rightfully, I think, as nothing less than an additional and quite wondrous validation of his own life as a coach and teacher, not that he needed any additional validation of it in the game he loved (though as a college coach he always harbored a certain mostly covert suspicion of the professional game). Where the poverty of the America he grew up in had placed a certain ceiling on his own ambitions, his son, the product of a much more football-focused environment and a much more affluent, sports-driven society, attained the very highest level of the profession.

He was an exceptional coach himself, classically known within the hermetically sealed world of college coaches as a coach's coach and a truly great teacher. He was considered by many the ablest college scout of his era, first in the period before there was very much use of film and tape, and scouts had to do most of their work with nothing save their own eyes from the press box, to the coming of tape, where he still remained the master, someone who would run the tape back and forth countless times looking for one more clue about what an opponent was going to do.

"Steve had superior intelligence and intellect," Bill Walsh, the former San Francisco 49ers coach told me, "and he not only saw the game as very few scouts did, but as he was seeing it, he understood as very few scouts did."

He taught many younger men how to scout and how to watch film and how to prepare their teams for the next week's game, but his best pupil, fittingly enough for the Hollywood scenario, was his own son, who started watching film with him when he was all of 9 years old, and one of whose greatest skills as a coach to this day remains his ability to analyze other teams, figuring out both their strengths and their vulnerabilities, and shrewdly deciding how to take away from them that which they most want to do. In that sense, perhaps more than any other, Bill Belichick is his father's son.

Steve Belichick was active until the end, a crusty, zestful, honorable, amazingly candid man, someone uncommonly proud of his son's success. He both enjoyed it, and knew the limits and the dangers of it, and he was very shrewd when other coaches and writers spoke of his son as a genius. He knew the G-word was two edged, potentially something of a setup, that if they used it for you on the way up, they might just as easily use it against you on the way down. "Genius?" he would say. "You're talking about someone who walks up and down a football field." At the end of his life he still went down to the Naval Academy regularly to check in with younger coaches, active still, though somewhat irritated that a minor stroke now limited his ability to go surfcasting off Nantucket in the summer.

His life spanned an extraordinary era in American life, and in American sports. He entered the game after an exemplary career at Cleveland's Western Reserve University, enjoyed a very brief career—one season—as a professional player in 1941, playing the game when the rewards were, in the financial sense, at least quite marginal. He was paid about $115 a week during his brief tour with the Detroit Lions.

But even as he began his coaching career at the Naval Academy in 1956, Steve Belichick watched as television changed the nature and importance of football; both college and professional football moved to the very epicenter of American popular culture, and his son, as the most successful of contemporary professional coaches, eventually drew a salary of $4 million a year.

His was quite a remarkable American story. The name was originally Bilicic. But it was phoneticized, much to the irritation of his mother, by a first-grade teacher in Monessen, Pa., when his older sister entered school and the teacher seemed puzzled by how to pronounce Mary Bilicic's name. His parents were Croatian immigrants—his father could not read or write in his native language—who settled in the coal-mining and steel-making region of western Pennsylvania and eastern Ohio.

Steve Belichick was the youngest of five children, and because of the Depression, his father was unemployed during most of his high school years. As a high school student, though he was obviously very bright and got very good grades, he did not take college-track courses. The principal of Struthers (Ohio) High once pointed this out to him and asked him why he didn't take physics or chemistry. "Why should I take them?" Belichick answered. "I'm only going to work in the steel mills anyway."

"Well," the principal answered, "you never know—maybe there'll be something out there for you."

There was. He was a very good high school running back, a little small, playing at around 160 pounds, but fast with very good peripheral vision and exceptionally good hands. His parents never tried to stop him from playing football—but the importance of sport in the process of Americanization eluded them and they never went to see him play.

By chance, a local basketball coach connected him with a football coach named Bill Edwards, an old friend of the legendary Paul Brown, the greatest of Ohio coaches; because Brown was legendary, Edwards, his pal, was at least semi-legendary and he coached at Western Reserve in Cleveland, where he had to recruit the kids that the Big Ten schools did not go after. Bill Edwards, for whom William Stephen Belichick is named, offered him a scholarship and in time he became a star running back there. In the process, Edwards became a great family friend and a lifelong mentor.

For a brief time right before World War II began, Bill Edwards coached the Detroit Lions, and brought Steve Belichick, then waiting to go into the service, to the team, first as an equipment manager and then as a fleet fullback who could handle the ball better than the all-American who was supposed to play fullback. Steve Belichick played on the same team as the famed running back Whizzer White. Belichick averaged 4.2 yards per carry, had his nose broken repeatedly, once quite deliberately by a player named Dick Plasman, who played for the Chicago Bears, "the last player to play in the NFL without a helmet, if that places him for you," Steve Belichick told me.

He scored two touchdowns in one game against the New York Giants, and then in a game against Green Bay, a play he never forgot, and the details of which he could recount to his last day on this planet, he took a punt, got it on a perfect bounce, one he said that you dreamed about getting because you did not have to break stride, slipped to the outside with all the Green Bay defenders clustered in the middle of the field, and ran it back 77 yards for a score. During the war, he served with the Navy on merchant marine ships that made Atlantic crossings and then repeated trips from England to France after D-Day.

After the war, Bill Edwards helped him get a job as a coach at Hiram College in Ohio. There he met a young, vivacious instructor in Romance languages named Jeannette Munn. He asked her out and for their first date took her to a Western Reserve game. The date was not a great success. She thought she might learn a great deal about football, which seemed extremely important to everyone else in Ohio. But he did not talk very much during the game, and instead spent a lot of time smoking cigars.

After the game they went out for a sandwich, but all sorts of people kept coming up to their table—and he repeatedly failed to introduce her. At first she thought he had exceptionally poor manners, but it turned out that he simply did not know their names—they were fans who recognized him. He was, she realized, something of a local celebrity. He persevered with her. She did not think him particularly handsome, but there was something about him—his obvious raw intelligence, his fierce sense of purpose and his innate honor that she did admire.

In 1950 they were married, much, as he liked to say, to the surprise of all her friends who were not necessarily football fans and a bit more *raffin*, and he suspected looked down on him and his world.

As they grew older and they spoke of their Hiram days, it was like hearing two great comedians who had a routine down perfectly on the question of whether he had tried to get her to give his football players a break on their grades. "I never asked for anything for them," he would say.

"Yes, you did," she would answer, "but you did it subtly—you would ask about how the player was doing, but I knew what you wanted. You didn't fool me a bit."

"Okay, maybe I did," he would answer, "but you never helped any of them."

In 1949, Bill Edwards took the job as head coach at Vanderbilt and brought Steve Belichick along as an assistant. At Vanderbilt he was viewed as a tough, smart, extremely original coach and a brilliant scout—he always gave his players an edge with his scouting reports.

If anything, some of the players thought, he might have been a better, more gifted coach than the more laid-back Edwards. There was always something original in the way he went about his work. For one quarterback who did not keep his throwing arm high enough, Belichick built special wooden sawhorses, so that if the quarterback's hand ended too low at the end of his throw he would bang it on the sawhorse. He tried to get some of his running backs and receivers to improve their peripheral vision by first walking and then running down the field alongside them, and holding up different numbers of fingers, getting them to see more even as they ran.

Edwards and Belichick did reasonably well there, but Vanderbilt's coaches do not last a long time, and they were fired after four years. From there he went to North Carolina with Edwards, where they were part of another ill-fated coaching team before being let go.

With that, in 1956, he took a job at the Naval Academy. He and Jeannette loved Annapolis, the value system of the academy, the exceptional young men who went there and were so receptive to coaching, the feel of the entire community. He was, he remembered, paid about $7,000 a year when he started—assistant coaches did not get rich back then. He was shrewd about it, and in some way he sensed when he first arrived that he had found a permanent home; he had been shot down in two previous jobs and he was wary of the life of a coach, the abundant pitfalls and the ever-tricky politics that went with the game itself and above all with the job of head coach.

Within the profession his talents were hardly a secret and there were repeated offers to go elsewhere for a good deal more money, either in the college world or as a pro scout. But he had everything he wanted, and he was content to be an assistant and a scout; he had an absolute sense of the value and the quality of his work. He was also shrewd enough, on the advice of a friend, to get tenure as a physical training instructor. That meant that, as a family, the Belichicks had a permanent base, one that gave them immunity from the normal viruses that struck at men in the coaching world. He coached there until 1989.

For the shadow of that hard childhood, being an immigrant's son in the Depression, always fell on their home, even in Annapolis in an ever-more affluent America. In the home of Steve and Jeannette Belichick, the values were old-fashioned and came right out of Monessen and Struthers. Nothing was to be wasted. Nothing was to be bought on time. Anything that could be repaired was repaired. He ran a summer football camp each year, and the money saved from it went to Bill's education. When he scouted at another school and the trip was 1,000 miles, which he drove in his car, and the government was paying eight cents a mile, then the $80 expense check went into a separate bank account to be used for the next Belichick car.

One of his best players of the Vanderbilt era, Don Gleisner, was a farm boy in Ohio and recalled for me the day that Steve Belichick showed up to recruit him.

"I was," Gleisner told me, "very cocky back then and when Steve came to the farm, I said something like, 'Coaching, that sounds like a pretty good deal—is there any money in it?' "

Belichick proudly pointed to his brand-new car and said, "That's a '49 Chevy, son, and there's not a penny owed on it."

That extraordinary work ethic was passed on to his son, and is one of the reasons he has done so well in the same profession. Nothing with the son, as with the father, is ever to be wasted, least of all time.

In every book a writer does, there are side benefits—the bonus of dealing with people whom you come to like more and more as the book progresses. So it was with Steve Belichick for me with this book. If he had been a crusty man with a rather tough interior when he was younger, then the interior had long ago softened, in part because of both his own success, and that of his son, and the sheer richness of his life. I loved talking to him—there were always stories, and each story begat another story. We became, as my work on it continued, the most unlikely of pals.

In the months I worked on the book I dealt with him almost every day, and he got quite accustomed to my calls. Sometimes he would answer the phone and say, "I thought that was going to be you—why are you so late calling this morning?" There was always something more he had thought of, something more he thought I should know about the game, always something more to be learned and to be taught. I thought he was straight and smart and funny, and quite brilliant. Because he was so tough and so focused a person, I think many people did not realize how truly smart and original he was. If he did not get all the recognition he deserved himself, then it was his good fortune in his own lifetime to see his son recognized for the uses of his mind as he himself had never been.

THE FITNESS-GOERS

From *Vogue*, July 1987

WE WERE, I SUSPECT, A MOTLEY-LOOKING GROUP THAT FIRST gray morning at the rowing school. Nothing came even close to resembling a uniform, and our T-shirts advertised everything from soft drinks and resorts to prep schools and musical comedies. Our bodies, regrettably, were hardly advertisements for the new aerobically conscious America. By and large, we did not look like rowers; nor, in fact, did many of us look like athletes.

In addition, we were all, I suspect, like kids at the first day of some strange new camp, filled with all the long-forgotten fears of dealing with new faces in a strange setting. If that were not bad enough, there was an additional anxiety—that of successful middle-aged people about to expose themselves not just to failure but, even worse, to looking foolish in front of fellow adults. My wife and I and about a dozen others, ranging from a teenage rower from Deerfield Academy to a retired New York University professor of seventy, had arrived at the Florida Rowing Center in Wellington, Florida, for a brief course in sculling.

Jean Halberstam and I possessed different levels of skill and different levels of apprehension. I had rowed and sculled relatively well in college some thirty-two years back; had let my skills, such as they were, atrophy; then had come back to the sport in 1984, when I had written a book about America's best scullers. In 1985, I bought an Alden shell, a recreational boat that I had rowed with rare pleasure over the past two summers in Nantucket. Having written about the nation's best scullers, and become a friend of some of them, gave me additional anxiety. I was, at the age of fifty-two, exposing my true vulnerability; I did not want to make a fool of myself in front of these teachers as well as my fellow students.

Jean faced a somewhat more primal dilemma. She had never before rowed a stroke. She was about to be forty, and she wanted more control over her body and more strength. In the preceding seven months, she had gone to a demanding gym in New York City and by dint of exceptional diligence had gotten herself in excellent shape. She still had not found a summer sport that gave her much pleasure.

For years, I had bored Jean about the pleasures of sculling, about how good it made you feel about yourself, about how sweet it felt when you did it right with the entire body—shoulders, back, and legs—working as one, with the stomach as the linchpin; how you could do it on your own terms, to your own specifications, without needing anyone else; how it was probably, in terms of aerobics and body toning, the almost-perfect sport for someone approaching middle age. In addition, I had told her (and this, for a woman whose husband works at home, was particularly persuasive) that there was a solitude to rowing that was particularly attractive, a sense of being utterly by yourself and with nature that I found uniquely calming. Finally, not without considerable misgivings, she had agreed to lessons. In addition to the normal fear of a grown woman trying a relatively complicated sport for the first time, Jean had—and I never knew it before—a deep and abiding phobia of being on the water, stemming from a serious accident when she was young. She was about to enter a wonderful new sport which, for all the pleasures it can generate, has been known for how easily its boats can capsize. She was not just anxious, she was also terrified.

But the world of rowing has changed, as I repeatedly pointed out to her; and the boats, at least the ones for beginners, are more stable now. Until quite recently, it would have been impossible to have a camp like this. Sculling, an almost perfect aerobic sport, remained a sport for those who had come to it very early—by and large privi-leged upper-class Americans whose fathers had rowed, who had gone to a handful of selected prep schools or (as in my case) one of the few colleges in the country where rowing and sculling were im-portant. In the past, one rowed racing sculls—graceful, slim, paper-thin craft twelve inches across at the beam and weighing perhaps thirty pounds. They were exhilarating to row (on days when I was rowing at my best, I felt that the boat was not even touching the wa-ter), but they required considerable skill to handle. One bad stroke by even an expert oarsman and the scull could flip over. What changed—and democratized—the world of sculling was the arrival, sixteen years ago, of Alden recreational shells. Made of fiberglass, these are not as slim nor as fast as racing shells, and they are nearly impossible to flip; they are the almost perfect introductory craft for someone new to the sport or someone, like me, who has to row in relatively rough water off Nantucket. Now, with a minimum num-ber of lessons, many people who had once watched from a distance can learn to scull and get as much fun from doing it as a champion. Anyone with a lake, a pond, or a relatively tame river now can scull; hardier souls can even try the ocean. For that reason, Jean and I had finally gone to Wellington, just west of Palm Beach, to row on Lake Wellington, a small invented lake of protected water about a mile and a half long. While there we, like most students at the school, stayed at the Palm Beach Polo and Country Club.

The Florida Rowing Center is the brainchild of Arnold Guy Fraiman, a retired New York State Supreme Court justice. Judge Fraiman, who is sixty-one and looks about ten years younger, opened the center two years ago out of a lovely mixture of self-interest and altruism. A serious runner who had competed in forty-three marathons, he had found in recent years that his running had worn out his knee cartilage, that his days as a jogger were over. At age fifty-eight, he took up rowing. Evangelical about the sport, Fraiman thinks that every serious amateur athlete should learn to row; by opening the camp, he also now has a place to row during the winter.

At the camp, Fraiman is the founder, all-purpose manager, cheerleader, chief of operations, and reassurer of the parents of teenage students—responsibilities he handles with exceptional goodwill. Coaches are Peter Sparhawk, for fifteen years head coach of men's crew at Princeton University; John Marden, one of America's premier scullers; John Murphy, a young man with boyish good looks who was hoping to win the Canadian lightweight singles title this year; and Marlene Royle, an excellent young American sculler hoping to make the national team in the lightweight double shells. The club can handle sixteen scullers at a time. Students come for either three or five days. The routine at the school is simple: two lessons a day, the first one starting at 7:30 A.M.; then a break for breakfast. At a midmorning meeting, coaches show videotapes of the morning workout; then a late-morning session is followed by a voluntary row in the afternoon.

The first day is not an easy one for Jean. Normally a strong, confident person, she has grown increasingly nervous about the project, and this first morning she starts out with her heart in her throat. The day is not a complete success. The boat seems an adversary to her, not an extension of self; the strokes that seem so easy for some of the others come hard for her. She constantly thinks of flipping over; she repeatedly bumps into the shoreline.

I first try a Vespoli, a step up in speed from the Alden, and I do not row well. Frustrated, I try seeing myself through the strokes but it does not work. Later, I realize I have rigged the boat badly and that has significantly thrown off my strokes. During the videotape session, the coaches note that I am using my arms too much instead of letting them serve as hinges and using my shoulders and back to apply the power.

In the second session, I set the rigging right and row well. I am pleased. Out of the corner of my eye, I watch Jean. She is still struggling, and it is hard. I know this is not fun for her. A little later, at lunch, she is still uneasy. "But there was a moment when I did about four strokes in a row that were just right," Jean says, "and it was wonderful." Ah, I think, the first glimmer of the rower within. In the afternoon, I watch as Jean returns to row again. Already there is sign of improvement, more good strokes than bad. At the end of the day, she is more confident and talks less of flipping.

On the second day, there are beginnings of genuine cama-raderie. Bonded by our anxieties, comforted that no one in our group is either a super sculler or a boastful gamesman, we help put the boats in the water and begin to root for each other. Jean, with some misgiving, is rowing a Vancouver. The coaches have told her that they think it will be easier for her to handle but also a little eas-ier to flip, clearly a mixed blessing. She accepts it as such.

That morning I am not pleased with my own rowing. The coaches come by and critique me: I am still using my arms too much and am cutting off a major supply of power. When Jean comes back from the first workout of the morning, she is frustrated; she has run into the bushes on the side of the lake several times. But looking at her videotape later that morning, I am impressed: she is slow and self-conscious, but her strokes are strong and her form is good. I am watching a rower. By the end of the day, Jean says that rowing is very good for women like her, who fear any exercise that builds the upper body, particularly the shoulders and arms. Sculling, if done properly, strengthens not only the arms but the legs, the lower back, and the abdomen.

By the third day we can joke about our nervousness. The rain has no effect on me; I am finally rowing well. The last two days have served as a crash course of good, simplified instruction; the video-tape, a marvelous coaching instrument showing us how we row, not how we think we row. On what is, for me, surprisingly flat water, I am now doing twelve miles a day rowing a Schoenbrod, a sleek boat, virtually a racing shell; and I love it. I take twelve quick strokes, and it is like going back thirty-two years in time; I am row-ing as I had thought I might, and I am thrilled by the speed of the boat. I have pledged to myself that I will not be competitive, but I am rowing so well that I soon find my eye—not me, but my eye—measuring the distance between myself and some of the other equally experienced scullers, trying to see if I have opened any wa-ter on them. Shameful stuff. I also wonder privately whether it will be hard to go back to the slower Alden once I get back to Nantucket.

Captivated by the pleasure of my own rowing, I have paid no at-tention to Jean. As I row back to the dock, I spot another boat. A Vancouver, moving quite nicely. It is my wife, and she is putting her body into it. As she comes up to the dock, her pleasure is self-evident. These are real strokes, and this is real rowing.

Technically, the school has three- or five-day classes; but Fraiman and Sparhawk are nothing if not flexible, and Jean and I decide to stay for a fourth day. The wind is up, and it is a very hard day to row. I stay somewhat closer to Jean, and I am pleased; she is frustrated by the coming of the wind, a new adversary. On this hard day, I see a young woman who has gone from absolute beginner to novice; her strokes are not just good, they are strong and she drives her entire body into them.

When we reach the dock, there is a new confidence to her voice. "In three days," she says, "you can feel that you're doing it right and take real pleasure from it. That doesn't mean you're a great sculler yet—only that you are doing it correctly enough to take pleasure. If I were starting out in tennis at my age, it might take six months or more of very hard work before I felt good about a serve." When she gets back to New York, Jean says she intends to take swimming les-sons for people who have serious fear of the water. (She does.)

Everyone seems pleased as they leave, but I think I am most pleased of all. There may be few things as sweet in this world as watching the person you love come to appreciate and like the sport you love.

ACKNOWLEDGMENTS

THE EDITOR WOULD LIKE TO THANK THE FOLLOWING institutions and individuals who were of assistance in tracking down material and putting together this volume: John Dorsey, the Boston Public Library, Joe Farara, the Johnson State College Library, Meg Downey, Christine Irizarry, the Nashville *Tennessean*, John Seigenthaler, Rob Fleder, Richard Johnson, Howard Bryant, Leanne Garland, Deborah May, the Nashville Public Library, Amanda Hicks, Alex Belth and Nate Rau. Special thanks to editors Will Schwalbe and Brendan Duffy at Hyperion Books, John Taylor "Ike" Williams of Kneerim & Williams at Fish & Richardson, and Jean Halberstam for the opportunity to work on this book.

CREDITS

INDEX

I9781401323127
796 HAL
Halberstam, David.
Everything they had :

5/14/08

I9781401323127
796 HAL
Halberstam, David.
Everything they had :

DATE DUE	BORROWER'S NAME